Crimes of the Future

D1262402

Crimes of the Future

Theory and its Global Reproduction

Jean-Michel Rabaté

B L O O M S B U R Y

NEW YORK • LONDON • NEW DELHI • SYDNEY

Bloomsbury Academic
An imprint of Bloomsbury Publishing Inc

1385 Broadway	50 Bedford Square
New York	London
NY 10018	WC1B 3DP
USA	UK

www.bloomsbury.com

Bloomsbury is a registered trade mark of Bloomsbury Publishing Plc

First published 2014

© Jean-Michel Rabaté, 2014

Library of Congress Cataloging-in-Publication Data
Rabaté, Jean-Michel, 1949-
Crimes of the future : theory and its global reproduction / Jean-Michel Rabat?.
pages cm
Summary: "Crimes of the Future sees one of the world's leading literary theorists exploring the past, present and potential future of Theory"– Provided by publisher.
ISBN 978-1-4411-4634-2 (hardback) — ISBN 978-1-4411-7287-7 (paperback)
1. Literature—History and criticism—Theory, etc.   2. Criticism.   I. Title.
PN81.R13 2014
809–dc23
2013049294

ISBN: HB: 978-1-4411-4634-2
PB: 978-1-4411-7287-7
ePub: 978-1-4411-5563-4
ePDF: 978-1-4411-8616-4

Typeset by RefineCatch Ltd, Bungay, Suffolk
Printed and bound in the United States of America

Contents

About the Author

Jean-Michel Rabaté, who has been professor of English and Comparative Literature at the University of Pennsylvania since 1992, is a co-founder and curator of Slought Foundation, an editor of the *Journal of Modern Literature*, and a Fellow of the American Academy of Arts and Sciences. He has authored or edited more than 30 books and collections on: modernism, psychoanalysis, and philosophy; and on writers like Samuel Beckett, Thomas Bernhard, Ezra Pound and James Joyce. In 2013, he edited *A Handbook of Modernism Studies* (Wiley-Blackwell). Forthcoming in 2014 are *An Introduction to Literature and Psychoanalysis; A Companion to 1922*; and *The Value of Samuel Beckett*.

Acknowledgments

Earlier versions of four chapters have been published in collections or reviews. All of these chapters have been revised and rewritten for this book.

A version of Chapter 2 was published as "Theory: future, ancient, fugitive," in *The Conditions of Possibility, Theory@buffalo*, vol. 13, 2009, pp. 6–20.

A version of Chapter 5 was published as "The 'Mujic of the Footure': future, ancient, fugitive," in *Futures: Of Jacques Derrida*, Richard Rand (ed.). Stanford: Stanford University Press, 2001, pp. 179–200.

A section of Chapter 6 was published as "The death of Freud: what is to be preferred, death or obsolescence?," in *Qui Parle: Critical Humanities and Social Sciences*, vol. 19, no. 1, 2010, pp. 37–63.

A version of Chapter 8 was published as "Crimes against fecundity: style and crime, from Joyce to Poe and back," in *Style in Theory: Between Literature and Philosophy*, Ivan Callus, James Corby and Gloria Lauri-Lucente (eds). London: Bloomsbury, 2013, pp. 111–39.

I am grateful to the editors for granting permission to use these texts.

Introduction

Originally, this book's title was *Theory of the Future*. It was planned as a sequel to my 2002 book, *The Future of Theory*,[1] whose theses I wanted to revisit more than ten years after; also, I did not mind practicing the kind of verbal reversal in the tradition of Marx's chiasmic logic when he replied to Proudhon's *The Philosophy of Poverty* by publishing *The Poverty of Philosophy*. Yet, when I had to explain to friends and colleagues what I had in mind with this lofty title, they would invariably ask: "So, you have a theory about the future; well, what can you predict for the future?" I would answer by quoting Rabelais's quip: "I predict that the blind will not see, that the deaf will not hear, and that there will be crimes . . ." I was in no risk of being found wrong, but was also echoing another book title, that of *Given: 1° Art, 2° Crime*,[2] a book that discussed modernity as haunted by crime as much as by technology, and in which Marcel Duchamp and Man Ray became prime suspects. However, the exact formulation of my new title was brought to me when I re-read Knut Hamsun's classic novel, *Hunger*.[3]

Hunger games

In that extraordinary first-person novel, a true precursor of Camus, Kafka and Beckett—a novel that should be mandatory reading in all high schools since it allows any young student to identify with a totally dispossessed, alienated, at times homeless and above all frantically hungry young man—we follow the narrator as he wanders through the streets of Oslo battling with poverty and near-starvation. His only source of revenue comes from the articles he manages to sell to newspapers, although most of the time he cannot write because he is too sick or delirious, subsisting on the sale of remaining possessions that he pawns one after the other. Among his projects of articles with which he intends to make money from newspapers is a recurrent project of writing an essay entitled "Crimes of the Future." "... perhaps today, as a matter of fact, I would get an article started on 'Crimes of the Future' (*Fremtidens Forbrydelser*) or 'Freedom of the Will', something like that,

[1]   Jean-Michel Rabaté, *The Future of Theory*. Oxford: Blackwell, 2002.
[2]   Jean-Michel Rabaté, *Given: 1° Art, 2° Crime—Modernity, Murder and Mass Culture*. Brighton, Sussex: Academic Press, 2007.
[3]   Knut Hamsun, *Hunger*, Robert Bly (trans.). New York: Farrar, Strauss and Giroux, 1998.

something saleable enough so that I could get five kroner at least . . ."[4] As Robert Bly notes wryly, these abortive articles that he will never write would only get him less than five dollars.[5] A little later, however, having pawned his only coat, he gets a few coins to buy some bread and cheese—on which he almost chokes. His strength having returned, the writer now hopes to get ten kroner, and the topics that he intends to publish should be less obvious: "it was not enough any longer to write an essay on something so elementary and simple-minded as 'Crimes of the Future,' which any ass could arrive at, let alone read in history books."[6] Instead, the starving writer contemplates writing a three-part essay on "Philosophical consciousness," with which he plans to settle his accounts with Kant's "sophistries." Alas, when he wants to write, he realizes that he has left his stub of a pencil in the coat he has just pawned. I leave you to follow the endless peregrinations of Hamsun's *alter ego*, and will suggest that he is closer to the paradigm of the revolutionary subject of the future than Melville's Bartleby, also spectacularly abstemious even if never actually hungry.[7] What I share with Hamsun, moreover, is the idea that anyone is capable of writing an essay on "crimes of the future," provided one's hunger remains at the right level. The allusion to history books should suggest "crimes of the past" and not of the future; Hamsun knows very well that one understands the forthcoming crimes of the future by contemplating the annals of past crimes systematically consigned in chronicles and history books.

One of the most disturbing aspects of Hamsun's *Hunger* is that its main character looks like a criminal—he loiters in a distracted manner, follows cute women and addresses them with obnoxious remarks, he tells wild lies to strangers in parks, he is prone to hysterical fits, he spends nights in jail, etc.— yet he never stoops so low as to commit a crime. The result is that it is the reader who wants him to be a criminal, a thief at least, if not necessarily a rapist. When he is obliged to chew on soft wood to assuage his pangs of hunger (he hasn't eaten for three days), we want to scream to him: "Steal that loaf of bread!" We would like him to become like Jean Genet's *alter ego* in *Diary of a Thief*; even though Genet was hungry at times, these periods never

---

[4] Knut Hamsun (see footnote 3), p. 8.
[5] Knut Hamsun (see footnote 3), p. 243.
[6] Knut Hamsun (see footnote 3), p. 12.
[7] I am alluding to a recent fascination for Bartleby as a political subject uttering a forceful refusal of the dominant values in his emblematic "I would prefer not to," a fascination shared by Gilles Deleuze, Giorgio Agamben and Jacques Derrida. For a balanced critique of this common trope linking politics and an ethics of refusal, see Jacques Rancière, "Deleuze, Bartleby and the literary formula," in *The Flesh of Words*, Charlotte Mandel (trans.), Stanford: Stanford University Press, 2004, pp. 146–64.

lasted long, what with prostitution with older gay men whom he would then shake of their money, or downright burglaries. In fact, Hamsun's hero is entangled in bourgeois respectability to such a point that readers cannot help criticizing it while admiring the excess of his masochistic heroism.

Yet, if we take the idea of "crimes of the future" seriously, we guess why this topic comes to the imagination of a frantic, hallucinating would-be writer wildly spinning away from conventional modes of living. Hamsun's hero tackles a notion that has to do with the long-term historical evolution of two genres, one that could be called the poetics of modernity, the other the genre of the detective fiction. They had merged earlier, in the middle of the tenth century, and were theorized jointly half-a-century later, after Hamsun had been awarded the Nobel Prize in 1920. At that time, he was sheltered from hunger, if not from historical mistakes.[8]

History displays its Scotland Yard badge

Modernity and crime met via Walter Benjamin, who had attempted at some point to write a detective novel with the help of Bertold Brecht,[9] and in whose *Arcades Project* we find regular references to Régis Messac's compendium, *Le "Detective Novel" et l'influence de la pensée scientifique*.[10] Messac, the author of a book on Poe, insisted on Poe's eminence in his survey spanning the huge period from Biblical and Arabic storytellers to the inception of modernity. He defined the genre of the "detective novel" tautologically by the process of "detection," a process going back to the ancient art of examining traces left on the ground by animals, thieves or murderers. It implied the reconstitution of a temporal sequence from clues that have to be interpreted in the right order. The art of observing traces in the sand, in grass or in streets, and then of reconstructing an event that has taken place is germane to the art of

---

[8] If Hamsun was reviled after WWII for having given his Nobel Prize medal to Goebbels as a token of his sympathy for the Nazis, he also managed to deeply infuriate Hitler the one time they met by requesting that the Führer free Norwegian prisoners and treat the local people better.

[9] Benjamin wanted to write a detective novel with a French title, *La Chasse aux mensonges*, in which the criminal would be a psychoanalyst. He invented a character who was in the habit of hiding money inside the pages of his books and who, having to run away, desperately goes through his library looking for banknotes. He had planned a novel in which the murderer and the detective would be as intimate as Holmes and Watson. See Walter Benjamin, *Gesammelte Schriften*, VII, 2. Frankfurt: Suhrkamp, 1989, pp. 846–8.

[10] Régis Messac, *Le "Detective Novel" et l'influence de la pensée scientifique*. Paris: Honoré Champion, 1929. In the pages that follow, I rephrase and condense material taken from the third chapter of Jean-Michel Rabaté (see footnote 2).

examining animals to assess their qualities or defects, namely early physiognomy. Messac saw in the progress of "detection" in fiction a burgeoning scientific spirit that came to maturity with the Age of Enlightenment; yet he observed that, since the emergence of Dupin and Sherlock Holmes, one spoke of "deductions" to describe the reconstruction of a criminal's actions, whereas in fact this process ought to be called "induction."[11] Thus the genre of "detection" based on "deductions" is predicated upon a general category mistake in which inductions are taken for deductions.

If the rise of the "detective novel" was contemporary with the flowering of the scientific spirit in the nineteenth century, we understand why Poe often compares his detection games to mathematics. Poe's Dupin, the ancestor of all detectives, marks the triumph of the thinker who remains in a room, smokes and tries to identify with the criminal. As we know, Poe loved riddles: he praised Godwin for having written *Caleb Williams* in reverse in his "Philosophy of composition"; he guessed the correct *dénouement* of *Barnaby Rudge* while Dickens was still serializing it, and he concluded from an examination of Maelzel's mechanical chess-player that it could not be a machine but that a dwarf player was hiding in the automaton.

Developing Poe's paradigm, Messac presents the Dupin trilogy, "The murders in the Rue Morgue," "The purloined letter," and "The mystery of Mary Roget," as the foundation of the genre of the detective novel. There is a surprising element of Frenchness there. Dupin's very name was borrowed from Vidocq's spurious but famous *Mémoires*, in which we find the mention of "that great prognosticator M. Charles Dupin."[12] Indeed, we see Dupin engaged in endless calculations when not solving chess problems. Yet if Poe flaunts his scientific knowledge and mathematical computations, most of the time the only science Dupin relies on is psychology. Thus his endless supputations about schoolboys who play a game of odd and even (they have to guess whether the number of marbles held in one's hand is odd or even) are based on guesswork from the adversary's level of cunning: "It is merely an identification of the reasoner's intellect with that of his opponent."[13] Similar guesswork applies to the beginning of "The murders in the Rue Morgue," when Dupin reconstitutes the chain of thoughts of his companion by observing his face's expressions as they pass signs and posters in Paris streets.

[11] Messac (see footnote 10) explains, in his footnote on p. 34, that the idea for his book came from the surprise caused by this remark made by a philosophy teacher in 1913.
[12] Messac, see footnote 10, p. 350.
[13] Edgar Allan Poe, "The purloined letter," in *The Complete Tales and Poems of Edgar Allan Poe*. Harmondsworth: Penguin, 1983, p. 215. Hereafter, abbreviated as CTP and page number.

This psychology of imitation is indeed a physiognomy: by reading an expression on your face, I can reconstruct your chain of thoughts.

The psychological acumen needed by Poe's French sleuth derives from Vidocq's *Mémoires*, a book which acted as a perfect trigger. The fundamental thesis of "The purloined letter" is that one hides best by not hiding at all. For once, Dupin guesses this truth in an *a priori* manner as it were, when he hears that the police, despite a systematic scrutiny of the house, have been unable to find the letter hidden by the minister. This time it is truly a "deduction" that leads Dupin to conclude that the letter will be visible if he can enter the Minister's study. He pays a visit to the Minister, finds the letter upside down, the paper folded back and scribbled over with another address, steals it and replaces it with a similar-looking letter. He had heeded Vidocq's tip about hiding places: ". . . the most conspicuous place is quite often the place that no-one will want to search."[14] Here is the birth of the intellectual detective who remains in his study and reconstructs the laws that govern the appearance of the signs revealing a crime.

Such a process of detection was shared by Benjamin as a critical historian. In *The Arcades Project*, he enlists Ernst Bloch's utopian thinking under the banner of detection: "A remark by Ernst Bloch apropos of *The Arcades Project*: 'History displays its Scotland Yard badge.' It was in the context of a conversation in which I was describing how this work—comparable, in method, to the process of splitting the atom—liberates the enormous energies of history that are bound up in the 'once upon a time' of classical historiography. The history that showed things 'as they really were' was the strongest narcotic of the century."[15] The impact of this type of allegorical history will produce, in a strange historical anticipation, something comparable to the invention of the atomic bomb. By abandoning illusions of historical objectivity, the detective reads history patiently, materially and productively. The petrified ruins of history explode when their atoms are set to whirl in the light of a new sun; then a new mode of "detective" intellection has been launched.

Messac's book on detective fiction establishes a central thesis: murder stories, detective fiction narratives and penny newspapers' depictions of crime scenes transpose to an urban setting the frontier world of adventure and "tracking" invented by James Fennimore Cooper, with Indians as main protagonists. The immense resources of observation and sagacity deployed by Mohicans in forests where they interpret the signs left by the enemy are adapted to the new urban setting by the detective. The influence of Cooper

---

[14] E. F. Vidocq, *Mémoires*. Paris: Garnier, Ch. XLVI, Vol. II, p. 330, quoted by Messac (see footnote 10), p. 357.

[15] W. Benjamin, *The Arcades Project*. Cambridge: Harvard University Press, 2002, p. 463.

and Poe was much more important in France than in England, protected by its insularity, sticking to a tradition shaped by *Caleb Williams* and Dickens, later refined by Wilkie Collins.[16] The American authors are rigorously contemporaneous (in 1841, Cooper published *The Deerslayer* and Poe "The murders in the Rue Morgue"). Their combined impact lends to the famous *flâneur* of Baudelaire an air of private detective, as we can see in Poe's "The man of the crowd." Benjamin's reading of this tale stresses the element of detection that is not immediately clear to first time readers: "Poe's famous tale 'The man of the crowd' is something like the X-ray picture of a detective story. In it, the drapery represented by crime has disappeared. The mere armature has remained: the pursuer, the crowd, and an unknown man who arranges his walk through London in such a way that he always remains in the middle of the crowd."[17] The story is well-known. An unnamed convalescent man enjoys his regained health by indulging in other people's observation.[18] He looks at the London crowds from a café near a busy thoroughfare. At first, he observes the "tides" and "groundswells" of the crowd before narrowing his attention to details. He provides a kind of radiography of social classes, starting with clerks, glimpsing noble people, going down the social ladder to the lowest rungs with prostitutes and drunks. Then the narrator's gaze focuses on an older man whose countenance is different from all previous types. His features yield contradictory clues, shifting from "mental power" to "bloodthirstiness," from "coolness" to "terror" and "despair." Unable to pigeonhole the man, the narrator decides to follow him. He discovers that the man drifts about with the crowds, always choosing streets where there are throngs of people. He is not looking for something or someone in particular in his frantic wanderings; he simply craves the anonymous company of the mass. As the night wears on, he finds shelter in the red-light district of the East End, with its streetwalkers and gin palaces, until he is forced by daybreak to return to the center of the city. Exhausted, the narrator finally stares at the old man who does not even stop to return his gaze and hurries along. The narrator concludes: "This old man ... is the type and the genius of deep crime. He refuses to be alone. *He is the man of the crowd.* It will be in vain to follow; for I shall learn no more of him, nor of his deeds. The worst heart of the world is a grosser book than the 'Hortulus Animae,' and perhaps it is but one of the great mercies of God that '*er lasst sich nicht lesen.*'" (CTP, p. 481) Poe concludes as he had begun, with a German quote meaning: "He does not let himself be

---

16 Messac (see footnote 10), p. 553.
17 Walter Benjamin, *Charles Baudelaire. A Lyric Poet in the Era of High Capitalism*, Harry Zohn (trans.). London: Verso, 1997, p. 48.
18 CTP, p. 475.

read". The tale is thus a story of failed detection; we will never learn the man's secret. Poe suggests that it is better, since our "little garden of the soul" contains worse crimes and nightmares than the teeming horrors of the world around us.

As a story of detection, "The man of the crowd" repeats the pattern of "The purloined letter." Both follow a trajectory, a circuit devoid of content. In the first story, there is a circular displacement from the legitimate addressee to the intervening minister who steals the object, until Dupin steals it again. For the mysterious "man of the crowd," we have a wild goose chase with no resolution in view, but it is clear that the old man will continue his aimless quest. If we find a certain closure with "The purloined letter," even if the letter left by Dupin is not identical with the first missive, in "The man of the crowd" the only conclusion reached is an overarching principle: the pattern described implies the eternal presence of crime. The concept of "crime" is generalized until it becomes a metaphysical burden, the horror of existential solitude, which sends us back to La Bruyère's epigraph: "*Ce grand malheur, de ne pouvoir être seul.*" (CTP, p. 475) Is the old man who cannot live alone, and needs the bustle of the crowd as a sort of oxygen, in fact a *flâneur* as Baudelaire tends to think,[19] or something else? We keep the suspicion that the subject of modernity is never far from the figure of the criminal. If he is not a criminal yet, it is because he has not been hardened enough by life, or too sick. This is why the observer is a "convalescent," who lets his gaze float on the crowd until he finds an interesting character to follow. As he pursues the shady old man until the bitter end, the narrator's fever flares up. It looks as if the old man's anxiety had started contaminating him. Finally, he understands that the old man embodies the spirit of the crowd, insofar as a crowd is a reflexive entity, which often becomes a spectacle to itself. The crowd can become dangerous, especially when, in Benjamin's analysis, it turns into a revolutionary "mass." Then the idea of "crime" sends us to the notion of salutary revolutionary violence. Usually, the term of *flânerie* supposes leisure and quest, even if its object is a pretext for "distraction." Here, the process splits up into two motivations, a quest for nothing but human proximity, which can lead to crime out of pure boredom, and a quest for the identification of the criminal even before any crime has been committed. The fiction or fantasy of a "future crime" sustains the convalescent observer's interest and thus perpetuates his wish to remain alive. The crowd then comes alive both as machine and as Nature: the crowd is a "tumultuous sea of human heads," it turns into a sea, an ocean, it has its own laws of attraction, its regular ebbs and flows, but its

---

[19] Charles Baudelaire, *The Painter of Modern Life and Other Essays*, Jonathan Mayne (trans.). London and New York: Phaidon, 1995, p. 9.

rhythm is also measured by a social clock, and urban space turns mechanical. Above all, it is ultimately inscrutable: like the old man, "*er lasst sich nicht lesen*", the crowd is an opaque text whose riddle finds a solution via crime and its consequences.

Crime and the "aura"

If the crowd cannot be deciphered at first gaze, it can be reproduced by art, by literature and photography for instance. This is how Benjamin appeals to the Parisian photographer Eugène Atget, who becomes for him the most symptomatic artist of modernity. Atget announced the experimental art of the Surrealists who had in fact re-discovered him, above all because he cleansed the atmosphere that had been polluted by artsy and pictorialist efforts at cheap picturesque tableaux. Atget effectively "killed" the aura: "He was the first to disinfect the stifling atmosphere generated by conventional portrait photography in the age of decline. He cleanses this atmosphere— indeed, he dispels it altogether: he initiates the emancipation of object from aura, which is the most signal achievement of the latest school of photography."[20] To portraits, Atget preferred street scenes, buildings, or details of architectural ornament. His aim was primarily scientific: he wanted to capture a city that was changing fast, so that it could be reconstructed as such, with all its varied idiosyncrasies, if it was to disappear. He kept an eye for the old trades, fast disappearing rag-pickers and street-vendors, yet was never looking for the mere picturesque. In this, Benjamin sees a destructive critique of the *aura* at a time when it was no longer possible: "[Atget] looked for what was unremarked, forgotten, cast adrift. And thus such pictures, too, work against the exotic, romantically sonorous names of the cities; they suck the aura out of reality like water from a sinking ship."[21] The objects or people photographed by Atget have been purified from their romantic associations. They are brought closer to pure shapes without falling into empty formalism. The photographer selects the "refuse of history" just to make a point of immortalizing the most unremarkable objects or details—thus the uniqueness of each shape disappears, swallowed by the possibility of reproduction.

This cleansing role comes to the fore in Paris street scenes. Benjamin mentions a brothel with the number 5,[22] with two women, one leering from a

---

20 Charles Baudelaire (see footnote 19), p. 518.
21 Charles Baudelaire (see footnote 19), p. 518.
22 See Man Ray's album of Atget's photographs, in Susan Laxton (ed.), *Paris as Gameboard. Man Ray's Atgets*. New York: Columbia University, 2002, pictures 16 and 17.

window, the other in the door entrance, yet most pictures are devoid of people. Unlike Poe's "man of the crowd," Atget would take his pictures at dawn so as not to be disturbed, hence his streets often appear ominously empty. This is not a defect for Benjamin, on the contrary: ". . . the city in these pictures looks cleared out, like a lodging that has not yet found a tenant. . . . It gives free play to the politically educated eye, under whose gaze all intimacies are sacrificed to the illumination of detail."[23] Details are purified, clarified and finally illuminated (*Erhellung*) by the proximity of the element of crime. Atget has reconstituted the "scene of the crime" in his deserted urban landscapes. Whereas the analogy is given early in the "Work of art" essay, it provides a fitting conclusion for the "Little history of photography": "It is no accident that Atget's photographs have been likened to those of a crime scene (*eines Tatorts*). But is not every square inch of our cities a crime scene? Every passer-by a culprit (*ein Täter*)? Is not the task of the photographer—descendant of the augurs and haruspices—to reveal guilt and to point out the guilty in his pictures?"[24] It should be clear from this that "crime" is a general metaphysical condition, and that Atget's own postlapsarian "crime" is productive in that it fulfills an important ethical function. The essay concludes nostalgically on the enduring charm of the first photographs ever taken, which are called "beautiful and unapproachable," since they are illuminated "from the darkness of our grandfather's day." This only serves to stress the parricidal nature of the "crime" documented by Atget. Neither the *flâneur* nor the old man of the crowd is innocent. They may not know it, but when they wander in the streets of the metropolis, they are on the look-out for clues of innumerable and untold crimes, crimes of the past as well as crimes of the future.

Atget was able to reveal this historical process because he stood at the cusp between an archaic photographic technique requiring a long pause, and new hand-held cameras that worked much faster. He needed the time to let the image appear. Yet, even the apparently empty streets of Paris photographed by Atget compose a human comedy: if men or women are absent, houses and streets assume human faces. They stare at us, daring us to reconstruct the inexplicable murder mystery they reveal and conceal at the same time. Like Joyce representing Dublin fully just in case the city was destroyed in a civil war, Atget preserved a bygone Paris, keeping a document that would survive war and destruction. He also saw beyond these cityscapes the endless possibility of further transgressions.

The concept of "crimes of the future" derives from a tense relationship with a haunted past fraught with half-forgotten murders, sexual alienation

---

[23] Susan Laxton (ed.) (see footnote 22), p. 519.
[24] Susan Laxton (ed.) (see footnote 22), p. 527.

and social exclusion, as Hamsun suggested. One of its objects is a redefinition of aesthetics, provided we understand the term following Jacques Rancière— we will engage with his theory in Chapter 8, as a "partition of the sensible" or a "parturition of the sensible." Aesthetics is often taken to mean theories about beauty, but in the context of "crimes of the future" it is safer to think of aesthetics as the destruction of beauty. To exemplify this point, I will end this introduction with the survey of a controversial writer who also developed the idea of "crimes of the future." The idea of "future" usually entails a collective picture of what civilization will look like in the next decades. What if all this had to be negated in the name of a nihilistic motto like "No Future"?

The link between collective crimes and the destruction of persons, buildings and cities was made forcefully by Yukio Mishima in the context of post-war Japan. I will now turn to him also because Mishima remains scandalous today. This was caused by the highly dramatic and theatrical nature of his public suicide on November 25, 1970. Two films have been made documenting the last days of the writer, one by Paul Schrader in 1985, and one by Koji Wakamatsu in 2012. They were both presented at the Cannes festival in 1985 and 2012 respectively, but the first film is still banned in Japan, while the second only elicited adverse reviews.[25] I will now focus on one of Mishima's first novels, a novel that presents a real "crime," the burning of a jewel of Japanese architecture by a disgruntled Zen student in 1950. One will have recognized the plot of the *Temple of the Golden Pavilion*,[26] thought by most critics to be one of Mishima's best works. What could have been limited to a psychiatric case study of the convoluted reasons leading the young Mizoguchi to set fire to a temple that he took as an emblem of beauty becomes in Mishima's exalted prose a lyrical account of human perversity, a subtle probing of the death drive, of sexual inhibition, and the confession of an aesthetics of nihilism.

Crime and the abortion of the future

The sexual aspects are no doubt present: the young Zen monk had been traumatized by the vision of his mother having sex with a man while his

---

[25] *Mishima: A Life in Four Chapters*, directed by Paul Schrader, 1985, and *11:25, The Day He Chose His Fate*, directed by Koji Wakamatsu, 2012. Schrader's film includes a dramatization of the *Temple of the Golden Pavilion*. Wakamatsu's film focuses on the political aspects of Mishima's failed coup that led to his *seppuku*.

[26] Yukio Mishima, *The Temple of the Golden Pavilion*, Ivan Morris (trans.), New York, Random House, 1994 [1959]. Abbreviated as TGP and page number. I had discussed this novel and Mishima's aesthetics in *La Beauté Amère*. Seyssel: Champ Vallon, 1986.

father was dying nearby. Later, whenever he is sexually attracted to a girl or woman, the image of the Temple arises and prevents him from performing. Here, Mishima also plays with an obvious model, Dostoevsky's *Crime and Punishment*, to which he alludes indirectly when Mizoguchi finally manages to have sex with a young prostitute; when he goes to see her, he buys "*Crime and Punishment* by Bequaria" on the way (TGP, p. 229). He thinks he will impress her with his culture, and when she starts giving him commonsense lessons, he thrusts the book in her face, to no avail. Behind Beccaria's 1764 pamphlet urging for penal reforms and the abolition of the death penalty, we recognize the main literary model used by Mishima: his Mizoguchi is a variation on Dostoevsky's Raskolnikov. Although he did not depart from the real facts given to him by the Japanese chronicle, he inserts many of his own meditations about Zen, religion, Japan, politics and beauty. Mizoguchi accomplishes only one "crime" before his fateful arsonist acting out: as he is the doorkeeper to the beautiful temple, he is forced by a drunk American soldier to stomp on the belly of a Japanese prostitute. To his surprise, he enjoys this act too much, and feels in him "a bubbling joy" (TGP, p. 77): "I had never imagined that another person's flesh could respond like this with such faithful resilience." (TGP, p. 78) The American gives him two cartons of cigarettes to pay for this sinister service; Mizoguchi gives them to his Superior in order to atone for his deed. The prostitute has a miscarriage as a result of this horrible trampling by the temple acolyte, and then complains to the Temple administration. The Superior buys her silence by giving her money.

The story of prostitution and forced abortion provides an easily recognizable allegory of the fate of Japan under American domination as seen by Mishima, who was later to become a militant for a return to the pre-1945 status. He never accepted that the Emperor had abdicated by renouncing his divine status, never fully accepted the "abortion" of the defeat. At the same time, he chose to distance himself from what he saw as the feminine aspect of Japanese culture, always dominated by Western "devils." He thus chose to live in a Western-style house, with a huge and gleaming statue of Apollo in the garden, a wife and children, while having a second life as a gay man frequenting shady clubs, until he decided to invent his own political movement and start a neo-fascist militia. This Dionysiac side of his life was kept secret (Mishima knew Nietzsche quite well) until the moment when his group of the "Society of the Shield" decided to capture an officer in the Tokyo headquarters of the ground self-defense forces.

In *The Golden Pavilion*, however, the outcome is different: at the end, after the temple has been set afire, Mizoguchi plans to commit suicide, and yet cannot. The transgressive act leads to a Nietzschean affirmation: "I wanted to live." (TGP, p. 262) The student does not stop being ugly, stubborn and resentful, a stutterer dreaming of beauty in such a way that he needs to annihilate it in order to live freely. Once he has destroyed his own allegory of supreme Beauty, Mizoguchi finds reasons to live. His progression is the exact opposite of Mishima's evolution: in thrall to aesthetic ecstasies, having created enough "beauty" in his life and works. Mishima had to go further, and realize the "Harmony of pen and sword"[27] by first becoming a body-builder, then by destroying his newly acquired muscular body once he had turned into a man of action. Hence ritual suicide appeared as the only "beautiful" and "tragic" action left to him. Beauty would have to expose its underside of ugliness, the mass of flesh concealed by the shining form.

This fascination for the flesh inside is revealed in a curious passage of the *Temple of Golden Pavilion*, which ominously anticipates Mishima's fate. It is an incident from the last years of the war, when the young Mizoguchi believes that bombs will destroy the Kyoto temple any day, which never happens. Having then travelled to Osaka, he witnesses casualties of American raids, among which is a factory worker carried on a stretcher with his belly open: "What is so ghastly about exposed intestines? Why, when we see the insides of a human being, do we have to cover our eyes in terror? Why are people shocked at the sight of blood pouring out? Why are a man's intestines ugly? Is it not exactly the same in quality as the beauty of youthful, glossy skin? . . . Why does there seem to be something inhuman about regarding human beings like roses and refusing to make any distinction between the inside of their bodies and the outside? If only human beings could reverse their spirits and their bodies, could gracefully turn them inside out like rose petals and expose them to the spring breezes and to the sun . . ." (TGP, p. 58) Such a meditation does not tally with the usual drift of Mizoguchi's nihilistic reveries. We discover the seed of the psychotic logic exposed much later in *Sun and Steel*[28] from 1968, Mishima's disquieting memoir in which the fantasy of opening up his body to reveal the insides is unleashed fully. Only then will the proof of a "truth" be given, that is when beauty and ugliness are mixed up in blood and gore facing the cleansing sun. Mishima also confesses that his most tenacious belief, after having replaced a body of words with a body of flesh, was what he calls his "day-to-day world destruction." This program was enacted when he staged a political coup that could only end in failure—hence leading to his ritual seppuku. As Lacan stated, only suicide can be considered as a successful gesture—and Mishima wanted to atone for Mizoguchi's failure to kill himself after the destruction of the Temple.

[27] This is the title of Part 4 of Paul Schrader's film, and a motto in the later works of Mishima.
[28] Yukio Mishima, *Sun and Steel*, John Bester (trans.). Tokyo: Kodansha International, 1970.

We can see in Mishima's queer aesthetics a radicalized version of Lee Edelman's powerful meditation on the concept of "No Future." In *No Future*,[29] Lee Edelman attacks a thesis commonly held about the future: that children are our future, and that therefore gay men and women are condemned because of their anti-reproductive attitude. But beyond his excoriating compulsory futurism, the reproduction of the human race being taken as an unquestioned common good, an ideology that he finds among thinkers of the left and of the right, he voices his anger at recent crimes against gay men. Among the many victims he mentions, he focuses on the terrible fate of Matthew Shepard, a 21-year-old gay man who was violently beaten up by two Wyoming men in October 1998. They left him to die, bound up to a wooden fence for almost one day. His tortured body had been mistaken for a scarecrow by startled passers-by.[30] As Edelman explains, there is a curious homology between the accusation of sterility that unveils a common death-drive and this type of hysterical and murderous retaliation. Edelman's flawless and brilliantly written book is a warning to those who insist upon a redemptive futurity predicated on the possibility of having children, whether real or symbolic, since students also count as symbolic offspring. Hence, we could list countless crimes in the present that are caused by structural flaws in our ideologies. Hate crimes, crimes of intolerance, racist crimes, and the constant recurrence of the temptation to solve wars by ethnic cleansing; all of these are caused by beliefs in a "certain" future determined by a single race, creed or sexual orientation. Edelman's powerful hypothesis is that we need to get rid of a certain imaginary future as shaped by lethal clichés of dominant futuristic ideologies. Visions of a rosy "future" often condense major delusions, and a more realistic recognition of our drives is a first step toward the dispelling of such illusion. I will return to these discussions in the following chapters.

What happens then when the death drive and the issue of aesthetics coalesce? This is the question posed by Mishima. His solution was to stage his own suicide in order to leave a "gesture" to posterity. This gesture can be understood via Georg Lukacs's theory of gesture as outlined in *Soul and Form*. In this first collection of essays, Lukacs explains that his main concern is not style: he wants to launch a new vision of life.[31] If "destiny," the ultimate

---

[29] Lee Edelman, *No Future: Queer Theory and the Death Drive*. Durham, Duke University Press, 2004.
[30] Lee Edelman (see footnote 29), pp. 115–16.
[31] Georg Lukacs, *Soul and Form*, edited by John T. Sanders and Katie Terezakis, and with an Introduction by Judith Butler. New York: Columbia University Press, 2010. Hereafter, SF and page number.

questions about the motivation of life, determines form, then form is necessary to put a limit to such an abstraction: "... destiny lifts up things outside the world of things, accentuating the essential ones and eliminating the inessential; but form sets limits around a substance which otherwise would dissolve in the All." (SF, p. 23)

The dialectical opposition between form and life was best exemplified by Kierkegaard's life. The determining moment of the Danish philosopher's career was when he broke his engagement with his fiancée Regine Olsen in 1841. This act made him appear as a vile seducer in the eyes of their community; it changed his life forever; that was a "gesture" giving form and meaning to his entire life. Such a gesture cannot be explained away by any reductive interpretive system, it is meant to be as opaque as a poem and as final as a conversion. Its function is to have been posited as a fixed point in a life that is by definition mobile and fluctuating. It was upon such a private gesture that Kierkegaard founded a form and also his own philosophy, with the tiered succession of the aesthetic, the ethical and the religious. His sudden leap from the indefinite mixture of meaning and meaninglessness that constitutes everyday life into a defining gesture entailed a radical re-foundation: "This, then, was Kierkegaard's honesty: to see everything as being sharply distinct from everything else, system from life, human being from human being, stage from stage: to see the absolute in life, without any petty compromise." (SF, p. 48) In the end, the gesture became not a "gesture" at all, since it had become fully justified; it had become life itself.

It may be that Kierkegaard's tortured decision to break up with Regine was the highest form of love he was capable of. Yet, even this self-torture keeps something ridiculous about it, as Lukacs notes: "... because he is so infinitely remote, [Kierkegaard] barely avoids appearing comic to any woman who, for whatever reason, is not destroyed when he looms up on the horizon of their life." (SF, p. 53) What Kierkegaard presented as his own sacrifice can always be considered ironically—and this was of course the case with Mishima, who was taunted by the Japanese soldiers he was exhorting to be more like "true men" whereas they all thought he was psychotic. They were right. There is something psychotic in the very attempt to try and express the totality of life and death absolutely and all at once. This is can only be achieved by withdrawing from life altogether. This is the moment when a gesture points less in the direction of forms (either of beauty or ugliness) than in that of ethics, if by ethics we can understand something like a creation of something new that cannot be identified with any current form or actual result. However, such a gesture can point to the future, as Kierkegaard's fate has shown, or to the past, as in the case of Mishima's final *seppuku*. I write "final," since, in Mishima's case, we know that he had described this gesture in several stories, including the famous "Patriotism,"[32] he had acted it on stage, he had been photographed and filmed accomplishing the ritual disembowelment. But he had to enact it "for real," in his wish to radically merge with a mythical and heroic Japanese history that concealed the Lacanian Real. This could only be achieved by the nihilistic and deliberate dissolution of the subject.

A cat is being cut

In order to go beyond the dead end apparently brought by such nihilism, we may turn toward the philosophical core of Mishima's novel. It lies in a famous *koan* that keeps being quoted and interpreted differently throughout the text. The parable provides a key with which the narrator wants to solve the riddle of Mizoguchi's negativity. Here is the Zen *koan* in the *Mumonkan* version:

> Nansen Oshō saw monks of the Eastern and Western halls quarrelling over a cat. He held up the cat and said: "If you can give an answer, you will save the cat. If not, I will kill it." No one could answer, and Nansen cut the cat in two.
>
> That evening Jōshû returned, and Nansen told him of the incident. Jōshû took off his sandal, placed it on his head, and walked out. "If you had been there, you would have saved the cat," Nansen remarked.[33]

The first time this Zen *koan* is quoted, it is by the Temple Superior to provide an oblique political commentary on the surrender of Japan after the two atomic bombs have been dropped on Hiroshima and Nagasaki. This would become the major historical trauma that Mishina would try to abolish in his later years. We saw that Mizoguchi expected the golden temple to be destroyed by American bombs; let us note that the firebombing of Tokyo in March 1945 killed about 100,000 people, many more, that is, than in either Hiroshima or Nagasaki at first, but the shrines of Kyoto were deliberately spared by US bombers.

Among the surprises that the story has in store is the fact that Nansen does not explicitly voice any question that would have to be answered adequately to save the cat. It is therefore fitting that the only answer is a mute gesture of humility. We have here the bare bones of a story without any

---

[32] Yukio Mishima, *Patriotism*, Geoffrey W. Sargent (trans.). New York: New Directions, 1966.

[33] *Two Zen Classics: Mumonkan and Hekiganroku*, Katsuki Sekida (trans.). New York and Tokyo: Weatherhill, 1977, pp. 58–9.

psychology, similar in that respect to the legend of King Psammenitus quoted by Walter Benjamin in "The story-teller."[34] We never learn why the Egyptian king, who has seen, without being moved, the execution of his son and the debasement of his daughter, starts crying upon seeing an old servant among the prisoners.

The story of Nansen and the cat receives several interpretations in the course of *The Temple of the Golden Pavilion*, and one can divide these into several levels. There is first a logical level: since the cat divides the community of the monks, the cat has to be divided as well. Then, there is an aesthetic level, upon which Mishima insists: the cat should stand for beauty, hence aesthetics; yet, at the outcome of the parable, beauty has to yield facing ethics, and ethics has to yield facing religion. There is also a political level: the harmony between the two groups of monks has been shattered, by cutting the object of division the superior reestablishes unity and order. The glosses provided by the *Mumonkan* and the *Hekiganroku* all stress a mystical reading in accordance with Zen teachings (Mishima was not extremely interested by this type of interpretation). Thus, by cutting the cat in two, Nansen exemplifies radical detachment from base matter and from the senses. Also, he displays a wholesome indifference to ethical issues. In Kierkegaardian terms, Nansen appears as a true religious subject, an Abraham who would not hesitate to cut Isaac's throat provided he was sure that this was what God requested of his faithful servant.

Let us note a slight discrepancy between the version of *Mumonkan*, in which we hear of only one sandal, while there are two sandals in *Hekiganroku*.[35] The first story is more reverential when it states that the disciple took only one sandal. In Zen *koans*, sandals are symbols of walking, traveling, migrating, they call up a progression though which one changes oneself for the better. We have seen that there were two groups of fighting monks and one cat split into two halves. Jōshū takes one sandal out of two in a calculated gesture of protest against the spreading division. By reaffirming the principle of One over the principle of Two, he combines a gesture of humility (the sandals are in contact with the humus of the earth) with a gesture of love, since love aims at a fusion with the One. Moreover, this gesture quotes the legend of Bodidharma, the founder father of Zen Buddhism who brought his teachings to China from India. According to the legend, Bodidharma died having reached the age of 150 years and yet, three years after his burial, he was spotted by an official of the Wei kingdom walking, wearing only one sandal,

---

[34] Walter Benjamin, "The Story Teller," in *Illuminations*, Harry Zohn (trans.). New York: Schocken, pp. 89–90.
[35] *Two Zen Classics* (see footnote 33), case 64, p. 320.

saying he was going back to India. He predicted the imminent death of the local king, which turned out to be true soon after. His tomb was opened, and Bodidharma was found to have been buried with only one sandal. Here, the faithful Jōshû reenacts the *topos* of a walking dead man wandering with a single sandal in order to undo the scandal of the cat's killing. If, on the other hand, it is the version of *Hekiganroku* that is right, we must imagine the faithful disciple trying to balance two sandals on his head while walking out—was he walking backwards then? How did he steady the dirty soles on his shaved head? Being modest, he can even find an excuse: "I like walking with my shoes on my head, they last longer this way." We are indeed in the domain of slapstick and non-sequiturs so often associated with popular versions of Zen, and can imagine Jōshû walking away with the syncopated gait of a Charlie Chaplin, just to make fun of Nansen's superior indifference to life and death.

So far, we have assumed that Jōshû's gesture "responds" to Nansen's unspoken question; yet this may not be simply a response but a rebuttal. Jōshû walks out, which means that he wants to abstain both from the internecine rivalries between groups of monks and from the rule of a pitiless leader. Yet, it would be too easy to denounce Nansen as a sadistic autocrat. After all, he had left a chance to the monks who didn't even try to say anything, which should teach them a lesson. Nansen is closer to Lenin when he prefers to act quickly and drastically in order to solve a crisis.[36] Or he can be seen as a Lacanian analyst forcefully destroying a fetish by producing a bold "cut" in words and deeds—the cat clearly plays the role of a fetish for the monks— which is why it is replaced by a dirty sandal in the disciple's gesture of atonement. At that point, cat fetishism will be undone by a parody of shoe fetishism. What Jōshû shows to his Superior, thus upping the ante, is that one can destroy fetishistic beauty with more equanimity, discreetly, humbly, and with no blood spilled.

We may be tempted to compare this *koan* from *Mumonkan* and *Hekiganroku* with the Biblical story of the judgment of Solomon in 1 Kings. There, as we know, the King only pretends to cut the baby in two in order to let the true mother reveal herself. Cutting the child in half is a decoy, the threat leads the evil prostitute (or sister-in-law, according to some interpretations) to expose her bitter envy of the living baby's mother. And yet, at a philosophical level, one may argue that it is not always possible to "split differences" in this manner. If the issue is life or death, and not just conscious rationalizations and unconscious desire, there is no way one can divide a

---

[36] See Slavoj Žižek, "Afterword: Lenin's Choice," in *Revolution at the Gates*, Slavoj Žižek (ed.). London: Verso, 2002, pp. 167–336.

subject with a sword. Alain Badiou has often stated it, following Lacan's intuitions: truth can only be produced by a cut in the real. He would have approved Nansen's drastic and irreversible decision to cut the Gordian knot directly on the tender flesh of a cat. We will develop some of the figures that this cut can take. To return just for a last second to Nansen and his doomed cat: what words would *you* have said to save the poor animal?[37]

---

[37] I'll suggest here that one adequate response to this question was provided by Soseki Natsume's title, when he published his famous novel, *I am a Cat*, in 1905 (Tuttle: North Clarendon, 2002).

1

How Global Should Theory Be?

We children of the future, how could we be at home in this today? We feel disfavor for all ideals that might lead one to feel at home even in this fragile, broken time of transition; as for its "realities," we do not believe that they will last. The ice that still supports people today has become very thin; the wind that brings the thaw is blowing; we ourselves who are homeless constitute a force that breaks open ice and other all too thin "realities."[1]

I think we ought to read only the kind of books that wound and stab us. If the book we are reading doesn't wake us up with a blow on the head, what are we reading it for? . . . But we need the books that affect us like a disaster, that grieve us deeply, like the death of someone we loved more than ourselves, like being banished into forests far from everyone, like a suicide. A book must be the axe for the frozen sea inside us.[2]

My two epigraphs play variations on the trope of a piece of ground compared to the surface of a frozen lake or sea; for Nietzsche, it entails a vision of the future as impending catastrophe, an ecological catastrophe that doubles as a metaphysical collapse, a total decentering for those who think that they had their "home," an impending fall from which they are blissfully unaware. For Kafka, the frozen sea is within us, it allegorizes our paralyses, inhibitions and neuroses; the effect of powerful writing is the unleashing of an affective storm that will shatter subjective isolation. These texts are not stating contradictory theses: they both call for a new wisdom of the future, a new literary and philosophical experience that will destroy the illusions of having a "ground," replacing it with an abyss. Happiness and homeliness are delusions, one should prefer the pathos of bewildering suffering that will put an end to contemporary alienation. The future may bring more pain but the passions it harbingers will bring better relationships with oneself and others.

[1] Friedrich Nietzsche, *The Gay Science*, Walter Kaufman (trans.). New York, Vintage, 1974, p. 338.
[2] Franz Kafka's letter to Oskar Pollak, *Letters to Friends, Family and Editors*, Richard and Clara Winston (trans.). New York, Schocken, 1977, p. 16.

My hope is thus to explore the state of what Nietzsche calls "homelessness," a term that he uses to repudiate once and for all the temptation of a nationalist resourcing of the self:

> We who are homeless are too manifold and mixed racially and in our descent, being "modern men," and consequently do not feel tempted to participate in the mendacious racial self-admiration and racial indecency that parades in Germany today as a sign of a German way of thinking and is doubly false and obscene among the people of the "historical sense."[3]

Talking to this new "European" modernity capable of accepting mixity and hybridization, Nietzsche parts ways with the composer whom he calls the "Musician of the Future." This is of course Wagner, to whose *Zukunftsmusik* ("music of the future") I will return later. Nietzsche does not believe in progress and rails against the "sirens who in the market place sing of the future."[4] He cannot believe in socialism and equal rights for all, he distrusts the cult of "humanity," bringing to these pious notions an air of danger and abrasive skepticism. The wind bringing a warmer air and thawing the ice is not a tropical breeze but, to quote Benjamin, a "storm blowing from Paradise" pushing the Angel of History forward: "This storm irresistibly propels him into the future to which his back is turned, while the pile of debris before him grows skyward."[5]

We have glimpsed with Poe's "man of the crowd" a different series of tropes, with Poe's complex conceptual knot binding together the idea of crime, the idea of an uncertain future with new scientific theories to be elaborated, along with another version of the new subjectivity, a "homeless" subjectivity to be sure, which is contemporaneous with modernity. Modernity generates the thrills deriving from the expectation of a crime before it is committed, and leaves room for a general destruction of ancient values. The "crime," as we have seen with Benjamin, is inescapably linked to the process of modernization and exploitation brought about by the development of international capitalism. It seems that here is our unavoidable future, even though we may be uncertain as to its precise forms, and being warned by films like *Minority Report*, we know that one will not solve the conundrum by preventing murders to come. Should we believe in Communism as a healthier alternative, as Slavoj Žižek and Alain Badiou argue? Or should we aim for a

---

[3] Nietzsche, see footnote 1, p. 340.
[4] Nietzsche, see footnote 1, p. 338.
[5] Walter Benjamin, "Theses on the Philosophy of History," *Illuminations*, Harry Zohn (trans.). New York, Schocken, 1968, pp. 257–8.

more ethical society, more aware of the violence perpetrated against minorities, animals and those we call "deviants"? These are huge questions, and I can only tackle them from the point of view of Theory as it fits into a larger cultural picture. Theory should not be taken as attempting to discuss tricky issues beforehand, as if the simple fact of thinking about future crimes could contain or prevent them. No, unhappily, there will be new crimes, we can be sure of this, and in some of them, like organ thefts, identity thefts, the computer hacking of citizens by entire governments, drone killings, we recognize the lineaments of a very threatening futurity. And such a future is already there, and it seems underpinned by the inexorable logic of globalization. This logic has been described clearly by Marx and Engels.

Global cultural capital

In *The Communist Manifesto*, Marx and Engels had written those prophetic words in 1847:

> The bourgeoisie has through its exploitation of the world-market given a cosmopolitan character to production and consumption in every country. ... In place of the old local and national seclusion and self-sufficiency, we have intercourse in every direction (*ein allseitiger Verkehr*), universal interdependence of nations. And as in material, so also in intellectual production. The intellectual creations of individual nations become common property (*Gemeingut*). National one-sidedness and narrow-mindedness become more and more impossible, and from the numerous national and local literatures, there arises a world literature (*Weltliteratur*).[6]

This world-literature emerged in full view of the European public when the first Nobel prize in literature was given to a non-European writer, Rabindranath Tagore, in 1913. Tagore became a self-conscious and determined bridge between traditions hitherto deemed incompatible. In those often quoted sentences, Marx and Engels are less completing Goethe's idealist and universalist project of a universal literature than showing the changes brought about by the new material conditions of the market of ideas. It is also in culture that private property will be abolished, as they state. This

---

6 Karl Marx and Friedrich Engels, *The Communist Manifesto* [1847], in Karl Marx, *Selected Writings*, David McLellan (ed.), Oxford: Oxford University Press, 1977, pp. 224–5; and *Das kommunistische Manifest*, reprint, Vienna: Volksbuchhandlung, 1930, p. 14.

is an idea that has been developed by Jacques Derrida in an interview
with the French-Korean artist Soun-gui Kim.[7] Taking his cue from the
untranslatable phrase of "*par-dessus le marché*" (meaning roughly "on top of
all that," "in supplement") with which the artist had begun interrogating him,
Derrida explains that one cannot jump over the market or pretend that it
does not exist. However, he expresses multiple reservations facing those who
praise "globalization" as a new panacea; for him, indeed, globalization is
nothing but the widespread effects of the domination of international
capitalism. He answers Soun-gui Kim thus:

> One can begin by suspecting this concept because, very often, it is used,
> manipulated by some people who want you to believe that the world
> population has an immediate access not only to all the commodities, all
> the ideas, all the resources created by labor, but also to all the works of
> art. But we know that is merely a slogan.

In the rest of the conversation, Derrida refers to his analysis of
"globalatinization," a portmanteau-word that he had coined in "Faith and
Knowledge" to describe the uniformization of the world along lines fixed by
the laws of the Roman Empire and the subsequent conflation of Christianity
and imperialism.[8] Yet, "Latin" is a slight misnomer since it has been replaced
by Anglo-American as the vehicular idiom of globalization. If one is to prefer
the term of "*mondialisation*," as Jean-Luc Nancy and Emily Apter have argued,
going back to a series of post-Heideggerian thinkers like Eugen Fink and
Kostas Axelos who, like Heidegger, connect a thinking of the world as a whole
entity with pre-Socratic questions such as one finds in Anaximander,
Heraclitus and Parmenides,[9] it is in the hope of avoiding the double bind of a
transnationalism predicated on a projection of today's balance of powers.[10]

---

[7] Jacques Derrida and Soun-gui Kim, "Par-dessus le marché, un art à l'époque de la
mondialisation," interview of March 7, 2002; film shown at the Art Biennale of Gwangju,
South Korea, Spring 2002. Conversation partly translated into Korean in the journal
Yolkan Misul, July 2002.

[8] See Jacques Derrida, "Faith and Knowledge," in *Acts of Religion*, p. 50, note 7, in which the
translator explains the difference between Derrida's "*mondialatinisation*" and his
translation by "globalatinization." See also *Acts of Religion*, pp. 66–7.

[9] See Eugen Fink, "Spiel als Weltsymbol" [1960], in *Gesamtausgabe*, Vol. 7, Freiburg: Alber,
2010; Kostas Axelos, *Vers la pensée planétaire*, Paris: Minuit, 1964; and *Le jeu du monde*,
Paris: Minuit, 1969.

[10] See Emily Apter's excellent chapter "Keywords 5: 'Monde,'" in *Against World Literature:
On the Politics of Untranslatability*, London and New York: Verso, 2013, pp. 175–90; and
Jean-Luc Nancy, *The Sense of the World*, Jeffrey Librett (trans.), Minneapolis: University
of Minnesota Press, 1997.

In order to avoid the leveling impact of globalization, Derrida prefers paying attention to idiomatic differences in works of art, all the while accepting that there is an undeniable need for circulation and reproduction. He hopes that artists will combine "poetical and political" forms of resistance to the drift of globalization: "Artists have the responsibility to create works of art that, through their strength, forbid the impoverishing leveling or homogeneitization. Often I associate homogeneity with hegemony." In order to resist "hegemo-homogeneitization," artists should not only think of building new communities but also, at times, of withdrawing from the frantic circulation of cultural commodities:

> And to use the word of "world" (*monde*), or *mondialisation*, at times there is a more powerful "*mondializing*" or "universalizing" adventure when someone is alone, locked up in a studio, who does not travel or circulate works, but creates things that acquire the power of universality.[11]

As an antidote to the illusion that one is a "global artist" because one's works travel between Paris and New York, Derrida opposes Paul Celan's *Meridian*, with the idea of a "secret of the encounter" (*Geheimnis der Begegnung*). This implies a certain silence, allied with an openness to the other, both of which are often disregarded in view of a fascination for rapid international exchanges and successful distribution of works via endless reproduction.

I have quoted Emily Apter's excellent book on the politics of translation, and agree with her insistence that there is "untranslatability" in many texts, words, concepts. Yet, I would argue that even if one should not erase differences in a mistaken belief that we have to be more "global," the new cultural communism brought about by world-wide technology and instant access to all sorts of databases entails that if theory will have to become a theory of translation, it will presuppose the possibility of translation. In the same way as today, Marxism has split between a historical balance-sheet in which one can oppose failures and successes, and a body of texts dating from the second half of the nineteenth century, texts in which our modernity is still inscribed, and we may see the new theory of the twenty-first century as a sort of cultural communism—a communism of ideas, which does not mean an idealism. This has to do with the possibility of translation that is implied by the very fact that we observe that there is something that is untranslatable.

When Derrida constantly reminds his translators that he is playing with untranslatable idioms (like "*mondialisation*"), whenever he asks: "How will

---

[11] Jean-Luc Nancy, see footnote 10, p. 6.

you translate this?" it is because, in fact, he expects a solution—or if not, at least a discourse about the impossibility of translation. I will allude here to two philosophers who apparently hold opposite positions on translation, Alain Badiou, who refuses the idea of the untranslatable, and Heidegger, whose later philosophy turns into a meditation on the untranslatable etymologies of various languages.

Intranslations

In March 1954, Tomio Tezuka, a Japanese Germanist who was translating Hölderlin and Trakl, came to Freiburg to visit the German philosopher Martin Heidegger. Tezuka and Heidegger talked about the difficulties of translating poetry, about aesthetics in German and in Japanese, and also about the definition of language in general. This led to the dialogue written by Heidegger, "A dialogue on language."[12] In his version, Heidegger is simply "the Inquirer" and Tezuka, a "Japanese." They reminisce about a common friend, Count Kuki, who knew many languages. They try to reach a deeper understanding of the other language's linguistic nuances, since both know that one only thinks in one's language. The difficulty is thus to distinguish concepts from idioms, and it may not be possible. The remark is made early enough by "I":

> I. Here you are touching on a controversial question which I often discussed with Count Kuki—the question whether it is necessary and rightful for Eastasians to chase after the European conceptual system.
> J. In the face of modern technicalization and industrialization of every continent, there would seem to be no escape any longer.
>
> (OWL, p. 3)

We see how globalization was perceived by Heidegger in the fifties: it is predicated upon the accelerated industrialization of the world in the name of newly unleashed technology. Here, though, the remark comes from the Japanese; his country had begun its industrialization at the turn of the century, taking Germany as a model. The use of the conditional tense leaves

---

[12] Martin Heidegger, "A dialogue on language between a Japanese and an inquirer," in *On The Way to Language*, Peter D. Hertz (trans.). San Francisco: Harper, 1971, pp. 1–55 (hereafter abbreviated as OWL and page number); and "Aus einem Gespräch von der Sprache, Zwischen einem Japaner und einem Fragenden," *Unterwegs zur Sprache*, Pfullingen: Neske, 1959, pp. 83–155.

some hope: perhaps one will pay attention to the singularity of certain terms and idioms, reaching in a dialogue a mutual understanding of their untranslatable specificity. The main danger to avoid is presented in those terms: "The language of the dialogue constantly destroys the possibility of saying what the dialogue was about." (OWL, p. 5) In order to avoid this pitfall, the two interlocutors heap up methodological precautions and discuss techniques of interpretation, from Biblical hermeneutics to philology via phenomenology, discourses that had been brought together by Heidegger at the beginning of *Being and Time*. They also comment on a few phrases. One of these, "House of being," used to qualify language, belongs to Heidegger while others are purely Japanese. "I" and "J" comment thus on *Iki*, presented as a key to aesthetics (the alluring charm, the pure delight of beckoning stillness, etc.), *Kû* (emptiness, the sky or the "Open"), and finally the most tricky term, *Koto Ba*, which usually means simply "language" in Japanese.

After several preparatory etymological explanations that unpack meanings and images by teasing out the metaphorical fields of these terms, like the presence of leaves unfolding, "I" reaches a verbal equivalent of *Koto* in German that is accepted as adequate by "J": it is "the appropriating occurrence of the lightening message of grace," an opaque concatenation of words that makes slightly more sense in German: "*Koto* wäre denn das Ereignis der lichtenden Botschaft der Armut."[13] A more literal translation would be: "*Koto* would then be the event created by illuminating news that grace is near." Have we entered Heidegger's later philosophy of language, or is this a true "translation"? Indeed, this cannot be a successful translation since the two interlocutors will yet need to gloss other words, like *charis* in Greek and all its shadings, before realizing that the effort to talk about language brings them to a circle. Having come back to the principle of a hermeneutic circularity with which they had begun, they will both agree that it was language that spoke through them ("language speaks," *die Sprache spricht* being the leitmotiv of the whole book). But does language speak in German—with this untranslatable repetition of the etymon, or does it unfold its leaves in Japanese?

Both speakers end up conceding that *Koto ba* will finally turn into a "speaking legend," since it is made to signify *die Sage* or *das Sagenhafte*, literally the "legend" of a "legendary saying." Language speaks mostly through multiple "signs" or "winks" (*Winke*) that call up Being while being shared by its carriers and messengers. One would have to read the entire dialogue closely to attend to all its subtle ramifications, but one conclusion is certain:

while discussing untranslatable expressions in Greek, German and Japanese, the two discussants have managed to translate series of words into different languages while testifying to a creative performativity of language, a performance from which meaning derives and is not preexisting to it. What Heidegger has achieved in this atypical Platonician dialogue about language comes very close to what Alain Badiou has called a "hypertranslation."

This is a term that Badiou uses for his adaptation of Plato's *Republic*. In this remarkable book, Badiou provides a free translation of Plato's famous dialogue in which he takes huge liberties: he modernizes the time-frame, insets the French revolution and the Soviet revolution, often mentions Stalin, Hitler and Mao, he cuts passages he does not like; he combines several characters, for instance he changes a man into a woman, Amantha, who then plays a crucial role, and above all he rewrites important concepts. Thus, when Plato talks about the gods, Badiou translates into Lacanese idiom as the "big Other"; he replaces the theory of irrational numbers with discussions of algebraic topology, he changes the divisions of the text, he often uses colloquialisms and swearwords. Most purists and specialists would be horrified if this was presented as a straight translation, which is not the case. In fact, the result is funny, exciting, exhilarating and consistently thought-provoking. It is an "intranslation," whose aim is to make you think. Badiou also knows that this massive dialogue is rarely read in its entirety by students who are given a few well-chosen passages like the allegory of the cave, the criticism of mimesis, the refusal of poetic images that distort truth, the noble lie, etc. He rejects such an anthologization of Plato via culled excerpts, preferring to make us actively participate in the unfolding of a thought that has contemporary relevance. Plato thus keeps asking: What is the ideal political system? What is the value of truth? Why should we avoid falling into the traps of the Sophists and Cynics who reduce truth to subjective opinion? Is Communism still an option as a political regime today? Is mathematics linked to scientific discoveries? How can one be true to a life-changing event, such as falling in love or joining a political party? Indeed, these questions sketch the contours of Badiou's system, founded as it is on Plato, Lacan, Sartre and Frege.

In order to be more precise, I'll give an example; it's one of the passages that triggered most negative comments about Plato's fascism and totalitarianism: the exclusion of the poets from the ideal city. Here is what this becomes in Badiou's freewheeling version:

> If a poet of that type, who's adept at captivating us by constantly transforming language expressions, shows up on our country's doorsteps, we'll give him a stirring public tribute. We won't hesitate to declare that

he's a holy and miraculous being, a wizard of life. We'll anoint him with all the perfumes of Araby and crown him with laurels. And then we'll escort him back to the border, explaining to him that there are no men of his kind in our country and that there never can be any, because we've created a more sober, less obviously appealing kind of poetry, which is closer to prose, or even to mathematics, by adapting it to our overall project and to the type of education that goes along with it.

That's all very well and good, said *Amantha*, but our country won't *have* any doorsteps or borders! You'll be well aware that its project is purely internationalist in scope. The proletariat has no country. A communist border agent would be a pathetic oxymoron!

Which only proves, *Socrates shot back*, that what I was suggesting was an *image*; that I was speaking metaphorically. Trust me, this vision of the poet, banned from the city, will become famous!

Oh, then *you*'re the poet with the deceptive language and the enticing images!

Well, *concluded Socrates*, I entrust you with the task of personally seeing to my deportation.

They all burst out laughing.[14]

What is generally a scene of philosophical consternation becomes here a joyful moment of dialogical one-upmanship. Badiou is aware of the fact that the trope of "poets excluded from the Republic" will be known to most students, and he decides to play with it, adding at the same time a paradox: how can the poet be excluded from an international and cosmopolitan "republic" in which all men and women would be able to choose between many social roles? He redoubles the paradox by showing how much of a poet and mimetic artist Plato was, which implies that he should have had to exclude himself from his perfect utopia. Is he thus both faithful to Plato's original meaning (poets are dangerous and should be excluded from the *polis*) and twists it in a series of dialectical reversals.

Another example of the strategy of "intranslation" would be provided by Badiou's essay on Beckett's last trilogy, a text that Beckett had despaired of translating into his "other" language, French. For Badiou, there is nothing so idiomatic that one could not think with it or through it, and to prove it he works from the French translation provided by Elizabeth Fournier after Beckett's death, *Cap au Pire*. Thus starting from a translation, and one that

14 Alain Badiou, *Plato's Republic: A Dialogue in 16 chapters*, Susan Spitzer (trans.), New York: Columbia University Press, 2012, pp. 88–9.

hadn't been revised or authored by Beckett, he treats the text as a set of philosophical theses—the main maxim being "the imperative of saying."[15] Badiou approaches *Worstward Ho* by comparing it with Heraclitus's poetic maxims, with Plato's *Sophist* or with Mallarmé's *Un Coup de dés*. The essay Badiou devotes to Beckett's text in *Handbook of Inaesthetics* defines it as a "short philosophical treatise, as a treatment in shorthand of the question of being."[16] Of course, Badiou's reading is intensely abstract and philosophical, yet, once translated into English by Toscano, one can verify that it has managed to recycle—to quote literally—most of the terms, words, concepts and phrases found in Beckett's text. Beckett's text begins in typically terse, abrupt and idiomatic manner:

> On. Say on. Be said on. Somehow on. Till nohow on. Said nohow on. . . .
>   All of old. Nothing else ever. Ever tried. Ever failed, No matter. Try again. Fail again. Fail better. . . .
>   No future in this. Alas yes.[17]

We know that Beckett himself had tried to translate his own text into French, and failed, at length concluding that this was utterly impossible. For instance, there is no way one could find a French equivalent of the perfect poetic and philosophical reversal of "On" into "No."[18] This does not deter Badiou, who boldly breaks down *Worstward Ho* in a series of theoretical propositions (that I slightly rephrase or condense):

1. "On" marks the imperative of saying, which is the first and only law of the text.
2. Being is equated with the "void" in a systematic exercise in disappearance.
3. We readers are inscribed in being (or in ontology) as are the characters in the text: the one of a woman, the two of an old man and a child. For them, the universe is a void infested by shades. "Dimness" is a condition of being, thus being is defined as that which can "worsen". Hence, existence is a constant "worsening" brought about by language, since it is always possible to say "worse" what has already been said badly. Yet language cannot be swallowed by the absolute nothing.

---

[15] Alain Badiou, "Being, existence, thought: prose and concept," in *Handbook of Inaesthetics*, Alberto Toscano (trans.). Stanford: Stanford University Press, 2005, p. 91.
[16] Badiou, see footnote 15, p. 90.
[17] Samuel Beckett, "Worstward Ho," in *Nohow On*. London: John Calder, 1989, pp. 101–3.
[18] See James Knowlson, *Damned to Fame: The Life of Samuel Beckett*. New York: Simon and Schuster, 1996, p. 601.

4. Thought is the recollection of (1) and (3). It is produced in a head or skull in whose confines the old drama of the Cartesian *cogito* is replayed endlessly.
5. The exercises in worsening are of three types, thus generating three "shades": they can bear on the one, they can bear on the two, and finally they can bear on the head or brain or skull. In the exercises in worsening that testify to the sovereignty of language, addition is equivalent to subtraction.
6. Worsening is a labor that demands courage, the courage to articulate the truth. Since there will be no end to language, this courage is founded upon a rapport between words and truth.
7. Since the void is unworsenable, worsening aims at getting always closer to the void. The void can only be crossed in an event that remains unspeakable.
8. What has been gained by exercises in worsening is first a rigorous definition of the "two" of love as the root of migration and change, and then a sense of joy and beauty deriving from the link posited between words and truth.
9. Finally, on the last page, there is something like the irruption of an event, similar to the way a "constellation" appears on the page (and in the sky) at the end of Mallarmé's poem *Un Coup de dés*. Here, the old woman has turned into a grave, it seems, but the imperative of language remains and all must begin again.[19]

Even though I cannot follow this reading to the end, since I am not convinced by the last point and cannot see why any final "event" should mark the last page, I have to confess that I admire the way Badiou reads the most untranslatable poetic text Beckett ever penned. He makes sense when he presents *Worstward Ho* as a philosophical treatise bridging the gap between the ontology of "worsening" and basic issues of ethics. On this reading, Beckett would make readers participate in an ethical act, having them struggle with meaning and with truth, a difficult truth to which all his writings testify. Such courage is not abstract since it is concretely embodied in the most opaque words. Badiou finally concludes that Beckett's method is the inversion of Husserl's phenomenological "suspension of the world" to reach the structure of subjectivity. What Beckett achieves is a method of subtraction, in which the subject is suspended to see what happens to being, and being is suspended to see what happens to subjectivity. It is truly a

---

[19] Badiou, see footnote 15, pp. 97–120.

Husserlian cogito turned upside down.[20] Badiou's double strategy finds a justification there: on the one hand, he quotes the very words provided by Beckett (such as "worsening"), and on the other hand, he articulates them in his own ontology, following his own abstract schemes and logical categories. For instance, it is his personal culture that makes him superimpose *Un Coup de dés* and *Worstward Ho* (there is no visible allusion to Mallarmé in Beckett's text.) In the end, his commentary's length is more than the double that of Beckett's prose poem. It includes it almost entirely while incorporating it forcibly into his philosophical system—a rare feat of close reading allied with a radical "translation."

Compensation

My two examples, Badiou and Heidegger, should converge on one main point. The role of theory is to compensate for the numerous "untranslatables" that abound in literature and philosophy. These would go from the most obvious, like the impossibility of translating into English Heidegger's major conceptual couple, the opposition between *Sein* (Being) and *Seiendes* (being), whereas it can be done in French with *être* and *étant*. We have a similar problem with Freud's concept of *das Unheimliche*, usually rendered as "the Uncanny." We lose something that is dense and paradoxical in *Unheimlich*, a term that echoes the "home" (*Heim*) and yet cannot be translated as "unhomely." By using "uncanny," we can at least play on a couple like canny vs. uncanny, whereas the French equivalent "*l'inquiétante étrangeté*," neatly poetic as it is, will not allow this.

Translation issues can be more topical or historical. I had to refer to the influential *Cahiers Marxistes–Léninistes* launched in Paris 1964 so as to discuss the context of May 1968 in France. I remembered that each issue quoted the same sentence from Lenin as an epigraph: "*La théorie de Marx est toute-puissante parce qu'elle est vraie*," "Marx's theory is all-powerful because it is true." A translator might hesitate before rendering "*toute-puissante*" as "all-powerful," since one may require a stronger adjective conveying more than "powerful." Yet, if the French ring of the term is religious—a true equivalent would be "almighty"—a translation by "almighty" would look too ironical or aggressive. If the adjective invokes a power typically granted to God and religion, a literal translation would sound like a critique: French

---

[20] Badiou, see footnote 15, pp. 117–18.

Maoists were all Catholics in disguise (many of them were). Thus, "all powerful," by no means highly idiomatic, is a better option.

Such problems become more acute when authors deliberately play on the poetic resources of the languages they use; here Lacan comes readily to mind. When I edited the *Cambridge Companion to Lacan*, I had to decide whether I would let Charles Shepherdson develop certain plays on signifiers as Lacan did when comparing "*étrange*" (strange) and "*être ange*" (being an angel), or when the formula for "*nécessité*" (necessity) was based upon "*ce qui ne cesse de s'écrire*" (what does not stop being written). In the first case, there was no doubt: the pun could be explained simply, a short gloss was sufficient.[21] Yet, when it came to the complex logic of contingency and necessity introduced by Lacan in Seminar XX, we decided not to stick to the letter of the argument; one of its hinges rests on the homophony between "*nécessité*" and "*ne cesse pas*,"[22] which as such does not make sense in English. On the other hand, its meaning—there is one—can be rendered by purely logical means. A simple diagram illustrating the four Aristotelian modalities served this aim better. It was used by Shepherdson to provide a brilliant commentary of Lacan's logics of sexuation.[23] Similar echolalic plays on signifiers like "*amour*" and "*amur*" were discussed, although in a different context, by Diana Rabinovitch. In the end, these puns could not support the weight of a long analysis.[24] In the same way, what may appear as one of the most intractable terminological problems in Lacanian theory, his decision to leave his concept of "*objet a*" untranslated, ended up being easy to solve, since one can understand it in English as "object a." The fact that this "a" derives from the "a" of "*autre*" and that the "big Other" (in English) is written capitalized "A" in French (and at times in English) because of "*grand Autre*" is similarly a hurdle that can be pointed out. The task of theory is precisely to make sense of all the obstacles; the simple fact of becoming aware of some difficulty, opacity or total loss will require a supplement of commentary, which in the end may entail a certain gain at the theoretical level.

The terms call up those used by Stéphane Mallarmé who, in a famous prose text, deplored the fact that individual languages do not always provide the best sounds for emotions or objects we would like them to evoke. Thus in

---

[21] See Charles Shepherdson, "Lacan and philosophy," *The Cambridge Companion to Lacan*, Jean-Michel Rabaté (ed.). Cambridge: Cambridge University Press, 2003, p. 139.

[22] See Jacques Lacan, *Séminaire XX, Encore*, Jacques-Alain Miller (ed.). Paris: Seuil, 1975, p. 86; and *Encore, On Feminine Sexuality, The Limits of Love and Knowledge*, Bruce Fink (trans.). New York: Norton, 1998, p. 94.

[23] Shepherdson, see footnote 21, pp. 144–6.

[24] See Diana Rabinovitch, "What is a Lacanian clinic?", see footnote 21.

French, *"jour"* (day) sounds dark and sullen, whereas *"nuit"* is light and brilliant. Most words are pesky contrarians, they tend not to sound like the meanings we ascribe to them, or they hesitate between contradictory suggestions. But as Mallarmé argues, here is the true source of poetry: poetry attempts to make these words sound different thanks to a linguistic machine that modifies them. This ultimately derives from the fact that there is no "absolute" or perfect language.

> Languages are imperfect insofar as they are many; the absolute one is lacking: thought considered as writing without accessories, not even whispers, still *stills* immortal speech; the diversity, on earth, of idioms prevents anyone from proffering words that would otherwise be, when made uniquely, the material truth. (. . .) *Only*, be aware that *verse would not exist*: it, philosophically, makes up for language's deficiencies, as a superior supplement.[25]

Here, Mallarmé has written *"rémunérer le défaut des langues"*: this presupposes a certain economy, which sends us in the direction of translation. It is in the domain of translation that one speaks commonly of "losses," "gains" and "compensations." What poetry achieves is a "refund" or "supplement," that is a general "compensation" in which one can place art as such. Ontologically, it compensates for the "natural" deficiencies of languages and idioms. What is true of poetry is even more relevant of theory. Mallarmé had been right to use the word "philosophically," and he was aware of the huge stakes of his theory; he had not only invented a theory of thought that anticipated Derrida's grammatology (we think by writing silently), but also ushered in a poetics of dialectical "sublation"[26] or sublimation. Thanks to the work of art, words become Things: not simple counters to be exchanged, but works of beauty to be admired.

Even if it often fails on the level of aesthetics and pure beauty, theory accomplishes a similar "sublation" when it translates concepts into other concepts while remaining aware that not everything is transparent or immediately translatable. In that sense, it opposes the ideology of globalization that believes everything to be translatable immediately or without loss. By

---

[25] Stéphane Mallarmé, "Crisis of Verse," in *Divagations*, Barbara Johnson (trans.). Cambridge, MA: Harvard University Press, 2007, pp. 205–6.

[26] I am quoting Derrida's famous translation of Hegel's concept of *Aufhebung* as "relève," which has then been rendered as "sublation." See Derrida's essay on "Qu'est-ce qu'une traduction relevante?" Paris, Editions de l'Herne, 2005. Translated into English by Lawrence Venuti as "What is a 'relevant' translation," *Critical Inquiry*, vol. 27, no. 2, Winter 2001, pp. 174–200.

insisting upon the effort of its "compensations," theory displaces the unique idiom, the incommensurable etymon toward a certain discourse in which differences are talked through. Its objects are not poetic images, as in Mallarmé's examples, but concepts and logical chains of reasons inserted in a specific context determined by history, language and culture. This is why it has to face squarely the problem posed on the one hand by the systems of thought that we call "cultures" and today's general drift toward homogenization in the name of globalization. At the same time, just as for Mallarmé there is no absolute language embodying truth immediately, in the case of theory we know that there is not absolute discourse that can be taken as a unique foundation. Thus, when I translated the meaning of a Zen *koan* into the dialectic of three realms, the aesthetic, the ethical and the religious, all borrowed from Kierkegaard, it was not simply because I had quoted the Danish philosopher just before. It is because these notions are better known to most Westerners than the dialectics of emptiness and negation typical of classical Buddhism.

This is why one sees more and more projects that attempt explicating huge foundational differences between concepts and cultures. I want to mention François Jullien's *Entrer dans une pensée, ou des possibles de l'esprit.*[27] The book, whose title could be translated as "How to enter into a Thought, or the possibilities of Spirit," attempts to compare three foundational beginnings: the first statement of the *I Ching, or Book of Changes*, the Hebrew Bible and Hesiod's *Theogony*, pointing out enormous problems of translation, as for the term of Qian, meaning "creative force" in the *I Ching*, and comparing it with *"Bereshit"* (in the beginning) as well with the first invocation to the Muses of the Helicon: Μουσά ων Ἑλικωνιά δων ἀ ρχώμεθ᾽ ἀ εί δειν.

By focusing on the initial impetus for change, the force or originary power that moves to impel the world or song, thus the initiation of the process of creation, Jullien knows that he is tackling huge semantic problems of correspondences. I cannot detail here his patient analysis, and will limit my remarks to his decision not to talk about different "traditions" and prefer the term of "inner heterotopias" that he borrows from Bruno Latour.[28] To the term of "tradition," he opposes the epistemological opening that each network of idiomatic terms will bring about. If he can observe that Chinese thinkers are more attuned to the idea of process, while Western poets, prophets and philosophers still like to think in terms of creation, the point is less to conclude to inbuilt differences than to open new possibilities for thought. This

[27] François Jullien, *Entrer dans une pensée, ou des possibles de l'esprit*. Paris: Gallimard, 2012.
[28] Jullien, see foonote 27, p. 165.

leads Jullien to the postulation that "translation is an ethical position."[29] It is a similarly ethical position that I tend to see as the first requirement of a new theory in an expanded field partly reshaped by globalization.

Theory in an expanded field

Today, globalization is best illustrated by one of Slavoj Žižek's jokes: it is wrong to say that the American working class has disappeared; it still exists, but it is in China. It is expressed more seriously in *Revolution at the Gates*: "Today, two superpowers, the USA and China, relate more and more as Capital and Labour. . . . The irony of history is that China fully deserves the title 'workers' state': it is the state of the working class for American capital."[30] Indeed, as soon as we buy commodities in the US, from clothes to electronics, it is no longer possible to ignore that we live in a globalized world. This cannot but impact theory and literary studies. But the consequences of globalization are multiple. A number of crucial events, among them the fall of the Berlin wall, the attack of 9/11, the Color Revolutions in the former Soviet world, the rise of economic leadership of China, and the changes brought to the Middle East by Arab uprisings, have radically altered the landscape of international politics, and a similar process is visible, although with a certain time-lag, in the world of global theory.

Moreover, the demise of most of the visible French or German philosophers who had for some time produced texts and concepts that triggered debates, then to be processed by the classical relays of Theory, has led to drastic revisions and starker assessments. There has been a time for mourning, and now we can gauge better the influence of canonical Theory's tenets on younger generations, capitalizing on the pedagogical potential of this varied corpus. It includes the later work of Derrida and deconstruction, and encompasses the lasting inheritance of Deleuze, Lacan, Levinas and Althusser.

One has asserted that the days of Theory were over, but this has not been verified. Theory is still being taught systematically in most American universities, and there is no indication that this will change in the future. The need has always existed; it was not systematically attended to at all times; by now, however, we have a series of protocols of reading, pedagogical tools (among which films play an important role), and excellent anthologies that

---

[29]   Jullien, see foonote 27, p. 177.
[30]   Slavoj Žižek, "Afterword: Lenin's Choice," *Revolution at the Gates*, p. 290.

fulfill their aim adequately. It is true that our new Theory has modified its syllabi and changed its tone. Perhaps the second factor is most visible, and I address this phenomenon in the next chapter when defining a new "fugitive theory." On the whole, globalization has been the most obvious factor to modify the selection of texts studied. For instance, today, it would be impossible to exclude from the syllabus of Theory Achebe's thoughtful but violent questioning of Conrad's latent racism in *Heart of Darkness*. I see as a sign of progress and a drift toward globalization the fact that this text has been added to the second version of the *Norton Anthology of Theory and Criticism*.[31]

This essay, written in 1975, draws on the anger felt by the Nigerian novelist when discussing the undeniable presence of racist elements in Joseph Conrad's canonical story *Heart of Darkness*. Up to this ferocious attack, most readers assumed that Marlow was a well-meaning liberal who observed with some dismay past colonial crimes perpetrated by Kurtz. They opposed his British sensibility to what is denounced as Belgian greed and terror tactics in Congo. By quoting a few passages in which Marlow betrays a certain disgust or horror at the idea of a "distant kinship" with those he calls "savages" and cannibals, Achebe introduced a redoubtable simplification in our reading habits; it was not enough to try and dissociate the author, Conrad, from the Victorian prejudices of his character. There were a few passages that any African person could find offensive. The debate that this position has generated is fascinating, and other African or Caribbean writers like Wilson Harris disagreed with Achebe's strictures (see NATC, p. 1612).

Another sign of a quiet revolution, was the introduction of two texts by Asian writers in 2010. The Chinese Li Zehou and the Japanese Karatani Kōjin are represented by very different essays, yet they both agree that the philosophy upon which they want to buttress their literary insights is a combination of Kant and Marx. Li Zehou introduced the concept of "sedimentation" as a way of showing artworks as the products of material labor (NATC, p. 1754), which is very close to the younger Marx's philosophical ideas. To this, he adds medium and form, and focuses on the idiomatic *qi*, life energy, vital force, or *pneuma*, and compares it with the Romantic idea of "genius". (NATC, 1758) Like Li Zehou, Karatani Kōjin believes in a fusion of the thoughts of Marx and Kant. The Anthology only reproduces a section

---

[31] Vincent B. Leitch (General ed.), *The Norton Anthology of Theory and Criticism*. New York: Norton, 2010. Abbreviated as NATC and page number.

of his survey of modern Japanese literature, in which he duly pays his respects to his master, Natsume Sōseki, one of the great inventors of Japanese literary modernity. As I am a great fan of Sōseki, I always assign this passage, although I have to confess that it is felt as too foreign by American students who have never read one of his novels. My ideal anthology would have replaced this text with a passage from the groundbreaking *Transcritique: on Kant and Marx*,[32] a more theoretical synthesis. Even if the articulation between the philosophy of transcendental idealism and Marxist historical materialism feels at times creaky or forced, I believe that the project of a "transcritique" describes adequately the new direction in theoretical studies. Karatani Kōjin is right to see his effort as a "pronounced parallax," in which Marx's thought is revitalized by its numerous inner breaks.[33] He captures well the contemporary relevance of Marx's *Capital*: "We should read *Capital* not as a classic written before the time of heavy industry and state capital, but as a text that can be revived in our age of neoliberalism and global capital."[34] The idea of "transcritique" combines the disciples of what can be called "comparative philosophy," leading to productive cross-fertilizations within a single field (here, say, post-critical German philosophy) and a moment of dialogical confrontation between different cultures and communities.

We are now more attuned to such great movements of thought, movements that can once more correspond to "translation" in a broader sense, as when Buddhism was imported to China and Japan from India, as we have seen. Other such moments of cross-fertilization were the spreading of Christianity to distant parts of Europe, as with the arrival of Saint Patrick in Ireland, or the dissemination of Islam in the Middle East and in Africa after the seventh century. We are here indeed closer to religious studies, but we should not forget that for more than a century, literary hermeneutics was based upon techniques used for Biblical studies. Literary theory has always progressed by absorbing other disciplines, especially in the domain that used to be called "literary criticism," a set of converging discourses that had been generated by the secularization of techniques of reading used for Biblical exegesis and sacred hermeneutics. During the twentieth century, the domain of Theory has incorporated poetics, rhetoric, aesthetics and all the various formalisms in linguistics and poetry, while looking for more foundational problematics by opening itself to broader issues deriving from continental philosophy.

[32] Karatani Kōjin, *Transcritique: on Kant and Marx*, Sabu Kohso (trans.). Cambridge: MA: M.I.T. Press, 2005.
[33] Kōjin, see footnote 32, p. 4.
[34] Kōjin, see footnote 32, p. 284.

What has changed today? The knowledge that we live in a multiethnic and decentered world has destabilized the primacy that used to be granted to classical studies and a purely Western canon.

It is crucial to help students acquaint themselves with the fact that, for instance, Confucius was articulating definitions of humanity and ethics at the time of Heraclitus, the first philosopher of absolute becoming, who died at about the same time. Plato was still writing about Socrates when Mencius was born. The thought of Aristotle would not have reached the Western world in the Middle Ages without the Arab translations of Averroes. Saint Augustine, one of the founders of the Christian church thanks to his perfect command of Latin rhetoric, was a rather dark-skinned African. The notion of "empire" was not born with the British Empire but existed much earlier in China and Africa, albeit with different inflections. The Japanese modernization of the Meiji era entailed inviting an American philosopher to teach Tokyo students the thought of Hegel; this philosopher, Ernest Fenollosa, ended up saving old Buddhist shrines that had been condemned as old-fashioned. He would be forgotten today had not Ezra Pound decided to found his poetics of the image on Fenollosa's linguistic theories about ideograms, even though they were terribly flawed. Thus, to reframe a humanistic approach to literature and culture in a globalized context, we need to pay more attention to issues of imperial domination and subjection, of racism and cosmopolitanism, of the various ways in which communities can be kept together. This entails not neglecting ethical concerns for an environment determined by global warming, the endangered ecology of the natural world, the extinction or massive killing of some categories of animals, the uncertain insertion of disabled subjects in urban settings. Moreover, the perspective of a unified world has forced us to confront a broader geography and a longer history, of which the figures of Antigone, Aristophanes' androgynous creatures, or the voice of the thunder in the Upanishads are just examples. Even traditional concepts of literary criticism such as comedy and tragedy, beauty and the sublime, the collective or individual nature of interpretation will have to be reinterpreted in such an expanded framework.

Decompensation

At the same time, there is a need to explain to students the meaning of different traditions. The moment has passed when it seemed that the point of theory was to debunk ancient traditions. Such a mistake has been illustrated by the insightful and hilarious memoir written by Walter Kirn about his undergraduate years at Princeton. In *Lost in the Meritocracy*, Kirn exposes the dangers of being instructed on how to deconstruct a "history of metaphysics" that no student had any knowledge of. Kirn, who majored in English as an undergraduate, read first a collection of essays called *Deconstruction and Criticism.* Awed by the verbal extravaganza of Jacques Derrida, he reached puzzling words like "heteronomous" and "invagination." Here is his account: "But real understanding was rare with theory. . . . Even when a poem or story fundamentally escaped me, I found that I could save face with terminology, as when I referred to T. S. Eliot's *The Waste Land* as 'semiotically unstable.' By this I meant 'hard.'"[35] One blames this on the clever tricks, the use of highfaluting words corresponding to a sophomore's short wisdom. Kirn has a deeper grudge against theory: it had become just a fashion, a fad.

> We recognized one another instantly. We toted around books by Roland Barthes, Hans-Georg Gadamer, and Walter Benjamin. We spoke of "playfulness" and "textuality" and concluded before we'd read even a hundredth of it that the Western canon was "illegitimate," a veiled expression of powerful group interests that it was our duty to subvert. In our rush to adopt the latest attitudes and please the younger and hipper of our instructors . . . we skipped straight from ignorance to revisionism, deconstructing a body of literary knowledge that we'd never constructed in the first place.
>
> For true believers, the goal of theory seemed to be the lifting of a great weight from the shoulders of civilization. This weight was the illusion that it was civilized. The weight had been set by a range of perpetrators—members of certain favored races, males, property owners, the church, the literate, natives of the northern hemisphere—who, taken together, it seemed to me, represented a considerable portion of everyone who had ever lived. Then again, of course I'd think that way. Of course I'd be cynical. I was one of them.[36]

Even if Kirn was not a "true believer" in Theory, this reproach rings true. The wish to deconstruct a whole tradition one has not been acquainted with in any depth is a typical temptation for students who suddenly discover an array of powerful weapons, new concepts used like catapults with which they can shoot at old bogeys. Thus they vent their rage at a world which includes the

---

[35] Walter Kirn, *Lost in the Meritocracy: The Undereducation of an Overachiever.* New York: Doubleday, 2009, p. 120.
[36] Kirn, see footnote 35, p. 121.

high culture that is force-fed to them. This happened to Kirn, who felt more and more alienated, moved from one pose or trend to the other, all the while painfully conscious of the lack of grounding in what he was doing. It did not help that he had been socially excluded by well-off members of his cohort. He ended up falling into a grave depression, a pure crack-up. One of his symptoms was aphasia, heralding a total breakdown of his personality. Here was a perfect illustration of what psychiatrists call "decompensation." Of course, we will not worry too much when reading the memoir: we know that Kirn overcame his dissociation, that he regained his language and fought successfully against social and cultural odds. He did not become an academic but went on writing novels, including this vengeful memoir full of unforgettable galleries of weird teachers and crazy students. Yet his critique of the wish to engage with "ideology critique" at any cost has a point. The denunciation of literature, opera and philosophy as a grand conjuration masterminded by a handful of great white males belongs to a period marked by "politically correct" idioms and culture wars. Hence, the recurrent nostalgia for something simpler, a bedrock of facts determined by history, affects, quantitative mappings; there is even an attempt to remain at "surface readings," content summaries devoid of philosophical or ideological questioning. Yet, as soon as one engages with the thinking that underpins texts, these domains appear in all their real complexity.

Thus I would want to argue that what matters is more to expand the knowledge of foundational texts—for instance, teaching Confucius next to Plato builds such a broader basis—rather than be running after the latest trends in contemporary schools. It is good to hear that "eco-criticism" or disability studies have been invented, and such interesting new schools need to be known, but one should not neglect the fact that most of their insights derive from a close confrontation with foundational texts. Therefore, I will be practical and pragmatic, and provide a list of those texts, hoping that their rationale will appear. I want to be precise about the choices of authors and texts. Here is a draft of an aborted anthology of literary theory on which I worked a few years ago—abortive above all for financial reasons: the rights to pay for each text were so high that such a book would have cost too much to the publisher, or would have been too expensive for students to buy. My proposed title was "Global Theory, an anthology."[37] I reproduce the table of contents here; I believe that "show and tell" works better than long explanations.

---

[37] I want to thank Avi Alpert, who had helped me prepare and compose this anthology. He gave me a number of invaluable suggestions in the selection.

A Modest Proposal ...
GLOBAL THEORY, a projected anthology

1. **Cosmopolitanism, Autochtony, Exchange Systems**
    Confucius, on the rectification of names, from the *Analects* (3 pages)
    Lao-Tse, *Tao-te king* (3 pages)
    Plato's "noble lie," *The Republic*, III, *Collected Dialogues*, pp. 414–15
    Diogenes of Sinope, cynicism and cosmopolitanism (3 pages)
    Marx and Engels, from *The Communist Manifesto, Selected Writings*,
        pp. 222–6
    Marcel Mauss, from *The Gift*, pp. 8–14
    Georges Bataille, from *The Accursed Share II*, in The *Bataille Reader*,
        pp. 302–6
    Kwame Anthony Appiah, from *Cosmopolitanism*, pp. 128–35
    Immanuel Wallerstein, from *World-System analysis*, pp. 23–30
    Paul Gilroy, from *Postcolonial Melancholia*, pp. 63–5 and 73–5

2. **Universal History and World Literature**
    J. W. Goethe on World Literature, *Princeton Sourcebook in Comparative
        Literature*, pp. 21–5
    G. W. F. Hegel, from *Introduction to the Philosophy of History*, pp. 20–4
    Ezra Pound, "Praefatio ad lectorem," *The Spirit of Romance*, pp. 3–5
    Walter Benjamin, "Theses on the philosophy of history," *Illuminations*,
        pp. 253–64
    Franco Moretti, "Evolution, world-systems, Weltliteratur," *Princeton
        Sourcebook in Comparative Literature*, pp. 400–8
    Pascale Casanova, from "The world republic of letters," *Princeton
        Sourcebook in Comparative Literature*, pp. 331–40
    Pheng Cheah, from *Spectral Nationality: Passages of Freedom from Kant
        to Postcolonial Literatures of Liberation*, pp. 235–40 and 243–7
    Rey Chow, from *The Age of the World Target*, pp. 80 and 88–91
    Takeuchi Yoshimi, from *What is Modernity?*, pp. 70–3

3. **Tradition, Authority and Awakening**
    "Nagarjuna's Stanzas on Awakening," in Giorgio Agamben, *Idea of
        Prose*, pp. 131–3

Ibn al-Rawandi and Abu Bakr Al-Razi, in Jennifer Michael Hecht, *Doubt: A History*, 2003, pp. 223–9

Spinoza, "Biblical hermeneutics and non-Mosaic authorship," *Tractatus Theologico-Politicus*, 2007, Cambridge, pp. 98–9 and 121–2

Stéphane Mallarmé, "Crisis in verse," *Divagations*, pp. 205–6 and 208–11, a letter to Cazalis on being dead

T. S. Eliot, "Tradition and the individual talent" (Part 1), *The Sacred Wood*, pp. 47–53

"Mikail Bakhtin on heteroglossia," *Four Essays*, pp. 269–75

Walter Benjamin, on Awakening, from "K: Dream city and dream house, dreams of the future, anthropological nihilism, Jung," *Arcades Project*, pp. 388–96

Roland Barthes, "The death of the author," *Image–Music–Text*, pp. 142–8

Michel Foucault, from "What is an author?", *Language, Counter-Memory, Practice*, pp. 121–38

4. Empire and Imperialism

Bartolomé de las Casas, from *Short Account of the Destruction of the Indies*, pp. 9–15

Denis Diderot, "Principles of colonization," *Political Writings*, pp. 175–77

Jose Marti, "Our America" (1891)

Leo Frobenius, "On the morphological method," from *On African History, Art and Culture*, pp. 24–7

W. E. Du Bois, "The African Roots of War," *The Atlantic Monthly 1915*, pp. 707–14

Antonio Gramsci, from *Cultural Writings*, pp. 220–2, 246–7, 255

Mahatma Gandhi, "On the verge of it," from *Selected Political Writings*, pp. 43–4

Michael Hardt and Toni Negri, from *Empire*, pp. 304–9

Kwame Nkrumah, from *Neocolonialism: The Last Stage of Imperialism*, pp. 239, 245–7, 252–4

5. Civilization and Difference

Victor Segalen, *Exoticism; Essay on the Aesthetics of Diversity*, pp. 18–21

Natsume Sōseki, "My individualism," from *Theory of Literature*, pp. 248–52

Sigmund Freud, *Civilization and its Discontents*, pp. 65–73

Marguerite Duras, *Hiroshima My Love*, opening sequence, script
pp. 15–21

Gilles Deleuze, "A Theory of the Other," *Deleuze Reader*, pp. 59–68

Edward Said, from *Orientalism*, Norton, 2010, pp. 1869–72, 1875–81,
1884–8

Paul Virilio, "State of Emergency", *The Virilio Reader*, pp. 46–57

Michael Davidson on disability studies, from *Concerto for the Left
Hand*, pp. 25–30

Giorgio Agamben, from *States of Exception*, pp. 32–7

6. Sexuality and Power; Intimacy and Transgression

Plato, from the *Symposium, Collected Dialogues*, pp. 542–5 and 555–8

Vatsyayana, *Kama Sutra*, "The Art of Kissing," pp. 62–8

Sigmund Freud, from "The Uncanny", *Writings on Art and Literature*,
pp. 216–29

Emmanuel Levinas, "Phenomenology of Eros," *Totality and Infinity*, IV, B

Judith Butler, from *Gender Trouble*, pp. 134–41

Ann Stoler, from *Carnal Knowledge and Imperial Power*, pp. 42–9

Leo Bersani, "The gay outlaw," from *Homos*, pp. 165–81

Tim Dean, "Introduction" to *Unlimited Intimacy*, pp. 1–6

Jean-Luc Marion, from *The Erotic Phenomenon*, pp. 123–8

7. Laughter and Society

Chuang Tzu, in *Chinese Wit and Humor*, pp. 17–19

Jonathan Swift, "A Modest Proposal" (1729)

Immanuel Kant, *Critique of the Faculty of Judgment*, Pluhar (trans.),
pp. 203–7

Freud on "cynical jokes," from *The Joke and its Relation . . .*, pp. 106–11

Samuel Beckett, Arsene on dianoetic laugh, in *Watt* (Grove Press),
pp. 46–8.

Hélène Cixous, from "The laugh of Medusa," *New French Feminisms*,
pp. 252–7

Ted Cohen, from *Jokes: Philosophical Thoughts on Laughing Matters*,
pp. 25–8

Octavio Paz, the meaning of "*chingar*," from *The Labyrinth of Solitude*,
   pp. 74–81

Alenka Zupančič, "Against Bergson's *Laughter*", *The Odd One In*,
   pp. 111–12

8. Ethics and Criticism

"Hegel on Antigone," *The Phenomenology of Spirit*, pp. 281–9

Thomas de Quincey, from *On Murder . . .*, Oxford, OUP, pp. 8–13

Charles Baudelaire, "Counterfeit" and "Beat up the poor," *Paris Spleen*,
   pp. 58–9, 101–3

Hermann Broch, "Evil in the value-system of art," in *Geist and Zeitgeist*,
   pp. 3–9

Maurice Blanchot, from "Literature and the right to death," *Station Hill
   Blanchot Reader*, 1999, pp. 359–5

T. W. Adorno, passages from *Minima Moralia*, pp. 101, 111–13,
   233–5, 247

Emmanuel Levinas, "Peace and proximity," *Basic Philosophical Writings*,
   pp. 162–9

Jacques Lacan on Antigone, *Ethics of Psychoanalysis*, pp. 247–8, 278–83

Judith Butler, from *Antigone's Claim*, pp. 68–72

9. Beauty and the Sublime

Plato on enthusiasm, from *Ion, Collected Dialogues*, pp. 219–28

Longinus on sublimity, Norton, 2010, pp. 136–46

Alexander Pope, from "Peri Bathos," *Selected Poetry and Prose*,
   pp. 307–31

Immanuel Kant, *Critique of Judgment*, Norton, 2010, pp. 433–40

Charles Baudelaire, from "The painter of modern life," *The Painter of
   Modern Life and Other Essays*

Junichiro Tanizaki, from *In Praise of Shadows*, pp. 3–6, 8–9

Jean-Luc Nancy, "The sublime offering," in *Sublime: Presence in
   Question*, pp. 49–53.

Christine Battersby, "Terror, terrrorism and the sublime," from
   The Sublime, Terror and Human Difference, pp. 21–24

Slavoj Žižek on *Vertigo*, from *Looking Awry*, pp. 83–7

10. Ideology and Subjectivity

Marx and Engels, from "The German Ideology," *Marx–Engels Reader*, pp. 127–30.

Thomas Carlyle, "Statistics of imposture," *Sartor Resartus*, Oxford, OUP, pp. 86–7

Friedrich Nietzsche, " 'Ressentiment,' asceticism and the 'pathos of distance,'" *Genealogy of Morals*, Cambridge, CUP, pp. 12–13, 34–6 and 107–11

Roland Barthes on Myth, in *Mythologies*, pp. 111–19

Louis Althusser, on Ideology, Interpellation and State Ideological Apparatuses, from *Lenin and Philosophy and other Essays*.

Ernesto Laclau, "Universalism and particularism," *Emancipation(s)*, pp. 22–35

Jacques Rancière, "The distribution of the sensible," *The Politics of Aesthetics*, pp. 12–19

Sianne Ngai, from *Ugly Feelings*, pp. 43–8

Heather Love, from *Feeling Backward: Loss and the Politics of Queer History*, pp. 1–3, 5–7, 8–10

11. Globalization and Postcolonialism

Edouard Glissant, "Transparency and Opacity," from *Poetics of Relations*, pp. 111–18

Homi Bhabha, on mimicry, from *The Location of Culture*, pp. 85–9

J. Achille Mbembe, "Aesthetics of vulgarity," *On the Postcolony*, pp. 102–10

Arjun Appadurai, from *Modernity at Large*, pp. 32–5, 37, 41–3

David Scott, from *Conscripts of Modernity*, pp. 3–8

Rosemary Marangoly George, from *The Politics of Home*, pp. 1–9

Sankaran Krisna, *Globalization and Postcolonialism: Hegemony and Resistance*, pp. 121–30

Gayatri Spivak, from *Death of a Discipline*, pp. 71–6

Robert Bernasconi, *African Philosophy's Challenge to Continental Philosophy*, pp. 188–92.

12. Technology and Domination

The Ikhwan al-Safa (Brethren of Purity), *The Case of the Animals versus Man before the King of the Jinn*, pp. 51–5

Alexandre Kojève, "Master and Slave," *Introduction to the Reading of Hegel*, pp. 43–51

Walter Benjamin, from "The Work of Art . . ." (revised version), pp. 20–7 and 36–42

Martin Heidegger, "The question concerning technology," pp. 4–6, 12–18, 33–5

Jürgen Habermas, "Technology and science as 'Ideology,'" from *Towards a Rational Society*, pp. 104–8, 110–13

Friedrich Kittler, from *Literature, Media, Information Systems*, pp. 31–4, 123–5

Peter Singer, "All animals are equal," from *Animal Liberation*, pp. 2–9

Lawrence Buell, from *Writing for an Endangered World*, pp. 2–6

Dorothy Roberts, from *Killing the Black Body*, pp. 247–8, 269–72

13. Religion and Community

Upanishads, "What the Thunder Said"; and Eliot, part V of *The Waste Land*.

Vico, "God's thunder and the genesis of religion," *New Science*, pp. 144–8

Nicholas Fyodorov, "The Common Task," *Russian Philosophy III*, pp. 37–45

Elias Canetti, "Catholicism and the crowd," *Crowds and Power*, pp. 154–8

Alain Badiou, from *Saint Paul*, pp. 98–106

Jacques Derrida, from *Acts of Religion*, pp. 50–60

Roberto Esposito, "Nihilism and community," from *Communitas*, pp. 135–49

Saba Mahmood, *Politics of Piety*, pp. 1–5, 10–17

Simon Critchley, "Mystical anarchism," in *Public*, No. 39, pp. 139–47

14. Translation and Subjectivity

Benjamin, "The task of the translator," *Illuminations*, pp. 69–82

Kafka, "Introductory talk on the Yiddish language," in *Wedding Preparations in the Country*, pp. 418–22

Freud, "Moses an Egyptian," from *Moses and Monotheism*, pp. 4–6, 50–3, 72–5

Jorge Luis Borges, "Pierre Ménard, author of the Quixote," *Collected Fictions*, pp. 88–95

Antoine Berman, "The manifestation of translation," in *The Experience of the Foreign*, pp. 1–9.

Vlad Godzich, on emergent literatures, from *The Culture of Literacy*, pp. 284–92

Michael Cronin, "Translation and the global economy," from *Translation and Globalization*, pp. 8–16

Naoki Sakai, *Translation and Subjectivity*, pp. 3–10

Lawrence Venuti, "Translation, community, utopia," from *The Translation Studies Reader*, pp. 468–77

The anthology that I had planned in 2010 had 14 sections, hence 14 thematic clusters. Why 14? Ideally, each of them would be treated in a week, following the usual division of the year in semesters of 13 or 14 weeks in most American universities. Each section would have averaged 50 pages of printed text, a demanding but not excessive requirement for the preparation of two or three weekly class meetings. Each section would have begun with a short introduction explaining the rationale of its grouping, followed by a bibliography listing further readings. The number of nine texts per section imposed itself pragmatically. Nine theses provided a rich series of dialectical interactions, and there was the benefit of giving enough textual ammunition to instructors teaching three times a week.

Moreover, in today's digitalized world, most of these texts can be found on the web, along with detailed information about their authors. Thus there was no real need to provide my own "Wikipedia" introductions; a minimum is necessary indeed, but most of this aspect can be left as a task that students will perform for themselves. If this becomes an assignment along with oral presentations, it forces students to explore a little more of each author; texts, in fact excerpts only most of the time, should be taken as a point of departure, an intersection between several ongoing conversations, rather than as the perfect fragment exemplifying a total system. Many professors have deplored the fact that the pedagogy of Theory is most of the time based on Readers, Anthologies, Guides and Introductions. Inevitably, each of them creates a certain vulgate of Theory, and my heuristic effort is no exception. The obvious drawback is the reduction of important concepts to ready-made "power-tools." One has to be aware of the risk, and the use in class discussion as a non-reductive moment of collective elaboration. The best solution to the problem I have found is to rely on students' participation. It is crucial to make them see that all these texts belong to a larger whole. Their creativity is stimulated if they agree to take each text as the emerging tip of downloadable textual icebergs. The tension between on-line archives, virtually infinite, and the few pages of their hand-outs can become a productive constraint. It is good to keep hard copies, printed pages that all participants in the class will have in their hands, rather than their computer screens if one wishes to generate constructive in-class discussions. Even difficult readings, if they have been done by all, lead to issues of terminology; with theory, it is crucial that one insists on the clarity of expression. Only extreme terminological precision can prevent the type of fashionable window-dressing that Walter Kirn had described.

If concepts have been adequately discussed by the class, they play the role of verifiable references in writing exercises and papers. I tend to encourage short writing exercises that take place in class and re-explore the basic definitions. Once the concepts have been mastered, it becomes easier to ask students to bring examples for the next class. Thus in a class on "Fashion Theory," I asked all students to define terms such as "aura," "allegory," "style." These were to be tackled not in themselves but in the context of Walter Benjamin's *Arcades Project*. These definitions usually took less than a page. Then, students had to bring their own examples to illustrate these abstract terms. Examples consist of photographs, video-clips, songs or written passages from authors of their choice. When they gave oral presentations, they would remain short, but always accompanied by a hand-out mapping clearly the semantics implied, and providing a frame for the historical references.

In this particular case, the idea of fashion was extremely useful to address the concern voiced by Kirn. How can we avoid the desperate quest for the next wave, the new concept, the terminology that will appear sexier? The only way to oppose this is to remind students that literature "thinks," and that the aim of Theory, if it is also to help reading texts, is to show as clearly as one can, *how* they think. One can achieve the same results in a pedagogical setting by highlighting texts that are not so readily marked off as "philosophical." But if we take the notion of fashion seriously, we need to turn to Fashion Theory, whose founder was the German sociologist Georg Simmel. Simmel was the first to outline the paradox of fashion: a style of dress bespeaks one's sense of belonging to a group, a profession or a generation, yet one always tries to use dress in order to enhance singularity, originality and creativity. As we will see in the next chapter, Walter Benjamin goes further in his notes on fashion in *The Arcades Project* when he notes that each generation sees in the preceding generation's fashion the most ridiculously anti-erotic cultural productions.[38]

---

[38] W. Benjamin, *The Arcades Project*. Cambridge: Harvard University Press, 2002, p. 64 and p. 79.

Yet all these attempts to dress oneself in fixed or codified ways correspond to a similar grappling with a death seen or suggested as lurking inside bodies. These ideas can apply directly to Theory. By choosing certain theories, one will generally want to belong to group discussion or to a given community of interpreters, yet one always entertains the hope that one will find an original voice through this conversation. We tend to see the previous generation's set of references or its ideal library as ridiculously outdated, yet we all grapple with the erotics of a renewed struggle with issues such as death, finitude, survival and an ethics of liberation. It is in this sense that we can see why Theory matters today. It will always be more than "literary theory" or the "methodology" we use to read texts. Theory accompanies the way in which literature thinks. Its outreach into the most varied domains of life and the real world is shaped by all the forces that bring us closer to the future.

Untimely theories of the future

It is now time to return to the "Theory of the Future." This term was used at the same period by a composer and a philosopher, Richard Wagner and Ludwig Feuerbach. Nietzsche knew this, reserving his barbs for his former friend:

> Recall how enthusiastically Wagner followed in the footsteps of the philosopher Feuerbach in his day: Feuerbach's dictum of "healthy sensuality"—that sounded like the pronouncement of salvation to the Wagner of the 1830s and the 1840s, as to so many Germans—they called themselves "*Young* Germans."[39]

Nietzsche alludes here to Feuerbach's *Principles of a Philosophy of the Future*, a short philosophical treatise published in 1843. Wagner, who had read it, was indeed enthusiastic, and then dedicated his own "The work of art of the future" (1849) to Feuerbach. This was followed by Wagner's essay on "Music of the future," first published in French in 1860 as "*La musique de l'avenir*," then in German in 1861 as "*Zukunftsmusik*." What united Wagner and Feuerbach in the 1840s was their rejection of a certain type of "absolute" in music and philosophy. For Feuerbach, of course, the thinker of the "Absolute" was Hegel; for Wagner, the musician of the "Absolute" was Beethoven. If E. T. A. Hoffmann had already analyzed Beethoven's *Fifth*

---

[39] Friedrich Nietzsche, *On the Genealogy of Morality*, Carol Diethe (trans.). Cambridge: Cambridge University Press, 1998, pp. 74–5.

Symphony in terms of its sublime and self-referential medium, since it was an autonomous music that did not illustrate anything but itself, it was then Wagner who claimed that Beethoven's *Ninth Symphony* exemplified "absolute music." This meant that it had to be rejected as a model.[40]

In philosophy, Feuerbach, considered as the leading "Left Hegelian," was attempting to move beyond the confines of the Hegelian system. His philosophy tried to create an ethical dynamism at a time when Hegel seemed to have closed up "absolute knowledge" upon itself. Feuerbach's weapons were the critique of religion, and a consistent appeal to the sensual body of men and women. I can only be brief and will merely note that the rediscovery of Feuerbach in France was due to Louis Althusser.[41] Feuerbach's philosophy of the future can be summed up in the idea of the "humanization" of theology: the God of a previous era has now to be replaced by Man. All the ancient attributes of God should now be given over to a new anthropology. Hegel, whose system was the culmination of all the previous philosophies, and who taught his disciples to think "absolutely," must be overcome; any philosophy of the future will begin by levering a radical critique of Hegel.[42] Thus Feuerbach saw in Hegel's idea of an "absolute knowledge" the remainder of the old theology: "So does absolute philosophy externalize (*entäussert*) and alienate (*entfremdet*) from man his own essence and activity! Hence the violence and torture it inflicts on our minds." (PPF, p. 37)

Nevertheless, it was Hegel himself who provided the means of his own undoing, given his thought that "overleaps its otherness." (PPF, p. 44) In that movement that aims at including the Other via regulated negativity, one can find a lever for the overcoming of abstraction; the abstraction of the concept will be replaced by the concrete determinations of life. Man will find in "self-activity" a new link with reality. (PPF, p. 51) The philosophy of the future should turn into a philosophy of sensuous embodiment, stressing sense data, feelings and also love (PPF, p. 52): "Only in feeling and in love does 'this'—as in 'this person' or 'this object,' that is, the particular—have absolute value and is the finite the infinite; in this alone, and only in this, is the infinite depth, divinity and truth of love constituted." (PPF, p. 52) Feuerbach's sensuous apprehension of life entails an account of love as a non-religious passion; in his writings, one finds a new tone that announces Emmanuel Levinas's meditations on radical Otherness:

---

[40] For all these debates, see the excellent book by Carl Dahlhaus, *The Idea of Absolute Music*, Roger Lustig (trans.). Chicago: University of Chicago Press.

[41] See the discussion of Althusser in the Conclusion.

[42] Ludwig Feuerbach, *Principles of the Philosophy of the Future*, Manfred Vogel (trans.). Indianapolis: Hackett, 1986, p. 31, par. 19, Hereafter, PPF and page number.

Love is passion, and only passion is the hallmark of existence. Only that exists which is an object—be it real or possible—of passion. Abstract thought that is without feeling and without passion cancels the difference between being and nonbeing, but this difference—which for thought is an evanescent difference—is a reality for love. Love means nothing other than becoming aware of this difference.

(PPF, p. 52)

The philosophy of sensuous awareness aims at abolishing any difference between essence and existence—a theme that will be taken as very original by Jean-Paul Sartre one century later. Art is the site of a fusion of truth and sensation (see PPF, p. 57).

The philosophy of the future clashes with the ancient philosophy's repressive abstraction—here, Feuerbach anticipates Nietzsche and Freud: the old God was supposed to be "a being apart from mind and thought, a real, objective, that is sensuous being; it was confessed only in a manner that was hidden, conceptual, unconscious, and reluctant, solely because it was coerced." (PPF, pp. 54–5) Thus religion enacts the repression of human desires, and our bodies contain more "truth" than our ideas. In the end, man is not ontologically different from animals—it is only language, hence thinking, that introduces a different order. Man is not only a thinking animal, but also an eating animal, and philosophy should begin with the stomach (see PPF, pp. 69–70). This thesis became simplified later in an evocative but reductive thought-rhyme: "*Der Mensch ist, was er isst*" (humanity is what it eats).[43] It would be absurd to sum up Feuerbach's materialism with this shorthand phrase. Its ramifications go much further, as witnessed by this statement: "The true dialectic is not a monologue of a solitary thinker with himself; it is a dialogue between I and thou." (PPF, p. 72)

Marx and Engels had no difficulty in poking fun at Feuerbach's well-meaning, generous but all too vague intuitions. Even though Feuerbach had allied himself with the Communists, his philosophy of sensuality had missed, they felt, its concrete historical applications. Feuerbach was still too pious in his wish to overthrow a divine religion in the name of the cult of the human. The fundamental sensuous activity from which any man seems divorced is not a social practice, it is not connected with any social and historical activity. Here lies Marx's and Engels's reproach against all the Left Hegelians: they believed that they had moved away from the circularity of the concept to

---

[43] Feuerbach used the phrase in a review of a book by a Dutch doctor, Jakob Moleschott, one of the inventors of a science of nutrition with *The Theory of Food* (1850).

attain "real life," and yet they were stuck in pure ideas, they generated even more "hypostatized abstractions." The only way to move closer to concrete history was to think through a human praxis defined as production and social activity. For instance, the link established by Feuerbach with animals missed its mark. Marx writes:

> Men can be distinguished from animals by consciousness, by religion or anything you like. They themselves begin to distinguish themselves from animals as soon as they begin to *produce* their means of subsistence, a step which is conditioned by their physical organization. By producing their means of subsistence men are indirectly producing their material life.[44]

Marx's concept of production, a key to his thinking, also includes reproduction via sexuality, and thus gives a more precise meaning to Feuerbach's abstract rhapsodies on love: "This production only makes its appearance with the *increase of population.* In its turn this presupposes the *intercourse* (*Verkehr*) of individuals with one another. The form of this intercourse is again determined by production."[45] The reappearance of the term of *Verkehr* already encountered in *The Communist Manifesto* is symptomatic: it is the young Marx's way of linking his analysis of bourgeois society and capitalism with the gradual homogenization of the world population. In another analysis devoted to Feuerbach, Marx writes:

> ...this development of productive forces (which at the same time implies the actual empirical existence of men in their *world-historical,* instead of local, being) is an absolutely necessary practical premise, because without its privation, *want* is merely made general, and with *want* the struggle for necessities would begin again, and all the old filthy business would necessarily be restored; and furthermore, because only with this universal development of productive forces is *universal* intercourse between men established, which on the one side produces in *all* nations simultaneously the phenomenon of the "propertyless" mass (universal competition), making each nation dependent on the revolutions of the others, and finally puts *world-historical,* empirically universal individuals in place of local ones.[46]

---

44 Karl Marx and Friedrich Engels, *The German Ideology, I, Feuerbach,* in *Collected Works, Vol. 5, 1845–1847.* New York: International Publishers, 1976, p. 31.
45 Marx and Engels, see footnote 44, p. 32.
46 Marx and Engels, see footnote 44, p. 49.

This view leads Marx and Engels to state that communism will only be possible when the development of the productive forces creates a "world-market" doubled by a "world intercourse" binding all men and women together. This would be the very foundation of the idea of communism. Only a world-wide revolution can create a humanity for which essence and existence are one and the same thing: it is when one creates a classless society.[47] This should help make sense of Marx's famous XIth thesis on Feuerbach: "The philosophers have only *interpreted* the world in various ways; the point, however, is to *change* it."[48] The first Marxist philosopher who was bold enough to criticize this famous motto was Louis Althusser, as we will see later. Very sensibly, Althusser points out in his autobiographical memoir that all philosophers since Plato and Confucius have desired to change the world.[49]

To be true, most of the time, they failed in their endeavors, which is why they still had time to continue teaching, researching and writing. Let's take Plato, who had gone three times to Sicily, where Dion, the brother in law of Dionysius the tyrant of Syracuse, had become his disciple. The first stay ended badly, Plato barely avoided being murdered, and then he was sold as a slave. Later he came back from Athens to assist Dion in his struggle against Dionysius II. He had written in a famous passage of Letter VII written in 353 BC: "Let not Sicily nor any city anywhere be subjected to human masters—such is my doctrine—but to laws,"[50] which was taken as an attack on tyranny. His general philosophy aimed at replacing dictatorship with a state of law. This was also Confucius's program, in another context of course. When in 498 BC Confucius was named first "Minister of Public Works" then, with a more sinister label, the "Minister of Crime" in the Lu state in which he had been born, he decided to fight against corrupt officials, and also to put down the houses of fractious noble families. He succeeded in the first task: he managed to get a "false" and "evil" government official arrested and beheaded—to the approval of Ezra Pound who praises this action in Canto 53; there, Pound gives the French transliteration of the beheaded official as C. T. Mao, a.k.a. Shao Ching-mao, as he quotes a history of China written in

---

[47] Marx and Engels, see footnote 44, p. 58.
[48] Marx and Engels, see footnote 44, p. 8. See the original manuscript p. 9. See also Warrren Breckman, *Marx, the Young Hegelians, and the Origins of Radical Social Theory.* Cambridge: Cambridge University Press, 1999.
[49] Louis Althusser, *The Future Lasts Forever: A Memoir*, Richard Veasey (trans.). New York: The New Press, 1993, p.172. I will return to this in the Conclusion.
[50] Plato, *Letter VII, Collected Dialogues including the Letters*, Edith Hamilton and Huntington Cairns (eds). Princeton: Princeton University Press, 1973, p. 1583.

French by de Mailla.[51] Unhappily, Confucius was less successful in curbing the arrogance of three noble families. They fought back, multiplied intrigues; finally he lost his war, and was forced to resign his official post. Thus in 497 BC, Confucius began his years of exile and wandering through China.

A basic principle that needs to be reiterated if we want to read Plato and Confucius side by side is that we will have to "translate" heftily. This principle leads me to reformulate Marx's XIth thesis on Feuerbach: Up to now, philosophers have tried to change the world, and they have failed. Now, it seems, the task is to translate it; this, of course, in the hope that, if we translate better, searching for more precise and exact idioms, respecting all the startling idiosyncrasies of concepts in their original languages, we will bring about a momentous change. There should be more *Verkehr*, in other words, in the three meanings of "traffic," "communication," and "intercourse." Moreover, theory should make room for exceptions—in this case, it would be that of Kafka, or at least of his *alter ego* Georg Bendemann, the doomed son of the only short story Kakfa had felt proud of, "The Verdict." At the end of the narrative, let us not forget, Georg is condemned to death by his father, and as he lets himself fall from a bridge, the narrative states blandly that urban traffic happens to be at its most intense. The last word of the story is *Verkehr*.[52]

To bring a future change, a theory of exceptions will be needed, along with a rethinking of the older modes of "absolute" thinking. In that sense, Nietzsche would agree with Marx, at least when he accuses his former role-model, Wagner, of having forgotten his "music of the future" to become a Hegelian: "Hegel is a *taste*.—And not merely a German but a European taste.—A taste Wagner comprehended—to which he felt equal—which he immortalized.— He merely applied it to music—he invented a style for himself charged with 'infinite meaning'—he became the *heir of Hegel*.—Music as 'idea.'"[53] Nietzsche's book on Wagner was finished just a few days before Nietzsche's total collapse in a street in Turin. At the end of his pamphlet, Wagner turns either into Circe, bewitching naïve sailors and companions of Odysseus, or

[51] Ezra Pound, *The Cantos*. London: Faber and Faber, 1986, p. 273. I have discussed Pound's mixture of Confucian and Heideggerian ethics with respect to the "Chinese Cantos" in *Language, Sexuality and Ideology in Ezra Pound's Cantos*. London: Macmillan, 1986. See also Homer H. Dubs, "The political career of Confucius," *Journal of the American Oriental Society*, vol. 66, no. 4, Oct–Dec. 1946, pp. 273–82.
[52] The last sentence of the story is: "In diesem Augenblick ging über die Brücke ein geradezu unendlicher Verkehr." Franz Kafka, *Meistererzählungen*, p. 22. Stanley Corngold translates perfectly: "At that moment, the traffic going over the bridge was nothing short of infinite." Franz Kafka, *Selected Stories*. New York: Norton, 2007, p. 12.
[53] Friedrich Nietzsche, "The Case of Wagner," in *The Birth of Tragedy and The Case of Wagner*, Walter Kaufmann (trans.). New York: Vintage, 1967, pp. 177–8.

the Minotaur who lures to their death the maidens of Greece. At any rate, Wagner is not "modern," which is a serious indictment for a philosopher who, two years earlier, had once more quoted Feuerbach when adding to *Beyond Good and Evil*, the subtitle "Prelude to a philosophy of the future" (1886).

To say that the problematic of a philosophy of the future belongs to the second half of the nineteenth century would tend to suggest that we are not so much the heirs of the Enlightenment, as Habermas believed, as the continuators—by other means—of the program launched by the Left Hegelians. We pursue their various lines of flight when they rejected the mythology and absolute theology elaborated by the German Romantics and, differently, by Hegel. In the chapters that follow, I will first follow the lead of Jacques Derrida, in whom I see another critical successor of Hegel, to whose phenomenology of the Spirit he added the dimensions of paradox and subversion. For my praise of translation should not be taken as leaving aside any critical investigation. Theory, in the sense of a "theory of the future," would be on a quest for problematizations of the present, and not for its legitimation. This had been once more well expressed by Nietzsche, who quotes Emerson and Diogenes in the third "untimely meditation." He quotes from Emerson's 1841 essay on "Circles":

> Beware when the great God lets loose a thinker on this planet. Then all things are at risk. It is as when a conflagration has broken out in a great city, and no man knows what is safe, or where it will end. There is not a piece of science but its flank may be turned tomorrow; there is not any literary reputation, not the so-called eternal names of fame, that may not be revised and condemned.[54]

Emerson goes on to compare the emergence of a new culture with a whole revolution. But it is Diogenes of Sinope, the first true Cynic, who condenses the issue most pithily; he is quoted as saying about another thinker: "How can he be considered great, since he has been a philosopher for so long and has never yet *disturbed* anybody?"[55] A more usual translation is: "Of what use is a philosopher who doesn't hurt anybody's feelings?"[56] Nietzsche's verb is *betrüben*, which can be rendered as "aggrieve." Nietzsche intended to antagonize people, and he did, beginning with Wagner. There was a streak of cynicism in him, especially as we may recognize in Diogenes the first

[54] Friedrich Nietzsche, "Schopenhauer as educator," in *Untimely Meditations*, R. J. Hollingdale (trans.). Cambridge: Cambridge University Press, 1991, p. 193.
[55] Nietzsche, see footnote 54, p. 194.
[56] Guy Davenport, *Herakleitos and Diogenes*. San Francisco: Grey Fox Press, 1979, p. 40.

"cosmopolitan" thinker—Diogenes would repeat: "I am a citizen of the world," a *cosmopolites*. However, cosmopolitanism will not suffice for theory to justify itself, to find a legitimation. We need to think a certain future combined with a quasi-hysterical demand for truth, a demand exemplified by Diogenes, also abundantly present in the work of Derrida.

After Derrida, theory cannot be defined as a meta-discourse that comes to legitimize certain philosophical or literary practices. The recurrent question posed by Derrida is this: in the name of what can one exclude this or that factor? Fundamentally, my book follows Derrida's questions, even if at times I will have to question his methods and his conclusions. Derrida's main legacy lies in the combination of a transcendental critique (posing the question: "in the name of what are you acting?") and of performative interactions that change texts and concepts, pushing issues always further until they turn into an impossibility, a pure paradox. The point, however, will be to let the "to come" of the future—as *l'avenir*, one of the French "untranslatable" terms inherited from him—still open. Derrida's plea for radical openness to the future is an ethical and political condition; it accompanies a plea for translation, since we have to speak and write in several languages at once. This is how we can claim the future, not to prepare it for another utopia, but as an ethical limit, even if it is always receding. This may entail looking for a certain state of silence. Our present is an extended "Now"[57] full of noises, a cacophony in which we attempt to find our balance; our past is made up of various polyphonies in which themes, voices and motifs keep crisscrossing or diverging. This is how we know that we do not share the same pasts even if we are together in the present. But the future is our resource of silence, a mute mouth from which all the rest proceeds.

---

[57] See Douglas Rushkoff's compelling account of today's "presentism" that has replaced Alvin Toffler's "futurism" from the seventies, in *Present Shock: When Everything Happens Now*. New York: Penguin, 2013.

2

Theory and its Lines of Flight

Future, ancient, fugitive

Lines of flight

In the Summer of 2001, I was completing a book on the future of literary theory when I was made to realize that the future had caught up with me sooner than I thought. I had barely finished the typescript of *The Future of Theory*,[1] a short "manifesto" for a series designed by Andrew McNeillie, and the writing pace had to be brisk. I mailed it to him on the last day of August 2001. On the date of September 11, 2001, I taught my first graduate class of the Fall semester in the morning. It was 9.00 a.m., and I had planned to begin by reading a passage from the book since it was a "pro-seminar" devoted to literary methodology. But then everything changed. Bravely, all the students insisted that we keep to the schedule in spite of the growing panic. I thus read a portion of a chapter discussing Plato's *Protagoras*. Socrates and Protagoras examine the question whether virtue can be taught. I had been fascinated by the way in which Socrates contradicts himself so much that, at the end, he exchanges positions with Protagoras. What role will the literary exegesis of an obscure poem about Virtue by Simonides play? Why is Plato attacking literary criticism so viciously? Needless to say, these questions, important as they are, fell on ears becoming more and more deaf; the students were too upset to continue the discussion, and my own dialectics fell upon them like a brick. This pedagogical experience has subsequently colored my apprehension of the "future" if not changed my position as defined in *The Future of Theory*. At the least, recent events illustrated the book's opening statement, in which I opposed theory to "life," with a true vengeance.

It was inevitable that the events of September 11, 2001, and the rapidly shifting world picture that they led to, forced us to reexamine our methodologies, our presuppositions facing the dwindling or withering role of Theory in the Humanities. I felt the need to compare the vision of the future contained in the last chapter of *The Future of Theory* with this changed

---

[1] Jean-Michel Rabaté, *The Future of Theory*. Oxford: Blackwell, 2002.

panorama, or to check the relevance of some of my analyses and predictions. I also wished to take a longer view so as to assess the specific temporality of Theory. I found my cue in an experimental novel by French writer Olivier Cadiot, *Futur, ancien, fugitif.*[2] Cadiot's playful and poetic text fancifully recreates linguistic games by going back to the Robinson Crusoe myth. Cadiot shows that any invocation of the "Future" will be fraught with dangers and attempts to provide useful advice. Here is how the blurb describes the book on the back cover:

> This book contains the complete list of what you need to do when you are in exile. Precise advice about the making of simple objects. A retrospective view of things that have taken place. A systematic manual of poetic exercises. A memento of table manners and polite usages. A rehabilitation of hidden memory. A description of different everyday lives. An analysis of potential recurrence. Observation techniques applying to people you know. A concentrate of individual sensations and their explanations. A method of one-voice dialogue. A plan to visit nature.

Had I in fact followed this hidden program when I had written a book on the future of Theory? Or did this describe the book I wished I had written? It was not just because I had felt that I needed to offer to my readers "a retrospective view of things that have taken place" along with "a rehabilitation of hidden memory" before dealing with whatever future I might perceive or invent. I had been striving to give my readers a "systematic manual of poetic exercises, a memento of table manners and polite usages"—not succeeding so well perhaps because I had remained caught up in my "method of one-voice dialogue." In my book, I had of course paid attention to a shifting paradigm— but it might have shifted somewhere other than I thought.

In my 2002 book, I had referred to Elizabeth Bruss's 1982 book, *Beautiful Theories,*[3] a book in which one witnesses the rapid emergence of the "Age of Theory" in America. Bruss describes how American universities perceived the "invasion" of foreign (mostly French and German) theoreticians in the early seventies. She analyzes how the annual bibliography of the MLA, which had only listed "aesthetics" and "literary criticism" until 1967, created the category of "Literary Criticism and Literary Theory," and how that list of publications grew from 200 to 600 in a few years. Bruss died before her book

[2]   Olivier Cadiot, *Futur, ancien, fugitif.* Paris: P.O.L., 1993.
[3]   Elizabeth W. Bruss, *Beautiful Theories: The Spectacle of Discourse in Contemporary Criticism.* Baltimore: Johns Hopkins University Press, 1982.

was published, which is sad, but spared her the spectacle of what followed: in the twenty-first century, Theory has lost most of its charms. It is not "beautiful" any longer, although not really ugly yet. Theory has proved amenable to the whims of various fashions, but as Walter Benjamin astutely observed in his *Arcades Project* book, there is nothing as anti-erotic as the fashion of a previous generation! "Each generation experiences the fashions of the one immediately preceding it as the most radical antiaphrodisiac imaginable."[4] Benjamin's original has the scary word of "*Antiaphrodisiacum*,"[5] which keeps medical, almost botanic overtones. These caveats are useful if we want to probe the changed temporality of Theory.

Hence, one should always begin with the future: it comes always earlier than we think. When designing *The Future of Theory*, I spent a lot of time designing a list of what I saw as the future trends emerging. This is the section that has triggered most disagreements and caviling remarks. Here is a rapid list of efforts that map out what I see as Theory's ongoing and future projects.

1. "New Arcades" taking Walter Benjamin as a point of departure for histories of material culture with a few original objects like clothes, hair, body parts, ornaments, excrements, monuments.

2. Technological criticism focusing on the interactions between humans and machines, and leading to concepts of the "posthuman," which includes the aesthetics of the technological sublime, and notions of virtual realities and possible worlds, collective dromologies, computerized gaming with "second lives" in virtual spaces.

3. Diasporic criticism taking as its main theme migrations and homelessness, studying displaced groups and emerging communities, analyzing notions like "home," exile and foreignness, leading to Globalization Studies assessing the transformations of nation-states in their literary versions, from trans-nationalisms to returns to nationalism, with sites of resistance and new utopias including ecological criticism.

4. Bio-ethical criticism revisiting bio-power and issues of sexual difference from the point of view of a theory of exceptions: from the ethics of otherness in sexuality, politics and literature to bioethical criticism, including animal studies and theories of animal rights.

5. Testimonial studies taking trauma, genocide and torture as limit-points from which one may map collective histories, archives or recovery testimonies, and autobiographical accounts of a non-literary genre.

---

[4]　Walter Benjamin, *The Arcades Project*, Howard Eiland and Kevin McLaughlin (trans.). Cambridge, MA: Harvard University Press, 1999, p. 79.

[5]　Walter Benjamin, *Das Passagen-Werk*, Rolf Tiedemann (ed.). Frankfurt: Suhrkamp, 1983, vol. I, p. 130.

6. Genetic criticism, a new way of talking about textual studies with objects such as drafts, archives and hypertexts. This corresponds to what remains of the institutions of literature in the age of electronic books.

7. Cognitive studies and the impact of brain mapping, which both have impacted literary studies along with studies of scientific themes such as chaos theory, fractal theory, catastrophe theory, complexity theory, Borromean knots; all these new scientific paradigms being applied to literary formalization.

8. Hauntology, the theory of tradition and ghostly influences pushing deconstruction to its limits, back to Freudian theories of the uncanny.

9. Hybridity studies, mixing race studies and gender studies, especially transgender studies; in the same way as "color" (whiteness, yellowness and blackness) appears as a social construct, sex and gender have evolved since the heyday of queer studies, in order to address issues of affect, displacement, legal segregations, etc.

10. Translation studies, from biblical studies to comparative studies of corpuses using close readings to redefine style and intertextual networks within the lingusitic techniques entailed by traductology.

For me, there were on top of these a few urgent agenda, special projects, or immediate concerns, some of which indeed emerged later. I have sketched a few that I see as relevant to these interests.

*   Reopening a dialogue between Lacanian and Levinassian ethics in the context of a redefined "post-humanism" and "post-feminism."
*   Critiquing historicism as Badiou has done when he assessed Deleuzian philosophy by moving away from its anti-foundationalism so as to point to interactions with science, film and politics.
*   Reopening the Nietzsche–Heidegger confrontation in terms of current controversies over bioethics and the need for a more rigorous definition of the human.
*   Rethinking technology as science and/or art, from a post-Derridian point of view or from the side of art-criticism.
*   Exploring the issue of emotions and affects, too often left to reductive psychology or traditionalist philosophy.
*   Rethinking Derrida's late turn to the religious and the notion of a "messianicity without a Messiah" as a critique of traditional conceptions of religion.

Like the previous one, this list is by no means limitative, it aims more at stimulating the imagination than providing a repertory. Its futurity is relative, as if it remains caught up within the "unaccomplished."

I have named Deleuze, yet should explain why the notion of "fugitivity" is not identical with Deleuze's and Guattari's famed "lines of flight," a notion that is recurrent in *A Thousand Plateaus*.[6] The term is often used in conjunction with the "rhizome" or with "nomadic thinking," which makes sense. Yet, even when they stress dispersion, decenteredness and deterritorialization, Deleuze and Guattari seem unaware that the term offers contradictory consequences: on the one hand, a "line of flight" can be defined by a "becoming animal" as evinced by Kafka's stories, or it can be contained within the optics of perspective as the "vanishing point" of an image. Deleuze and Guattari are intent upon not losing any of the three meanings collated by the French expression *ligne de fuite*: flight as fleeing; flight as flying; and line of flight determining an imaginary point that we need to suppose infinitely remote as the keystone of a perspective in order for its construction to hold. When Deleuze and Guattari discuss Barbarian invasions and migrations in one of the most fascinating chapters, "Micropolitics and segmentarity," Brian Massumi has a hard time translating "*fuite*": at times, it has to be rendered as "escape." "Then, on the horizon, there is an entirely different kind of line, the line of the nomads who come in off the steppes, venture a fluid and active escape (*fuite*), sow deterritorialization everywhere, launch flows whose quanta heat up and are swept along by a Stateless war machine."[7] No matter the mixed metaphors, a trademark of Deleuze and Guattari, we can follow here a double movement: the nomads also turn into settlers after a while, whereas centralized empires end up crumbling and generating new offshoots and mobile satellites. What happens then in an age of "planetary computerization," when all the "revolutions" in technology merge in a new capitalistic order defined by "information processing, telematics, robotics, office automation, biotechnology," and so on, until we are faced with a more powerful system of alienation and domination?[8] Isn't this our future, after all?

The issue of a deterritorialized globalization sends us to critics who sound a similar note, less however in the context of geo-politics than in the loaded context of academia, of its culture wars and endless reshufflings of intellectual and institutional territories. To exemplify this dimension, I will refer to Daniel O'Hara's *Empire Burlesque, The Fate of Critical Culture in Global America* (2003). O'Hara argues that globalization has had a negative impact on the culture that spawned Theory. In O'Hara's vivid account,

---

[6] Gilles Deleuze and Felix Guattari, *A Thousand Plateaus: Capitalism and Schizophrenia*, Brian Massumi (trans.). Minneapolis: University of Minnesota Press, 1987.

[7] Deleuze and Guattari, see footnote 6, p. 222.

[8] I am quoting here Felix Guattari's "Regimes, pathways, subjects," in *The Guattari Reader*, Gary Genosko (ed.). Oxford: Blackwell, 1996, p. 103.

globalization has led critical culture to a state of self-parody that leads finally to one main position: fugitivity. In a chapter devoted to a reading of class in Henry James, O'Hara uses Jon Elster's book, *Making Sense of Marx.*[9] Rather than stress class as a determinist function of social origins and rapports as in traditional Marxism, Jon Elster takes class as instable, emergent agency, which is always in transformation. This versatile and labile theory of class as a set of rule-governed games remains a collective actor while being endowed with a sense of radical mobility and improvization. O'Hara applies this model to a perceptive analysis of academics in their institutions. More precisely, he analyzes the "abjection" of the average American academic:

> Just as . . . we saw in Elster's rational-choice version of Marxism that any collective subject for intellectual workers can emerge in our global culture only fugitively, piece-meal, and thus repeatedly, with differential accumulations, so, too, I think that any critical vocabulary for analyzing and rectifying any current or foreseeable scene of instruction can be innovated only in a provisional and an improvisatory way.[10]

I quote this passage to give a sense of this new tentativity. It bypasses a facile opposition between the meta-narratives of a self-assured Modernism and the splintered, contradictory, localized mini-narratives typical of post-modernity to herald a sense of Foucault's limited-scale problematizations.[11] Here, I speak in my name, since O'Hara's book contains a violent attack on Foucault, who indeed should not matter much according to him. Of course, the Foucault he debunks is the American Foucault who has been taken hostage by cultural studies and historicism when both were deployed against Theory.

As Foucault stated in a 1984 interview responding to Rorty's objections, the issue was not to presuppose a collective subject that would be needed for any political action, but to ask questions in such a way that they will generate a "we," a collectivity capable of pushing questions left open in the wake of given problematizations. One can notice that "Fugitivity," whatever it is, has usually a bad press, from the stealthy spy planes sent in reconnaissance operations in Iraq to the Southern poetic and literary movement created in the late twenties to promote an early form of New Criticism, "The Fugitives."

---

[9]	Jon Elster, *Making Sense of Marx*, Cambridge: Cambridge University Press, 1985.
[10]	Daniel T. O'Hara, *Empire Burlesque: The Fate of Critical Culture in Global America.* Durham, Duke University Press, 2003, p. 166.
[11]	See "Polemics, politics and problematizations: an interview" in *The Foucault Reader*, Paul Rabinow (ed.). New York: Pantheon, 1984, p. 388.

It may be that we are too often afraid of anything that flaunts its transient nature. Lindsay Waters has compared Theory not just with a drug, but with the ultra fleeting impression of absolute knowledge that such a cheap drug can generate:

> Theory is to the academy what crack cocaine is to the ghetto: it gets you high real fast. You feel like the King of the World up there on your throne, taking it all in. And then you crash. It makes you feel like you understand everything, if only for a moment, and the hunger for that feeling is insatiable. In the end, theory, like crack, is nihilistic.[12]

Waters, a clear-sighted and ironic commentator, sums up the gist of Richard Rorty's attack on Theory in *Achieving our Country: Leftist Thought in 20th-Century America* (1998). Like O'Hara, Waters remained closer to Paul de Man, but both can only lament the triumph of a universal resistance to Theory.

Beings of flight

What does it entail to be be a "fugitive," then? For a detailed analysis of "flight" one can look at Proust's "The Fugitive," and we will not be at a loss for answers. It is of course Albertine who was famously defined as an "*être de fuite,*" a coining term for which "fugitive being" is a weak rendering, even before she becomes the "prisoner" of the narrator's jealous obsession. The rest is well-known: Albertine leaves the narrator for good, he tries to make her come back by sending her a tortuous letter in which he states that he wishes her to stay away. Then Albertine kills herself by falling from a horse; the narrator broods and mourns, accumulating more knowledge of her old betrayals and infidelities until he feels free to go to Venice on his own.

Beyond the jealous paranoia displayed by all of Proust's lovers, one realizes that Albertine's "*être de fuite*" is crucial to the love that binds her to the narrator. "Now this love, born first and foremost of a need to prevent Albertine from doing wrong, this love had thereafter preserved the trace of its origin. Being with her mattered little to me so long as I could prevent the fugitive creature ("*l' être de fuite*" between quotes in the original) from going to this place or to that."[13] (p. 442) Such being-fugitive stamps not only their previous love but also marks its limit:

---

[12] Lindsay Waters, "Dreaming with tears in my eyes", *Transition: An International Review*, no. 74, 1988, p. 87.

[13] Marcel Proust, *The Fugitive*, in *Remembrance of Things Past*, translated by C. K. Scott Moncrieff and Terence Kilmartin, New York, Random House, 1982, vol. III, p. 443.

Every woman feels that, the greater her power over a man, the more impossible it is to leave him except by sudden flight: a fugitive precisely because a queen. ("*Fugitive parce que reine, c'est ainsi.*") True, there is an extraordinary discrepancy between the boredom which she inspired a moment ago and, because she has gone, this furious desire to have her back again.[14]

Here is an obvious allegory. What Proust describes in obsessive detail over 400 pages about "fugitives" and their impact on those who remain in the same place applies all too well to our current relation to Theory. Theory can be considered as this "fugitive being," fugitive because a queen, boring when she is there with us but ardently desired once she has fled. Queen Theory reigns only when she is in flight, as she is now. The new fleeting being has fewer and weaker weapons than the older masculine model in which King Theory could always reign because it knew how to divide: "Disseminate, Differentiate, Wield difference to reign!" such would be the updating of an old motto.

Perhaps this is what impelled a mute and dying Benveniste to hand his scepter to Kristeva with the ominous letters: T-H-E-O. Let me quote the full context:

My friendship with Benveniste holds an important place in the period dominated by my participation in *Tel Quel*. . . . He secretly confided in me his belief that there were only two great French linguists: Mallarmé and Artaud. I can see him, some time later, at the hospital in Saint–Cloud, then later in Créteil, stricken with aphasia but surprisingly warm toward me, tracing with a trembling hand on a white sheet of paper the enigmatic letters T-H-E-O.[15]

Even though he was a world-renowned linguist, Benveniste evinced here a remarkably healthy skepticism facing language—and seems to have announced the current rejection of the myth of linguistics taken as a model of scientificity. More recently, Jeffrey Galt Harpham nailed the coffin of the myth of linguistics for Theory in his compellingly critical analysis, *Language Alone—The Critical Fetish of Modernity* (2002). Harpham shows that there has never been any consensus about language. A review of twentieth-century theories of language will prove that one can say almost anything about

---

[14] Marcel Proust, see footnote 13, p. 432.
[15] Julia Kristeva, "My memory's hyperbole," in *The Portable Kristeva*, Kelly Oliver (ed.). New York: Columbia University Press, 1997, p. 10.

language. Is not the mistake to transform something that still keeps a trace of the divine—*Theos*—into a science?

When Heidegger proceeded to examine the etymology of the word "theory," he had *theoria* derive from *theorein*, which calls up *thea*, the root of "theater," evoking looking, glancing and outward appearance, and from *horao*, which implies taking one's time in the contemplation. "Theory" was the supreme mode of existence for philosophers like Plato and Aristotle, a goal set to humanity in the *Nichomachean Ethics*.[16] Heidegger added a third derivation: *thea* and *orao* can be inflected to read *thea* and *ora*, and they lead to *Thea*, the goddess. Theory would entail the effort to behold the goddess *aletheia* in a contemplation that "keeps watch" over truth. In her study of "Theoria,"[17] Hannelore Rausch has gone beyond Heidegger, mapping various etymologies regrouped on the word, and she too stresses its religious overtones. Nevertheless, she points out an important meaning symptomatically omitted by Heidegger. Greek *theoria* was primarily connected with the noun *theoros*, meaning an "observer," a "spectator," someone who travels to see men and things; this is also an ambassador, an official witness sent by the city to represent it as a special envoy to religious ceremonies, in order to request an oracle, or to participate in special gatherings like games. The pledged deputy attested that important events had really taken place: a given theoros's reputation impacted on the renown of a whole city.

The meanings ascertained by Heidegger, the religious sense suggesting a vision of gods and goddesses, and the visual-epistemological beholding activity both converge in a function which is "political" in the strictest sense: the official representative who is sent as an eye-witness is more than a citizen on jury-duty, he is an ad hoc magistrate pledging his honor to the city's highest values; in his authorized gaze, everyday deeds will be integrated into a sacred "theater": there things will be seen under their most essential aspect, so that they can be recorded. Rausch has demonstrated conclusively that this meaning still adheres to the more philosophical usage found in Plato and Aristotle. Both agree essentially with Proust.

What can this teach us? First, that there is no site that has been reserved for Theory: the lessons we derive from life or fiction are fundamentally and essentially the same; one will indeed "make" theories from one's readings but also from one's loves, fears or chance encounters. What really counts is age, not old age necessarily but a certain passing of time leading to considerations

16 See William McNeill, *The Glance of the Eye: Heidegger, Aristotle and the Ends of Theory*. Albany: State University of New York Press, 1999.
17 Hannelore Rausch, *Theoria: Von ihrer sakralen zur philosophischen Bedeutung*. Munich: Wilhelm Fink, 1982.

of impending death and extraordinary survival in spite of all—often, American students who take a good theory class for the first time acknowledge that they have "aged a lot" in one semester. This is what Proust writes:[18]

> After a certain age our memories are so intertwined with one another that what we are thinking of, the book we are reading, scarcely matters anymore. We have put something of ourselves everywhere, everything is fertile, everything is dangerous, and we can make discoveries no less precious than in Pascal's *Pensées* in an advertisement for soap.

Proust confirms an insight that has been as crucial for Roland Barthes as for Slavoj Žižek.

I will return to the crucial role played by Albertine in Chapter 6, since I will connect her character with writing itself seen as an ultimate line of flight. Albertine will end up embodying perfect alterity, according to Levinas at least. Albertine, this being of flight, remains "other" even after her death. Her death has created a new depth, to be taken literally as a new verticality for the narrator. We find this in the penultimate page of *Time Regained*: "Deep Albertine, whom I saw sleeping and who was dead."[19] Even dead, she has fled: *mulier totalier aliter*. The Latin expression "*totaliter aliter*" (wholly other) comes from a medieval tale in which two monks, both from the same order, exchange visions of the paradise into which they will go when they die. Their imaginations differ greatly, and they promise to each other that whoever would die first, would come back to tell the other whether life after death resembles what they have imagined (*taliter*) or is different (*aliter*). Soon after, one of the monks dies. He duly appears in a dream to the surviving monk. He just says: "It is all different," ("*totaliter aliter*," completely different). Adorno uses this anecdote in order to condense in one striking formula Proust's major ambition: "'It's completely different,' could serve as the motto for Proust's 'search of lost time'—a body of research into the way it really was, as opposed to the way everyone says it was: the whole novel is an appeal at law filed by life against life."[20] Adorno compares this with the experience we may have that whatever is meaningful among our encounters with others seems to depend on an "author" who is behind and scripts our fates. Life judges itself

---

[18] Marcel Proust, see footnote 13, pp. 553–4.

[19] Marcel Proust, *Le Temps Retrouvé: A la Recherche du Temps Perdu*, Jean-Yves Tadié (ed.). Paris: Gallimard, Pléaide, vol. IV, 1989, p. 624, my translation.

[20] Theodor W. Adorno, "Short commentaries on Proust," in *Notes to Literature*, vol. 1, Shierry Weber Nicholsen (transl.). New York: Columbia University Press, 1991, p. 176. For the original, "*Revisionsprozess des Lebens gegen das Leben*," see Theodor W. Adorno, *Noten zur Literatur* II. Frankfurt: Suhrkamp, 1969, p. 98.

and appeals against itself in the name of Literature, following a process which can be historicized. Such a process corresponds to the end of the open society presupposed as a model by liberalism, since now we only live under a regime of "preestablished disharmony."[21]

Fears of flying

Adorno's joke on Leibnitz's phrase captures an essential character of the new millennium. The twenty-first century was born with a bang, not a whimper—the September 11 airplane attacks masterminded by committed and radicalized PhD students, and the subsequent wars it generated, leading to domino effects throughout the world, have marked the end of the optimism, albeit critical, about globalization still evinced by Hardt and Negri. Then, US state officials and pedagogues suddenly discovered that America lacked students trained in eastern or mid-eastern languages or people conversant with the emerging cultures that have arisen from the collapse of former colonial or commercial empires. The utopia of a peaceful hybridization of cultures that is dubbed "multiculti" belongs to a globalization project that had borrowed the late-Hegelian fantasy of the "end of History." This view assumes that history keeps repeating itself neither as tragedy nor as farce but as a bourgeois comedy whose democratic and capitalistic happy ending has been scripted in advance, at least since Kojève took upon himself to rewrite Hegel and since Fukuyama attempted to translate this into the idiom of the American right.

All this would be nothing more than a Western projection, the well-meaning entropic daydream of a world in which differences are not abolished straight away but blend harmoniously to produce more pungency and subtlety. Alas, in the variegated menu offered by "other" cultures that come with their original flavors, exotic spices turn to poisons when an uneven economic development leads to a struggle to death between antagonistic fundamentalisms and incompatible foundational creeds. It is then time to rethink the generous utopia underpinning multiculturalism, and assess whether we can still cling to a concept of "culture" (whether universalist or particularist) that would provide a safe haven protecting us from fanaticism, bigotry, intolerance and ethnic suspicion.

When I started teaching in the US, since it was known that I had been teaching for some time in France, the assumption was that I would be able to

---

[21] Theodor W. Adorno, "Short Commentaries on Proust," see footnote 18, p. 177.

"do" Theory the way Monsieur Jourdain spoke "prose" ... It took me some time to realize that a scholar who would refer to, say, Hegel, Derrida, Kristeva or Lacan would be enlisted quasi automatically in the camp of "Theory." So far, I and several French friends had entertained the illusion that we were just being a little more "modern" or perhaps "radical" in the etymological sense by contrast with an older "humanistic" way of dealing with literary discourse. When that battle had been won, since we were uncomfortably close to some major actors in what we would call just philosophical debates, we could not ignore important divergences between camps like those of the Deleuzians, the Derridians, the feminists, and the Lacanians—not to speak of the linguists and the phenomenologists. This is why it was more difficult to produce a syncretic or globalized notion of Theory as such, which seemed to be a uniquely American obsession.

The definition of fugitive Theory that I propose entails a philosophical awareness of possible moves facing literature, visual culture, comparative religion or history, each of these domains constituting a moving archive defined by a complex layering of institutions and texts. Yet Theory does not just correspond to philosophy. We need to distinguish once more between Theory with a capital T, the Theory that dominated in the seventies, the fugitive theory of today, and mere "theories" such as can be listed together in an Encyclopedia of Theories.[22] Yet such lists have little to do with literary Theory. During a discussion with Gregg Lambert on "The Future of Theory and Theory Today," a scientist in the audience alluded to Popper's "hypotheses" that would be tested or verified by facts. Some would be discarded and a new "theory" would be produced in their place. Were we alluding to this sense of theory? We had to distinguish between Theory as a contested field in the humanities and the scientific concept of theories about matter, dark holes, energy and our expanding or cooling universe. A Popperian model has little to do with what we were alluding to when talking about "Theory," by which we meant teaching Bhaba, Kristeva, Butler, Said and others ... Indeed, each discipline gives a specific meaning to "theory"—think for instance of the psychoanalytic sense of "infantile theories" about sexuality or the mathematical use of "meta-language." In the humanities, the field of what is commonly called "Theory," half-way between philosophy and aesthetics, cannot be predicted upon a principle of verifiability, precisely because it is a field created by "inventors of discursivity, to quote Foucault's famous expression.

---

[22] See for instance Jennifer Bothamley (ed.), *A Dictionary of Theories*. Farmington Hill: Gale Research, 1993.

In "What is an Author?" (1969) Foucault distinguishes his position from that of Roland Barthes who had argued one year earlier that authors had to be decreed "dead" as they could only play the part of bourgeois owners of a meaning that had to be given back to the crowd of readers. Without granting back the old privileges and the control over meaning to singular authors, Foucault explained that one needed these authors' names at least to put them forward as sign-posts and recognizable markers in historical discourses articulated in their wake. For Foucault, the author-function is absolutely indispensable if we want to write a historiography of culture. The concept is all the more crucial when we deal with what he calls "inventors of discursivity" or "initiators of discursive practices."[23]

Among them, Freud and Marx figure preeminently. Foucault describes how the necessary returns to foundational texts will not simply point out lacks or gaps but transform the discursive practice governing a whole field: "A study of Galileo's works could alter our knowledge of the history, but not the science, of mechanics; whereas a re-examination of the books of Freud or Marx can transform our understanding of psychoanalysis or Marxism." (LCP, 137–8) If Marxism and psychoanalysis do not have the status of hard sciences, it is because they are still in debt to the texts of a founder, a founder who leaves a legacy of future strategies that are both marked by future resemblances and future differences:

> [Marx and Freud] cleared a space for the introduction of elements other than their own, which, nevertheless, remain within the field of discourse they initiated. In saying that Freud founded psychoanalysis, we do not simply mean that the concept of libido or the technique of dream analysis reappear in the writings of Karl Abraham or Melanie Klein, but that he made possible a certain number of differences with respect to his books, concepts and hypotheses, which all arise out of psychoanalytic discourse.
>
> (LCP, 132)

Unlike scientific inventors, the "founders of discursivity" cannot be accused of error. Foucault even writes that "there are no "false" statements in the work of these initiators" (LCP, 134)—but it is precisely for this reason that their theories demand a constant reactivation. In fact, such theories are productive

---

[23] Michel Foucault, *Language, Counter-Memory, Practice*, Donald F. Bouchard (ed.). Ithaca: Cornell University Press, 1977. Abbreviated as LCP.

because of their "constructive omissions" which in their turn demand endless returns to the original text. Once more, it is not an origin that would be defined by truth procedures or verification. The textual origin is entirely porous, full of gaps and holes, and our serial returns are textual: the return "is always a return to a text in itself; specifically, to a primary and unadorned text with particular attention to those things registered in the interstices of the text, its gaps and absences. We return to those empty spaces that have been masked by omission or concealed in a false and misleading plenitude." (LCP, 135) Foucault made it clear that the "return" to Marx (with Althusser) or Freud (with Lacan) did not entail respectful imitation but a type of reading that is also a creative rewriting.

There is a "return" of Theory despite a demise that has been announced repeatedly in the press and academia, but one cannot resuscitate the unitary model elaborated by Althusser. Theory can no longer function as a unifying canon or set of concepts commonly shared so as to underpin the diversity of spoken languages and the infinity of "visited" cultures. Theory thus defined comes closer to Derrida's idea that what counts is to be able to speak at least two (if not more) languages at once. What counts is less our election of Levinas or Heidegger as "master thinkers" than our awareness that in their works, tensions, inconsistencies or divisions are more productive than systematic architectonics. A sense of inner division thus adheres to the schools emerging out of the demise of monologic Theory. Now that "'language" has proven inadequate as a founding paradigm and has shown that it was merely "an ideology of the science of language," Theory will have less qualms to go back to its origins, to the place where it was born, that is, philosophy. Wittgenstein will work as well as Heidegger, Pierce as well as Nietzsche, or indeed, as Proust knew, Pascal's *Pensées* along with some publicity. This does not mean calling for a return to philosophy as a stable site of discourse after all others have failed, but suggests that Theory should work through philosophy relentlessly, destabilizing it in the name of other discourses, among which literature will only provide one more path and not a weaker mode of readability. A model might be Socrates who loved nothing like wonder and seduction, and who, moreover, believed that any untaught slave could rediscover the principles of science provided the right questions be asked. These questions, if they can be articulated together, define a "problematic." That is what Foucault called the "problematizations" that allow one to mediate between the singularity of given texts and the generality of repeatable procedures based on definable concepts. Yet these concepts do not have to build a consistent totality. To exemplify this, I will allude to an influential manifesto written by Hélène Cixous, a "fugitive" manifesto to be sure, the well-known "Laugh of the Medusa."

Laughing at theory

Written in 1975, it hasn't lost its edge and bite.[24] Cixous's position was clear enough then: she allied herself with the politics of American feminists while rejecting their brand of identity politics. On the other side, she launched a new lesbianism that insisted on the possibility of giving birth.[25] One sees this in a digression on motherhood, a term that she refuses to abandon to masculine clichés.

> Bring the other to life. Women know how to live detachment; giving birth is neither losing nor increasing. It's adding life to another. Am I dreaming? Am I misrecognizing? You, the defenders of "theory," the sacrosanct yes-men of Concept, enthroners of the phallus (but not of the penis): once more you'll say that all this smacks of "idealism," or what's worse, you'll splutter that I'm a "mystic."[26]

To whom is this attack directed? No doubt, to the Lacanians and the Althusserians, too prompt to wield the term of "Theory" as an absolute weapon. Cixous's diatribe goes on: "And what about the libido? Haven't I read the 'Signification of the Phallus'? And what about separation, what about that bit of self for which, to be born, you undergo an ablation—an ablation, so they say, to be forever commemorated by your desire?"[27] Here lies the leitmotiv of this manifesto: a concerted critique of Freud's and Lacan's phallocentrism, the latter being recognized by the title of his famous essay published in *Écrits*.

This evokes the disintegration of a certain Freudianism–Marxism elaborated by Althusser and Lacan in the name of Theory. In 1973, Lacoue–Labarthe and Nancy published *The Title of the Letter*,[28] which Lacanians interpreted as an attack led by Derrideans against their own camp. In 1975, Jacques Derrida published "The truth factor" in *Poétique*, a review co-directed by Cixous. This time, the fall-out was manifest, as historians of structuralism

---

[24] See the recent republication with a new introduction: Hélène Cixous, *Le Rire de la Méduse et autres ironies*. Paris: Galilée, 2010.

[25] Hélène Cixous, "The laugh of the Medusa," Keith Cohen and Paul Cohen (trans), *Signs*, vol. 1, no. 4 (Summer 1976), p. 885.

[26] Cixous, see footnote 23, p. 891.

[27] Cixous, see footnote 23, p. 891.

[28] Philippe Lacoue-Labarthe and Jean-Luc Nancy, *The Title of the Letter: A Reading of Lacan*, François Raffoul and David Pettigrew (trans). New York: State University of New York Press, 1992.

like François Dosse and François Cusset have shown.[29] A certain branch of feminism was leaning towards Derrida, while Philippe Sollers and Julia Kristeva chose to remain faithful to Lacan, thus provoking further quarrels. Meanwhile, Lacanians were trying to score points in the aforementioned game of checkers by elaborating new "sexuation formulas," according to which a male or female subject could sexually position him/herself either as a man or as a woman.

"The laugh of the Medusa" took part in this debate, heralding the emergence of a specific French feminism. On one side, Cixous takes her American friends as models: "We will rethink womankind beginning with every form and every period of her body. The Americans remind us, 'We are all Lesbians'; that is, don't denigrate woman, don't make of her what men have made of you."[30] This evokes the history of militant feminism in the 1970s, marked by Ti-Grace Atkinson, Adrienne Rich and many others. If the allusion remains vague, it is because of the critique brought in by the next paragraph. The text summarizes the global struggles met by women in the US and the question of activists wondering if class-struggle-oriented involvement surpasses sex struggles: "This alteration is already upon us—in the United States, for example, where millions of night crawlers are in the process of undermining the family and disintegrating the whole of American sociality."[31] This self-satisfied outlook may appear overblown, and is nuanced in a note: "But this takes place within an economical-metaphysical closure whose limit, because it remains unanalyzed, un-theorized, will stop and block (unless there is a change, for now impossible to foresee) the impact of the movement quite soon."[32] Here Cixous adopts a more cautious tone and uses a critical vocabulary close to Jacques Derrida's. What prevails is a definition of femininity that is not limited to a struggle for power, that is not a direct political demand, because it seeks instead to bring about a radical disruption of language, of thought, of bodies and of sexuality. The aim is to avoid essentialism, to eschew a stable theory of feminine identity. Women's writing thrusts, steals and flies (*vole*) in order to undermine male domination—but finds its models in the writings of men like James Joyce and Jean Genet. This is how Theory will learn to fly or to be perpetually in flight.

---

[29] See François Dosse, *History of Structuralism*, Deborah Glassman (trans.). Minneapolis: University of Minnesota Press, 1997; and François Cusset, *French Theory*, Jeff Fort (trans.). Minneapolis: University of Minnesota Press, 2008.

[30] Cixous, see footnote 23, p. 881.

[31] Cixous, see footnote 23, p. 883.

[32] Cixous, see footnote 22, p. 50, note 1. However, this note does not appear in the 1976 English translation of Cixous's text.

To accompany the burgeoning of a feminist strain of Derrideanism, we have to resort to the oxymoron contained in the untranslatable French verb *voler*: it means both to steal and to fly; thieving and giving, flying high in the sky and fleeing low on the ground, multiplying lines of perspective without the classical binary of the Real and the Imaginary together. The classic Freudian vocabulary, with terms such as fantasy, the unconscious, repression, the uncanny, is replayed differently, recaptured creatively; it is diverted and made to a different use, rejecting Freud's canonical doctrine about the genesis of feminine sexuality. Hence writing consists in liberating one's gendered unconscious; this is an almost surrealist agenda, to which a phallocrat like André Breton would not have objected. Yet, the change lies in the link established between the unconscious and the body. This body is feminized and climaxing. If the rock of castration is being struck at its heart, as in Lacan's last works, what is highlighted concerns bisexuality. There is no bisexuality in Lacan's work while it is present in Freud's, and in Jung's too. This bisexuality is not to be understood as the Jungian fantasy of the totalizing of the two sexes, because it remains marked by *différance*. In short, this type of bisexuality does not cancel differences, but rather exaggerates them. In this quarrel against Lacanian psychoanalysis in the name of a feminized deconstruction, what ultimately prevails is the performative dimension. The gesture consists in reviving writing through atomic explosions. The Freudian drives atomize Theory with bursts of laughter and jubilant lyrical assocations. Following the lead of Medusa, we can trust a fugitive theory, a theory which will be less male-oriented and dominant, more ironical, more paradoxical, and finally more productive. A passage from the second book of Blake's *Milton* captures poetically such a link between fugitivity and fecundity:

> There is a moment in each day that Satan cannot find,
> Nor can his watch fiends find it; but the Industrious find
> This moment and it multiply, & when it once is found
> It renovates every moment of the day if rightly placed.

It behoves to us to discover "such a Period / Within a Moment: a Pulsation of the Artery," the point in time when both the "Poet's Work is Done" and "all the Great Events of Time start forth and are conceived."(*Milton*, 29: 1–3)

3

Investigations of a Kantian Dog

Investigations of a dog

The invocation of Milton will bring us closer to an array of animals, from snakes to dogs. To conceive fully what a human being can do for the future, we have to imagine what a dog can wonder about, if it is not food. I will begin by quoting a series of questions, anguished questions assuredly, questions coming from a dog who is not sure about the boundaries of his own species.

Where, then, are the fellows of my species? Yes, that is my complaint, that's it. Where are they? Everywhere and nowhere. Perhaps one of them is my neighbor, three jumps away from me; we often call to one another, and he comes to me as well, I do not go to him. Is he a fellow of my species? I don't know. To tell the truth, I don't recognize anything of the sort in him, but it's possible. It is possible, yet nothing is more improbable; when he's away, with the aid of all my imagination, just for a lark, I can discover in him much that is suspiciously familiar but when he stands before me, all my fantasies are a joke.[1]

The wording being very tricky, I quote the original, and let the ambivalence of "Genossen" (comrades) and "Art" (type, kind) appear:

Wo sind denn aber meine Artgenossen? Ja, das ist die Klage, das ist sie eben. Wo sind sie? Überall und nirgends. Vielleicht ist es mein Nachbar, drei Sprünge weit von mir, wir rufen einander oft zu, er kommt auch zu mir herüber, ich zu ihm nicht. Ist er mein Artgenosse? Ich weiß nicht, ich erkenne zwar nichts dergleichen an ihm, aber möglich ist es. Möglich ist es, aber doch ist nichts unwahrscheinlicher. Wenn er fern ist, kann ich zum Spiel mit Zuhilfenahme aller Phantasie

---

[1] Franz Kafka, "Researches of a dog," Stanley Corngold (trans.), in *Selected Stories*. New York: Norton, 2007, p. 147.

manches mich verdächtig Anheimelnde an ihm herausfinden, steht er dann aber vor mir, sind alle meine Erfindungen zum Lachen.[2]

I'll come back at the end of the book to Kafka's weird sense of humor and to his irrepressible laughter. What interests me in the context of theoretical discussions of "being human" and the theories of the exception is the rationale for these frantic investigations of a dog.[3] They are presented in Kafka's enigmatic tale that generated a series of superb exhibitions in Paris at the Maison Rouge and in other cities in 2010–2011.[4] Kafka's story dates from 1922, it is thus one of the last fiction texts that Kafka was able to complete, if it is indeed complete, since the text does not end on any sense of closure at the end. It belongs to the series of animal parables that culminate with "The burrow," this time a clearly unfinished text ending in mid-sentence. Like "The burrow," "Investigations of a dog" presents itself as a first-person narrative, and it is predicated upon the idea that the dog narrator can never understand or even perceive the presence or agency of mere humans. He can only see and know dogs, thus he can never fully grasp where his food comes from, why some dogs can dance and others not, and so on. He explains that it was the vision of a group of seven dogs dancing to the tune of an exotic music that launched him, a long time ago, on the path of scientific investigation. The strange humor of this story derives from a systematic application of dramatic irony—after we have re-read the tale, we will know that we know more than this dog, but we will also have sympathized with his thoughts even though they are produced by a thinking that excludes us. And yet, if the dog only perceives the existence of his brothers, he keeps interrogating what brotherhood means, a question that was of special relevance to Kakfa, especially when he had to define his own relationship to Jewishness. He wrote in his diary in 1914: "What have I in common with Jews? I have hardly anything in common with myself and should stand very quietly in a corner, content that I can breathe."[5] Unhappily for the dog narrator, he cannot stay quietly in a corner and has to exhaust himself in futile or abortive investigations of

---

[2]   http://de.wikisource.org/wiki/Forschungen_eines_Hundes
[3]   I am following the title of the Paris show. For a recent translation with that title, see Joyce Crick's version in Franz Kafka, *A Hunger Artist and Other Stories*. Oxford: Oxford University Press, 2012, p. 137.
[4]   "Les Recherches d'un Chien", exhibition curated by Paula Aisemberg and Noëligle Roux, La Maison Rouge and FACE Foundation, 23 October 2010–2016, January 2011.
[5]   Franz Kafka, *Diaries (8 January 1914)*, Martin Greenberg and H. Arendt (trans). New York: Schocken, 1975, p. 252. On this topic, see Vivian Liska's excellent *When Kafka Says We*. Bloomington: Indiana University Press, 2009.

what it means to be a dog, trying to get at the essence of "dogdom" (*Hundschaft*). One of the key issues that he hopes his investigations will solve is the source of the food provided to the dogs.

The initial experience that made him move from the state of being a mere "puppy" to that of an adult dog was his fateful encounter with seven *Musikerhunde*, a group of "music dogs" all seized by some kind of mystical ecstasy. Everything was music around them, even though they were "just dogs like you and me." (p. 135) Then, in spite of the bewitching music, the narrator discovers that these dogs walk on their hind legs, and thus look shamefully naked. (p. 134) The narrator concludes that he has discovered sin, and he wants to investigate it, while retaining his pure being. What he is after is the series of laws that govern the world and nature, and his nature is such that one basic law is "Wet on everything, as much as you can." (p. 139) The curious *petitio principi* of the narrator is that "all knowledge . . . resides in dogs." (p. 141) It is indeed a "dogknowledge" marked by desire—as soon as he thinks about food, he is seized by desire, and he knows that this desire will be shared by the others: "My howling and yours mingle and unite, everything aims at finding oblivion in ecstasy, but the one thing that you wanted to achieve above all—admission of knowledge—remains denied to you." (p. 141)

It seems that Kafka is rewriting Hegel's *Phenomenology of Spirit* as a quest for the "absolute" knowledge of a dog. Indeed, if we just look at a passage on animals, we can verify that Hegel had scripted this move when he discussed the only solid basis of knowledge—sensory experience. Hegel refers those who trust sensory certainty to the ancient Eleusinian mysteries, the rites of Ceres and Bacchus. Such ancient wisdom entails that whoever partakes of the rite will also participate actively by consuming the bread and the wine offered during the mysteries. Somewhat surprisingly, and also polemically, Hegel moves on to include animals in the awareness of such a basic truth:

> Even brute animals are not excluded from this wisdom but show themselves rather to be most deeply initiated into it. For they do not stand still before sensory things as existing-in-themselves, but despairing of such "reality," and with full certainty of the nothingness of sensory things, they help themselves without further ado and eat them up. And all of Nature celebrates, like these animals, those revelatory mystic rites, which offer instruction as to just what the "truth" of sensory things is.[6]

---

[6]   *Hegel's Phenomenology of Spirit*, translated and edited by Howard P. Kainz. University Park: The Pennsylvania University Press, 1994, p. 41.

It is not clear whether Kafka had read Hegel (although he may well have), but his parody of the constant trial by error that defines the progression of consciousness in *The Phenomenology of Spirit* also impregnates his dog's searches; his very style owes something to Hegel's syntax and terminology. It is as if Kafka was rewriting *The Phenomenology of Spirit* from the point of view of a dog devoured by the *libidio sciendi*. A good example might be this:

> People begin to produce reasons, to piece together some sort of rational foundation, they make a beginning, although they will not go beyond this beginning. But that is still something. And in the process something comes to light that, while not the truth—we will never get this far—intimates the deeprootedness of the lie. All the senseless phenomena of our life, and quite particularly the most senseless, can be rationalized in this way. Not completely, of course—that is the devilish joke—but just enough to ward off awkward questions.
>
> (p. 144)

The dog then veers off at a tangent to discuss a particular type of dog he calls "air dogs" (*Lufthunde*), idealistic people who like to speculate, homegrown philosophers and who are therefore more dependent on their "fellow dogs."

This is because the central issue is that of "fellow beings," and the notion of kinship in a given group of living beings. My preamble on Kafka should introduce us to Derrida's discussion of the disputed boundaries between humans and animals. This started at the Cerisy Conference devoted to "The autobiographical animal" in July 1997. Derrida was intervening in a debate concerning bioethics and the rights of animals that had been launched by Peter Singer, and he was also dialoguing with Elizabeth de Fontenay, whose extraordinary compendium was to follow.[7] Two years after the Cerisy conference, a vibrant and complex plea for animals was provided by J. M. Coetzee's *The Lives of Animals*, thus pushing these investigations into the domain of fiction as much as that of ethics. In July 1997, Derrida started from a homely experience: would he feel naked if he walked from his shower in front of his cat? This led him to a series of mediations and critical discussions published posthumously as *The Animal That Therefore I Am*.[8]

---

[7] See Elisabeth de Fontenay, *Le Silence des bêtes: La philosophie à l'épreuve de l'animalité*. Paris: Fayard, 1998.

[8] Jacques Derrida, *The Animal That Therefore I Am*, translated by David Wills, and edited by Marie-Louise Mallet. New York,: Fordham, 2008, hereafter abbreviated as TATTIA.

Bobby, the Last Kantian dog

The Cerisy conference has been published by Marie-Louise Mallet, and it offers an interesting viewpoint since it keeps the order of all the presentations. They include the talk that followed Derrida's long intervention, Alain David's lecture on Levinas and his dog Bobby.[9] Alain David, who happens to be an old friend of mine, gave a spirited commentary on "The name of a dog, or natural rights," a text that Levinas had published in 1975.[10] David comments on this atypical autobiographical narrative, in which Levinas meditates on an experience from the war. He had been a war prisoner in Germany, as Louis Althusser was at the time. Levinas had been spared from extermination as a Jew by his status as soldier in the French army. He had been captured on June 18, 1940, and then interned in a *stalag*, a prisoner's camp reserved for Jewish soldiers. All the biographers of Levinas agree that the experience he narrates really happened, even though it displays troubling coincidences. The Jewish commando bore the number 1492, the year of the expulsion of all Jews from Spain. It numbered exactly seventy prisoners, like the Septuagint, the pre-Christian translators of the Jewish Bible into Greek. In the eyes of the Germans who were around, these prisoners were not felt to be really human: they were "stripped of their human skin," "subhuman, a gang of apes."[11] One day, a wandering dog came to play with them and became their friend. As a game, the prisoners called him Bobby. Bobby, who had no master and survived at the outskirts of the camp, clearly recognized the French prisoners as full human beings. Levinas concludes his essay with a beautiful evocation of the stray dog:

> Perhaps the dog that recognized Ulysses beneath his disguise on his return from the Odyssey was a forebear of our own. But no, no! There, they were in Ithaca and the Fatherland. Here, we were nowhere. This dog was the last Kantian in Nazi Germany, without the brain needed to universalize maxims and drives. He was a descendant of the dogs of Egypt. And his fierce growling, his animal faith, was born from the silence of his forefathers on the banks of the Nile.[12]

---

[9] Jacques Derrida, "L'animal que donc je suis (à suivre)", in *L'Animal autobiographique. Autour de Jacques Derrida*, Marie-Louise Mallet (ed.). Paris: Galilée, 1999, p. 264, note 1.
[10] Emmanuel Levinas, *Difficile liberté*. Paris: Albin Michel, 1976, p. 199. Quoted by Alain David, "Cynesthèse: auto-portrait au chien," in Derrida, see footnote 9, pp. 303–18. See also Alain David, "Lecture de 'Nom d'un chien ou le droit naturel' d'Emmanuel Levinas," in *Mono kurgusuz labirent*, "Reflections on Lévinas", Istanbul, 2010, pp. 75–96.
[11] Levinas, see footnote 8, p. 153.
[12] Levinas, see footnote 11, p. 153.

Alain David rightly asserts that this is one of Levinas's most beautiful essays.[13] Nevertheless, it contains problematic assertions that Derrida will later question and deconstruct. We have seen how Levinas displaces the mythical parallels from Homer's Odyssey to the Bible: this dog is Egyptian and his barking calls up Exodus. Is he a particular dog or an allegory? David hesitates between a definition of the dog as "life without form, *bios* without *logos*"[14] in order to suggest that there is a part of animality in all of us, and a definition of the "dog according to the letter", a letter that would put him beyond any reductive characterization, since the letter always implies the "reduction of a *bios*, of a *zoê* to a *logos*".[15] I cannot sum up here this rich and moving essay, that expands Levinas's central insights, and simply note that such a deep and empathic commentary hardly prepares for Derrida's violent response to Levinas.

This is to be found in *The Animal That Therefore I Am*. Derrida begins by being astonished by the fact that Levinas never made much room for animals in his philosophy. He sees in this lack a symptom of Levinas's wish to situate himself in human problematics of the subject as endowed with a face and with speech. The animal would be excluded from the start given the restriction of the definition of what constituted an Other. Derrida's critique focuses on a key issue: for Levinas, an animal would be deprived of a face. Derrida quotes a dialogue between John Llewelyn and Levinas during which the latter insists upon the irreducible difference constituted by a human face. Levinas tells Llewelyn: "I cannot say at what moment you have the right to be called 'face'. The human face is completely different and only afterwards do we discover the face of an animal. I don't know if a snake has a face. I can't answer that question."[16] We can note Levinas's prudence when it comes to a snake, as opposed to a more anthropomorphic animal like a dog. As Levinas adds, we do not want animals to suffer because we transfer to them what we know of suffering.

In another conversation with Robert Bernasconi and David Wood, Levinas spoke of an extension of his ethics to animals as a "catachresis" corresponding to a figurative extension of ourselves.[17] Derrida discusses at length Levinas's inability to find a face in a snake. Derrida insists relentlessly:

> For declaring that he doesn't know where the right to be called "face"
> begins means that he doesn't know at bottom what a face is, what the

---

[13] David, in Derrida, see footnote 9, p. 310.
[14] David, in Derrida, see footnote 9, p. 317.
[15] David, in Derrida, see footnote 9, p. 312.
[16] Quoted by Derrida, see footnote 8, pp. 107–8.
[17] Quoted by Derrida, see footnote 8, p. 150. Cf. *The Provocation of Lévinas: Rethinking the Other*, Robert Bernasconi and David Wood (eds). London: Routledge, 1988, pp. 168–80.

word means, what governs its usage, and that means confessing that one didn't say what responding means. Doesn't that amount, as a result, to calling into question the whole legitimacy of the discourse and ethics of the "face" of the other, the legitimacy and even the sense of every proposition concerning the alterity of the other, the other as my neighbor or my brother, etc.?

(TATTIA, p. 109)

This would entail a whole recusation of Levinas's ethics and his phenomenology of otherness. As always, Derrida's gesture is that of philosophical rigor: he stops a demonstration before it can pan out as a humanism of the other because it has excluded an apparently trivial exception—the face of a snake. Deconstruction takes the frame of a system and focuses on the terms that have been silently excluded or occulted since the beginning.

This is why Derrida does not answer directly to Levinas's query, but simply quotes a poem by Paul Valéry, whose famous "Sketch of a Snake" ("*Ébauche d'un serpent*") turns the "face" of a snake into the image of seduction and even radical evil. A long tradition lies in wait, and one could think of Book X of Milton's *Paradise Lost*, in which Satan narrates his fight with God, and boasts of his main triumph: having seduced Eve disguised as a serpent. The fact that all reptiles have been spurned as inferior creatures subsequently is not a price too high to pay given the success of Satan's enterprise. Expecting to be cheered and applauded for these high deeds, Satan is surprised to see that all the demons he has gathered begin to hiss him. Their pandemonium turns into an animal cacophony, after which his own face loses its human contours and turns fully bestial:

> His Visage drawn he felt to sharp and spare,
> His Arms clung to his Ribs, his Legs entwining
> Each other till supplanted he fell
> A monstrous Serpent on his Belly prone . . .

(X, lines 511–14)

The loss of this "visage" entails the loss of speech:

> . . . *he would have spoke,*
> But hiss for hiss return'd with forked tongue
> To forked tongue, for now were all transform'd
> Alike, to Serpents . . .

(X, lines 517–20)

What follows is a catalogue of monstrous snakes whose final metamorphosis signifies the open revelation and the contagion of evil. However, this passage confirms Levinas's intuition that a face is indissolubly linked to speech. Speech does not have to be spoken by the animals, since it may be attributed to a human catachresis, the lending of a figurative trope when the literal meaning is lacking. Yet Derrida insists: Levinas would assert: "Where there is evil, there is face." (TATTIA, p. 110) One important consequence is that the category of murder can never apply to the animal. The prohibition "Thou shalt not kill" is reserved for the human face. Hence one can kill animals freely and without any guilt. Animal sacrifices are not prohibited by the Jewish Law, only regulated, and in these laws the dog often occupies a place apart. Levinas began "The name of a dog, or natural rights" with an epigraph from Exodus 22.31: "You shall be men consecrated to me; therefore you shall not eat any flesh that is torn by beast in the field; you shall cast it to the dogs."[18] Levinas opens with the Biblical prohibition about eating corpses—they can be left to the dogs. Man, even when he eats flesh in the fields is watched upon by God. In it is this loaded context that Derrida returns to Levinas's autobiographical narrative concerning Bobby.

His reading aims at disenchanting those who, like Alain David, allowed themselves to be seduced too easily by Levinas's superb rhetorics (TATTIA, p. 114). Very rapidly, he voices three fundamental reproaches. When Levinas writes: "For him, there was no doubt (*c'était incontestable*) that we were men,"[19] Levinas does not specifiy what is the ground for this absence of doubt. This does not define what makes "men" of these French Jews. Then the attribution to Bobby of a Kantianism that would be dead in Germany is less generous than it seems: Levinas doubts that Bobby has any reasoning faculty since he is "without the brain to universalize maxims and drives."[20] Let us note that the French original had "the maxims of his drives."[21] Derrida can then easily refute the thesis that Bobby was a true Kantian dog: ". . . how can one ignore that a Kantian who doesn't have 'the brain needed' to universalize maxims of 'drives' would not be Kantian, especially if the maxims in question are the maxims of 'drives' that would have made Kant bark." (TATTIA, p. 114) The attack is fierce, and Derrida has to apologize for having felt the need to "tear into" such a beautiful text. But tear he does. Finally, he examines the two exclamation marks that dot the end of Levinas's text. A double "But no! But no!" (in the original) implies a tremendous power of negation.

[18] Emmanuel Levinas, *Difficile liberté*. Paris: Albin Michel, 1976, p. 151.
[19] Levinas, see footnote 18, p. 153.
[20] Levinas, see footnote 18, p. 153.
[21] Levinas, see footnote 18, p. 216.

Such rhetorical violence would derive from a tension between Bobby, a particular dog, and the allegorical role he is made to perform. The exclamation mark has already accompanied an injunction at an earlier moment of the text: "But enough of allegories!"[22] Even earlier, Levinas has exclaimed: "But enough of this theology!"[23] Now the dog comes from Egypt, and not from Greece. Is he as Egyptian as Moses was, according to Freud, that is? Is he one of the dogs that accompanied Moses and the tribe of the freed Jews during Exodus? Derrida concludes that this dog is neither Biblical nor Kantian, but closer to Descartes's mechanical animals; he is a sort of machine that can never speak, hence never reach any transcendence, or, if he does, it will be only negatively.

How can we understand Derrida's violence facing a philosopher who has often inspired him? If he decides to proceed to this severe critique of the foundations of Levinas's ethics of the Other, it is because he finds behind Levinas another adversary who claims Levinas as his spiritual father, Giorgio Agamben. We see this better in Derrida's 2001–2002 seminar on *The Beast and the Sovereign*, in which all of this pertains to an annoyed reaction against Agamben's philosophical claims. Derrida is irritated by Agamben's grandiose attributions of preeminence and originality. He mocks Agamben's assertion that Hegel has been the "first philosopher" who thought language as both "inside and outside itself,"[24] or that Levinas has been the "first" to understand and denounce the complicity between Heidegger and Nazism (BS, p. 94). Levinas would also have been the first to replace Heidegger's political drift to the right in the perspective of biopolitics. Fundamentally, what is regularly ironized is Agamben's theory of "exceptions" as based on the thoughts of Carl Schmitt.

The twelfth session returns to Agamben's distinction between *zoê* and *bios*, a distinction upon which the entire problematic of *Homo Sacer* is founded.[25] Quoting both Heidegger and Aristotle, Derrida points out a real issue for Agamben: if the concept of *zoê* defines "bare life," how is it possible that Aristotle defines man as *zoon politikon*? (BS, pp. 326–31) At the end of a thorough philological demonstration, Derrida points out that the alleged dichotomy is much less rigorous than what Agamben states. Going further, he pushes Agamben towards a dramatic alternative: either he affirms, like Michel Foucault, that politics have become bio-politics in our late modernity, or one affirms, as

[22] Levinas, see footnote 18, p. 152.
[23] Levinas, see footnote 18, p. 151.
[24] Jacques Derrida, *The Beast and the Sovereign*, Vol. 1, Geoff Bennington (trans.). Chicago: The University of Chicago Press, 2009, p. 93. Hence, BS and page number.
[25] Giorgio Agamben, *Homo Sacer: Sovereign Power and the Bare Life*, Daniel Heller-Roazen (trans.). Stanford: Stanford University Press, 1998.

Heidegger does, that these notions have always been with us, at least since Greek philosophers invented them. In which case, they would underpin our "metaphysics" and our "ontology" since time immemorial. It is the entire notion of bio-power that is at stake here. In a contradictory manner, Agamben founds himself both on the later Foucault and on Levinas, assuming that Levinas would have already criticized Heidegger's Nazism. Levinas would have already seen the infamy of Heidegger's notorious remarks on the holocaust compared with the problems posed by the industrialization of farming. This is a huge debate—I sincerely think that Derrida wins it, even if it entails being rude to Levinas. I will now try to show that even if I side with Derrida in this debate, I think that Levinas's philosophy of the other cannot be cornered so easily into aporias. To do so, I will turn to Levinas's original account of his discovery of Bobby the German dog. This will allow me to return to a theme already discussed in Chapter 2, Albertine as a "being of flight."

From Bobby to Albertine

I will begin this section with two quotes from Levinas's *Captivity Notebooks* whose proximity may prove startling. From Notebook 2: "'This is not a dog. He abandons his master to run after whoever (*n'importe qui*),' Tramel said. 'But that is precisely what a dog is,' Mimi answered."[26] And here is the second quote, this time from Notebook 6: "The dog Bobby is nice and friendly (*sympathique*) because he loves us without any ulterior motives (*sans arrière-pensée*), outside all our distinctions and social rules." (*CC*, p. 150) If, as we have seen, Derrida is severe in his critique of Levinas's anthropomorphism facing Bobby, it was above all to debunk Agamben's idea that there could be a "bare life" exemplified by animals caught up between *bios* and *zoê*.[27] For Derrida, as long as an animal speaks, the animal has a face, an idea which could be accepted by Levinas; to this, Derrida adds as long as an animal looks at you, the animal has a face. This is why Derrida answers to Levinas's parable with his own allegory: it is the gaze of a cat looking at his own naked body that makes him reflect on the alleged divide between men and animals.

In fact, one could argue that this problematic is already in Levinas when he considers the divide between humans and animals. If being a dog entails

---

[26] Emmanuel Levinas, *Carnets de captivité*, suivi de *Écrits sur la captivité*, et *Notes philosophiques diverses*, Vol. 1, Rodolphe Calin and Catherine Chalier (eds), with a Préface by Jean-Luc Marion. Paris: Bernard Grasset et IMEC, 2009. Abbreviated as *CC* and the page.

[27] See Derrida, footnote 8, pp. 106–18.

both being free while looking for a master and also abandoning one's master, then Levinas's stray Kantian dog heralds Derrida's errant and masterless writing. Such a notion would have been launched earlier by Proust, who is the privileged object of Levinas's attention in his *Captivity Notebooks*. Since all three point to an alterity beyond the human, this modernist and theoretical otherness can be equated either with love or with literature. In the second quote, we recognize the lineaments of the autobiographical vignette—the theme is already a Kantian, or more precisely Hegelian, for that matter, "recognition" of the other as belonging to humanity. The first note insists on the theme of anarchy and the absence of a master. Why is it that Bobby has no master? Has he fled a bad and sadistic owner from Germany, has he lost a good friend gone to war? One will never know, but the question remains. A dog is not only the noble companion of man, he is also a being who runs around everywhere and feels no constraint except his whim, appetite and desire (what Levinas later called "the maxims of his drives," a phrase that should not be reduced so quickly, as Derrida had done, to an absurd oxymoron).

Such anarchy recalls what Jacques Rancière will call, as we will see in Chapter 9, the errancy or truancy of the letter. This could also evoke the free letter that Plato tried to reduce and subsume under a concept in *Phaedrus*. Derrida gave a wonderful reading of this dialogue in "Plato's pharmacy." There might be a similarly errant grammatology at work in Levinas's war notebooks. One finds a similar thought in one of the "Philosophical notes" of the same period, under the heading of Plato, when Levinas quotes *Phaedrus* 230 a: "Am I a more complex creature and more puffed up with pride than Typhon, or a simpler, gentler being whom heaven has blessed with a quiet, un-Typhonic nature?"[28] He adds a commentary that is a sort of developed translation: "Am I a peaceful animal without so many complications, and who, by nature, participates in a divine destiny untainted by the fumes of pride?"[29] Typhon had a hundred snakes' heads or dragons' heads, and this snake-like figure contrasts eminently with the doctrine of "know thyself" reached in this passage. Levinas does not develop this theme here, but in several notes he sketches a philosophy of the interconnectedness of humans and animals. There is a fraternity here because we have to acknowledge a part of animality in all of us.

By comparison with the toiling prisoners of the *stalag*, animals look happier: they do not work: "*Animals do not work*" (underlined, *CC*, p. 84.)

---

[28] Plato, *The Collected Dialogues*, Edith Hamilton and Huntington Cairns (eds). Princeton: Princeton University Press, 1973, p. 478 (modified to be closer to Levinas's own quote).
[29] Levinas, *Notes philosophiques diverse*, see footnote 26, p. 308.

Levinas may have forgotten horses and cows here, since he seems caught up in a Tolstoian reverie about a natural state. Yet, in spite of this idealized leisure, animals display another important characteristic: they leave traces. This refers apparently to wild game or hares, as the following notes prove; we meet here for the first time a key concept, that of trace: "Like the animal that flees and that precisely then leaves on immaculate snow the traces that will allow one to find it." (*CC*, p. 84) One page later: "Walking on a road where there is no human trace, only the footsteps of wild game." (*CC*, p. 85) The combination of these two remarks leads to a critical rethinking of Heidegger's philosophy, not just from the point of view of ethics, as is often said, but from the point of view of a general erotics. Levinas writes thus: "A crucial element in my thinking—which is how it diverges from Heidegger's philosophy—is the primacy of the Other. *Eros* as a central moment." (*CC*, p. 134). Thus, if one can show that the theme of the animal participates in this alterity, and if it can be linked with a certain eroticism, then Derrida's critique becomes redundant. Here are two notes that follow one another: "The nation as mode of access to reality. Heidegger's world" and "The human foot—its humble appearance, poor animal. These are the two legs ('pattes') that still occupy the function of the animal in man. Not so with the hands." (*CC*, p. 105). Thus, any human body contains a duality: we have animal feet and human hands!

Animal life combines traces and memories of an ideal sympathy with the world. Against Heidegger, who famously said that animals are "poor in world," for Levinas, marks an intimate proximity with the world. He sees this in a book he has just read, the *Book of San Michele* by Axel Munthe, an author whom he admires:

> The contact with life—a direct contact with life as an entity. Through the animal reign. . . . Book that highlights the limitations of social philosophy. The sympathy with the animal world has no place in social metaphysics. The latter defined the place of man in the world: things and men are pigeonholed easily. They are objects of needs, tools, and men are either exploited or exploiters. Animals in sympathy with him . . . are only life, cannot be shelved in such categories.
>
> (*CC*, p. 127)

We find here again the theme of "sympathy" that had characterized Bobby from the first moment; there can be a mutual sympathy between men and animals. In another passage, Levinas comments on what he perceives as the horror of animal sexuality in Tolstoy: "T. feels horror for those beings . . . those women . . . yet full of beauty—who are only cows who walk on hind-legs for him." (*CC*, p. 143) Animals want to be happy, and sexual beings too—

this is accepted as such by Levinas, in contradistinction with Tolstoy's aristocratic disdain for the "baser" functions of sexuality. It happens that humans intervene in a sadistic manner in the lives of their pets, too: "A cat loses all its dignity if you step on its tail. One thought this was a decorative appendix ... and now this appears full of nerves. The cat is a mysterious animal, a sorcerer—Baudelaire's cat screaming like an old hag." (*CC*, p. 168) Levinas often quotes "The cats" by Baudelaire and he mentions several times Poe's "The Raven." At one point, it is his own wife's family that morphs suddenly into a feline group: "Image: I am sitting at a table with my in-law aunt. Surprise! She is a bitch! The uncle is a cat. How can I penetrate their lives as dogs and cats, their habits, their customs? It is so animal—enemical—madness, madness!" (*CC*, p. 188) In this quasi-Surrealist vignette, it becomes impossible to tell humans from animals.

Space is lacking for a systematic survey of all of Levinas's *Captivity Notebooks*, in which one can see quite early the intertwining of philosophical and literary preoccupations. The war notebooks throw light on Levinas's attitude facing literature, not only because we see him planning several novels in 1939–1940, but also because he considers writing a book of criticism on Proust: he plans his "work still to be completed" as divided between the "Philosophical" which includes a book aptly titled *Being and Nothingness*, the "Literary" with two novels in the making, one called *Sad Opulence* and the other *Unreality and Love*, and the "Critical," with a planned book on Proust.[30] As stated, Levinas's *Captivity Notebooks* show him planning several novels in 1939–1940, and a book of criticism on Proust:

My work still to be completed:
Philosophical:

1. Being and Nothingness
2. Time
3. Rosenzweig
4. Rosenberg

Literary:

1. Sad Opulence
2. Unreality and Love

Critical:
Proust.

(*Carnets*, p. 74)

[30] Levinas, *Carnets de Captivité*, see footnote 26, p. 74.

All this is to be found in a section in which Levinas quotes many passages from *Albertine Disparue*. One entry in particular sketches the entire argument of a later essay, "The other in Proust" (*Deucalion*, 2, 1947):

> In Proust, poetry of the pure social element. The interest lies not in "psychology" but in the theme: the social. The whole story of Albertine as a prisoner—is the story of one's relationship to the other. What is Albertine (and her lies) if she is not the very evanescence of the other, its reality made up of nothingness, its presence made up of absence, of the struggle with the ungraspable? And next to this—the quietude felt facing Albertine when she sleeps, facing Albertine turned vegetal.
>
> (*CC*, p. 72)

In 1947 as in 1942, Levinas criticizes Sartre who had contemptuously declared that Proust's psychology was not even Bergsonian, but simply went back to Ribot, the psychologist who studied heredity, habit and forgetting. Thus the point is not to read fiction as providing better or worse psychological insights. In 1947, Levinas saw this clearly: "To recognize in Proust's psychology the mainsprings of empiric psychology is not to destroy Proust's work, for which theory is only a means, but to allow its charm to emerge."[31] One should not reduce Proust to psychology: sociology and eroticism are better themes to pursue.

Levinas explores the paradox of the proliferation of "theories" as "general explanations" found on every page of *La Recherche*. A serious reading of Proust will prove that, contrary to what is written in *Time Regained*, theory is not to be rejected because it is compared to a "price-tag" left on a gift—"A work in which there are theories is like an object which still has its price-tag on it."[32] Most commentators have noted that such an attack on theories appears paradoxical when it comes from a writer who develops theories about everything under the sun. Levinas knows that *La Recherche* is also a "philosophical novel" in which the narrative is constantly impeded by varied theories on art, beauty, jealousy, homosexuality, food, music, travels, drunkenness, memory, forgetting, perception, etc. However, Levinas sees the

---

[31] Emmanuel Levinas, "The Other in Proust," translated by Sean Hand, in *The Levinas Reader*, Sean Hand (ed.). Oxford: Blackwell, 1989, pp. 161–2. I will refer to this essay as OP and page number.

[32] Marcel Proust, *Time Regained, In Search of Lost Time*, Vol. VI, translated by Andreas Mayor and Terence Kilmartin, revised by D. J. Enright. New York: The Modern Library, 1999, pp. 278–9. I have developed this analysis in *The Future of Theory*. Oxford: Blackwell, 2002, pp. 118–23.

Proustian theory at work not primarily in the domain of ethics; he does not try to make us read Proust "ethically."

To be true to Proust's philosophical and literary intentions, we have first to explore the spiraling abyss of human perversion. And then, once Sodom and Gomorrah have been crossed, no ethical system can remain whole. There is no moral value that would be unscathed. Levinas calls this Proust's "*felix culpa*," a term that echoes with *Finnegans Wake*. (*CC*, pp. 71–2) Levinas develops this idea in the 1947 article:

> It is curious to note the extent to which Proust's amorality fills his world with the wildest freedom, and confers on definite objects and beings a scintillating sense of possibility undulled by definition. One would have thought that moral laws rid the world of such glittering extravaganzas more rigorously than natural laws and that magic begins, like a witches' Sabbath, where ethics leave off. The change and development in characters, some of them highly unlikely, feel completely natural in a world that has reverted to Sodom and Gomorrah, and relations are established between terms that seemed not to permit them. Everything is giddily possible.
>
> (*OP*, p. 162)

We are not far from Dostoevsky's momentous: "God is dead, everything is possible!" Yet, Levinas shows that Proust goes beyond the amoralism of Sade, Nietzsche or even Genet. The real key lies in the lesson brought home to the narrator by Albertine. It is a revelation of being as otherness.

There is a striking convergence between Levinas's reading of amorality in Proust and Samuel Beckett's earlier approach to Proust. When he wrote the first English monograph on Proust in 1931, Beckett also highlighted the total absence of moral sense in Proust's world: "Here, as always, Proust is completely detached from all moral considerations. There is no right and wrong in Proust nor in his world."[33] As Levinas will do ten years later, Beckett connects this lack of moral concerns with the emergence of Albertine at the end of the novel. He points out that the bewildering multiplicity of plural "Albertines" leads to the establishment of a "*pictorial* multiplicity of Albertine that will duly evolve into a *plastic* and moral multiplicity."[34] These contradictions in her being are in fact no longer "an effect of the observer's angle of approach rather than the expression of an inward and active variety, but a multiplicity

---

[33] Samuel Beckett, *Proust*, and *Three dialogues*. London: John Calder, 1970, p. 66.
[34] Beckett, see footnote 33, p. 47.

in depth, a turmoil of objective and immanent contradictions over which the subject has no control."[35] For Levinas, similarly, Proust's modernist fiction acquires a philosophical value that is exemplary; its power is that that it can achieve a radical break with classical philosophy understood as ontology. He thus concludes his 1947 essay with the idea that Proust "breaks definitively with Parmenides." (OP, p. 165)

Can this insight be generalized? I believe so, and would add here that the insight of a Proustian critique of ontology blends modernism and theory. As we have seen in Chapter 2, theory soon turns into a "fugitive theory" for which Albertine, Proust's eternal "Fugitive," provides the best model. Albertine is all the time defined as an "*être de fuite*," and remains so even when she accepts turning into the "prisoner" of the narrator's jealous obsession. It is thus tempting to compare the behavior of Bobby, a dog who is both free and lost at once, who appears as an "abandoned being," as Jean-Luc Nancy would have it, with the attitude of Albertine. Is Bobby looking for a master? Not really, he is happy to be in the company of a big group, of a multiplicity. No quarrel, it seems, marked his casual frequentation of the group. No prisoner tried to make him his pet, there was no need for a chief or kapo to threaten with cutting it in two. The dog does not care whether his friends are prisoners, Jews or German vacationers. If we look at Albertine in Proust's *La Prisonnière*, we see many commonalities. Curiously, this was the episode of *La Recherche* that Levinas discusses most, as he was no doubt thinking of his own situation. The proximity of the two "prisoners"—Albertine because of the narrator's jealousy; the dog, because he decides to share the predicament of the French prisoners, is troubling.

Did Levinas know that Proust had imagined a character called "Bobby"? Proust first baptized "Bobby Santois" the character who emerged as one of the most crucial second roles at the end, Morel. Morel is the son of Oncle Adolphe's valet but, despite his modest origins, he is ambitious and talented (he plays the violin very well) and he is also thoroughly bisexual. He is nicknamed "Charlie," as an echo of Bobby that keeps in line with all the "Charles" in the novel, including the notorious Charlus. Proust may have sensed that his earlier choice of "Santois" was too allegorical and transparent as a name: in "Santois", one can both hear "*sans toit*" (homeless) or "*sans toi*" (without you), which brings us closer to Levinas's concern with the Other. Whatever the reason may have been for the change of names, what stands out is that Albertine is a double of Bobby Santois/Morel. This is easily perceptible in the evolution of the two characters in the novel between 1914 and 1922:

---

[35] Beckett, see footnote 33, p. 47.

both come from the people, both are extremely seductive but also disappointing, both have dark hair, they have marked bisexual dispositions and an indefatigable urge to have as many lovers as possible; above all, both lie all the time in order to preserve their freedom.[36]

Bobby the dog thus puts Levinas on the trace, on the scent one might say, of Albertine; Levinas follows Proust like a dog in order to go beyond facile moral antinomies. The dog, combining freedom and slavery, flight and sympathy, allows Levinas to overcome the amoralism of a Marquis de Sade or of Nietzsche. What matters then is to be able to fuse freedom and otherness. This is the lesson given to the narrator by Albertine. In 1947, Levinas systematizes his assessment of Albertine: "The reality of Albertine is her evanescence within her very captivity, a reality made of nothingness. She is a prisoner although she has already vanished and has vanished despite being a prisoner, since despite the strictest surveillance she posseses the ability to withdraw into herself." (OP, p. 153) Or, to put it in a more condensed form: "The nothingness of Albertine discovers its total alterity." (OP, p. 164) This is why her very death gives access to a pure Eros, an Eros that is "ontologically pure" because it "has a direct relation to something that both gives and refuses itself, namely the Other as Other, the mystery." (OP, 164) Thus, better than any philosopher, Proust allows us to intuit being as radical alterity. Thanks to the multiplicity of the contradictory images and blurred traces left by Albertine after her final disappearance, one can both grasp what love really means and understand the link between the mystery of one individual as a "being of flight" and the community with which she interacts:

> Marcel did not love Albertine, if love is a fusion with the Other, the ecstasy of one being over the perfection of the other, or the peace of possession. Tomorrow he will break with the young woman who bores him. He will make the journey he has been planning for so long. The account of Marcel's love is doubled by confessions that are seemingly destined to put in question the very consistency of that love. But this non-love is precisely love, the struggle with what cannot be grasped (possession, that absence of Albertine), her presence.
>
> (OP, pp. 164–5)

Levinas's astute and profound reading makes us understand how Proust breaks with the tradition of Greek ontology by ushering in a thinking of the

---

[36] On this topic, see J. Hillis Miller, "The other's other: jealousy and art in Proust", *Qui Parle?*, vol. 9, no. 1, Fall–Winter 1995, pp. 119–40.

Other—an otherness first allegorized by Bobby, the errant dog, and then by Albertine. As he writes so well, with Proust, "despair is an inexhaustible source of hope." (OP, 165) Which does not exclude humor. When the narrator described the slow transformation of Albertine, from the cute *garçonne* of Balbec, who was a little foolish and untutored, to the more intellectual society girl in Paris, he shows that she can cultivate herself by reading. At the same time, she appears as less desirable, less beautiful; she begins appreciating literature, reads Dostoevsky, of whom she can state categorically: "It's interesting, but really, it might have been written *by a pig.*"[37]

Could writing itself be allegorized by an animal as impure as a pig? We would have to turn to Georges Bataille, who appreciated Proust's sadism and excess no less than Levinas, to continue on this way. The "becoming-animal" lies in wait for whoever attempts to follow the errant traces of writing to the end. It would prevent philosophers from turning into Levinas, a danger that lay in wait for Derrida, and against which he reacted a little too violently, as we have seen.

Robert Antelme and the "human species"

In conclusion, I would like to return to Derrida's refusal of Agamben's theories of the exception. As we have seen, Derrida rejected the opposition between *bios* and *zoê*, finding it too glib; this is not a sufficient foundation to rethink the boundary between men and animals. I will briefly adduce a text that describes another kind of war prison from that of Levinas, and it brings us back to the statement "I am a man," "I am a dog," or "I am a cat." The statement was made explicitly by Robert Antelme, the author of one book only, *L'Espèce humaine*.[38] Let us note that the title has been translated into English as *The Human Race*,[39] whereas, as Agamben insists rightly, it should have been *The Human Species*: "It is important that Antelme uses the technical term *espèce* here instead of referring to the more familiar one of *le genre humain*. For it is a matter of biological belonging in the strict sense ... not of a

---

[37]   Marcel Proust, *The Captive: Remembrance of Things Past*, Vol. III, C. K. Scott-Moncrieff and T. Kilmartin (trans). New York: Random House, 1982, p. 10. For the French original, *À la recherche du temps perdu*, III, Paris, Gallimard, Bibliothèque de la Pléiade, 1988, p. 528.

[38]   Robert Antelme, *L'Espèce humaine* (1947). Paris: Gallimard, 1957.

[39]   Robert Antelme, *The Human Race*, Jeffrey Haight and Annie Mahler (trans). Vermont: Marlboro, 1992.

declaration of moral and political solidarity."[40] Agamben quotes the beginning of Antelme's harrowing account of his stay in several concentration camps, Buchenwald, Gandersheim, then Dachau:

> To say that one felt oneself contested then as a man, as a member of the human race (*comme membre de l'espèce*)—that may look like a feeling discovered in retrospect, an explanation arrived at afterwards. And yet it was that that we felt most constantly and immediately, and that—exactly that—was what the others wanted.[41]

In several impassioned passages, Antelme claims just that—the unalienable fact of his being part of a common species. By enforcing the main law of the *Lager*, that the inmates are not men but *Schweine*, just pigs, the SS attempt to obliterate the commonality in a shared human nature.

Thus Antelme voices his resistance: "The SS cannot alter our species,"[42] he writes, meaning the phrase in the biological sense of a "mutation." Antelme does not simply assert a biological community—this is the foundation for a rejection of the Nazi desire to obliterate the humanity of those they intern, torture and kill.

> But we cannot have it that the SS does not exist and has not existed. They shall have burned children, they shall have done it willingly. We cannot have it that they did not wish to do it. They are a force, just as the man walking along the road is one. And as we are, too; for even now they cannot stop us from exerting our power.[43]

The man on the road is the passer-by who walks along the camp's barbed wires and cannot see the humanity of the prisoners. Even those who try to do their best, like the German woman who slips a chunk of bread to Antelme, or the Rhinelander who one day shakes their hands, are accomplices as long as they do not claim this common humanity fully and openly. There are no dogs in Antelme's narrative, the prisoners do not have that luxury. If there had been dogs, it is likely that they would have been confiscated by the SS's fake sentimentalism ferociously denounced by Reznikoff's poem *Holocaust*:

---

[40] Giorgio Agamben, *Remnants of Auschwitz: The Witness and the Archive*, Daniel Heller-Roazen (trans.). New York: Zone, 1999, p. 58.

[41] Antelme, *The Human Race*, see footnote 39, p. 5; *L'Espèce humaine*, see footnote 38, p. 11.

[42] Antelme, *The Human Race*, see footnote 39, p. 74; *L'Espèce humaine*, see footnote 38, p. 83.

[43] Antelme, *The Human Race*, see footnote 39, p. 74; *L'Espèce humaine*, see footnote 38, p. 84.

The SS man took the baby from her arms
and shot her twice,
and then held the baby in his hands,
The mother, bleeding, but still alive, crawled up to his feet,
The SS man laughed
and tore the baby apart as one would tear a rag.
Just then a stray dog passed
and the SS man stooped to pat it
and took a lump of sugar out of his pocket
and gave it to the dog.[44]

Antelme knows that even a dog becomes a historical object in times of duress and exploitation. Nevertheless, he keeps the courage to act, thus making ethical sense—by transforming biology into history—of the most insane system of terror and dehumanization:

> By denying us as men the SS had made us historical objects that could no longer in any way be the objects of ordinary human relations. These relations could have such consequences, so impossible was it just to think of establishing them without being aware of the enormous prohibition against which one had to rebel in order to do so; so completely had one to have withdrawn oneself from the community whose grip in wartime was stronger, so ready had one to be to incur the dishonor, the ignominy of desertion, even of treason, that these relations could hardly be begun without turning at once into history, as if they were in themselves the paths, narrow and obscure, that history had been forced to follow.[45]

---

[44] Charles Reznikoff, *Holocaust*. Los Angeles: Black Sparrow Press, 1975, p. 29. I owe this quote to my friend François Dominique. See Dominique's essay "We are free" in *On Robert Antelme's The Human Race*, edited by Daniel Dobbels, and translated by Jeffrey Haight. Evanston: Northwestern University Press, 2003, p. 171.
[45] Antelme, *The Human Race*, see footnote 39, p. 75; *L'Espèce humaine*, see footnote 38, pp. 84–5.

4

Divided Truths on Lies
Derrida with Hannah Arendt

It may look counter-intuitive to link the question of the future with that of the Shoah. Yet, this is a point repeatedly made by Derrida and by a thinker I now will turn to, Hannah Arendt: we need to prepare for the future by thinking through and through the conditions of possibility, ethically, politically, and philosophically, of such a historic horror. I will contextualize their debate in a rapid sketch of Derrida's legacy. Today, more than ten years after the untimely demise of the philosopher, there are three main ways of approaching his impact.

There is the biographical approach. Since 2010 for the French version, Benoît Peeters's excellent biography[1] has allowed us to reconsider Derrida's *oeuvre* in light of his personality. What makes Peeters's biography engaging and refreshing, is that we discover a different Derrida; he appears more driven, tormented, excessive, impassioned, than a successful and charismatic world-renowned philosopher. We are surprised to see a neo-Romantic thinker whose vaunting narcissism had to be kept in check and whose power of seduction seemed boundless, yet with a darker, brooding, melancholy side. He was obsessed by death, his own and that of his loved ones, but stuck until the end to a grueling schedule of international lectures that only an athlete in the physical and intellectual sense could carry through. It was not by chance that Peeters felt the need to publish along with his huge biography a slim volume in which he accounts for the difficulty of such a daunting task.[2]

This second book should be made available in English: one should read it side by side with a biography whose author all but disappears and erases his voice to let Derrida speak.

What makes Peeters's biography invaluable is its modesty and the thoroughness of its documentation. Peeters sums up countless letters, manuscripts and unpublished seminars that one can have access to (which is not always granted) by going to the Irvine University library. Thus, for

---

[1] Benoît Peeters, *Derrida: A Biography.* Cambridge: Polity, 2013.
[2] Benoît Peeters, *Trois ans avec Derrida: les carnets d'un biographe.* Paris: Flammarion, 2010.

instance, Peeters presents the context of the 52-page letter sent by Derrida to his school friend Pierre Nora who had published a scathing indictment of the French presence in Algeria. This letter, now added to the republished book by Nora, shows that Derrida sided with Albert Camus and Germaine Tillion, the "liberals" of the time, while remaining uncompromising on issues of ethics and human rights.[3] The debate about the rights of the French colonists to remain in Algeria or even to belong there throws a sharper light on Derrida's otherwise radical politics. This proves that there is a need to know more about Derrida's "secrets" hidden in his huge archive in which his private life, his theoretical positions and his ethical or political commitments are intermingled. I would include in this first category the books written by friends and disciples who want to honor his memory and testify to his charisma by making better sense of his ideas. This is the case of books by Nicholas Royle, Peggy Kamuf, Derek Attridge and Geoffrey Bennington.[4] They attempt to memorialize their mentor and disseminate his teachings while trying not "mourn" him too soon. These four books, written by excellent commentators who have important things to say about aspects of Derrida's theories, hesitate between personal memoirs and textual exegesis. They explain why Derrida is "hard to follow," in all the meanings of the expression.[5] Avoiding the dangers of hagiography, they testify to the pathos of a personal loss while making sense of the French philosopher's lasting legacy.

The second approach is what I would call a systemic interpretation of Derrida's philosophy. It is often provided by authors who were not as close to Derrida as the previous group. They attempt to rethink his concepts and methods from a distance and in their own vocabulary. What they are eager to eschew is the risk of mimetic ventriloquism, a danger faced by all those who grapple with Derrida's idiosyncratic readings of other texts. We see this in Peter Sloterdijk's *Derrida, an Egyptian*,[6] or in Alain Badiou's homage in his *Pocket Pantheon*.[7] Sloterdijk uses thinkers and writers, like Freud, Franz

---

[3]   Pierre Nora, *Les Français d'Algérie, édition revue et augmentée*. Paris: Christian Bourgeois, 2012. I will return to this book in Chapter 9.

[4]   Nicholas Royle, *In Memory of Jacques Derrida*. Edinburgh: Edinburgh University Press, 2009; Peggy Kamuf, *To Follow: The Wake of Jacques Derrida*. Edinburgh: Edinburgh University Press, 2010; Geoffrey Bennington, *Not Half No End: Militantly Melancholic Essays in Memory of Jacques Derrida*. Edinburgh: Edinburgh University Press, 2010; Derek Attridge, *Reading and Responsibility: Deconstruction's Traces*. Edinburgh: Edinburgh University Press, 2010.

[5]   Attridge, *Reading and Responsibility*, see footnote 4, p. 51.

[6]   Peter Sloterdijk, *Derrida, an Egyptian: On the Problem of the Jewish Pyramid*. London: Polity, 2009.

[7]   Alain Badiou, *Pocket Pantheon: Figures of Postwar Philosophy*, David Macey (trans.). London: Verso, 2009, pp. 125–44. This lecture was given in 2005.

Borkenau and Niklas Luhmann, to reach a central metaphor in Derrida's *oeuvre*, which would hinge around an inverted Egyptian pyramid. In this way, Derrida becomes if not immediately a Kafkaian figure, at least a Joseph-like interpreter calling up the hero of a novel by Thomas Mann. Badiou insists on the politics at work in deconstruction, since he chooses to see in Derrida a "man of peace," who destroyed all dichotomies, whether philosophical, like Being and being, racial, like Jew versus Arab; or political, like democracy versus totalitarianism, in order to reach an unstable and fugitive point of undecidability. Key in Derrida's thinking is a productive "indistinction" of distinction, which leads neither to confusion nor to pure difference. Even if there is a huge gap between Badiou's system and Derrida's proliferating texts, they can be joined by a similar concern for the notion of the undecidable. A similar but more sustained effort at rethinking the whole system of Derrida's thought has been deployed by Martin Hägglund in his groundbreaking *Radical Atheism*.[8] This book unifies Derrida's project and refuses the idea that Derrida would have moved from a "playful" mode of Nietzschean critique of all foundational concepts to a more "serious," that is more ethical or even religious concern with alterity, justice, messianicity and the dream of a democracy ever "to come." Going back to the earlier insights developed by Derrida when he launched the concept of writing as trace, deferral and active *différance* in the sense of the creation of a temporal as well as spatial distance, Hägglund posits the logic of "survival" as the key-stone of deconstruction. Thus there is only one Derrida, from his first essays to the moving last interview with Jean Birnbaum in 2004,[9] and he is the thinker of a radical finitude, the true heir of Heidegger and not a Levinassian in disguise.

Finally, a third group of authors discussing Derrida can be called dialogical. They aim at reopening various dialogues between Derrida and other philosophers or writers. The collection edited by John Sallis under the title of *Deconstruction and Philosophy*[10] provides a good model. Derrida is paired with Hegel, with Heidegger, with Kant, with Husserl, and contextualized within the discourses of metaphysics or ethics. Derrida appears hence as a "Left Heideggerian" (as one would speak of "Left Hegelians" to include Feuerbach, Stirner and Marx), that is as a revolutionary thinker who had had

[8] Martin Hägglund, *Radical Atheism: Derrida and the Time of Life*. Stanford; Stanford University Press, 2008. See also his application of the logic of survival to modernist literature in *Dying for Time: Proust, Woolf, Nabokov*. Cambridge: Harvard University Press, 2012. I will discuss it in Chapter 7.

[9] See Jacques Derrida, *Learning to Live Finally*, Pascale-Anne Brault and Michel Naas (trans). Brooklyn: Melville House, 2007.

[10] Jacques Derrida, *Deconstruction and Philosophy*, edited by John Sallis. Chicago: Chicago University Press, 1987.

the audacity to replace Heidegger's ontological difference with the "question concerning technology." The true audacity consisted in using Heidegger's main concepts against themselves. Of course, Derrida had to transform "technology" into "writing," a startling move toward the material, perhaps even to dialectical materialism, that made a world of difference. If ontological difference can be rewritten as technological difference, writing acquires a new valence, a new violence, and an almost unlimited power in the world of thought and facts. More recently, Leonard Lawlor went to the root of this replacement when he reopened the dossier of Derrida's critique of phenomenology in his superb *Derrida and Husserl*.[11]

It is within this group of dialogical approaches that one can place Raoul Moati's *Derrida/Searle: Déconstruction et langage ordinaire*.[12] Moati is less interested in the genealogy of the confrontation between Derrida and Searle about the true meaning of Austin's theory of the performative—one may note that it is rare to see such polemical ferocity on both sides in a philosophical discussion—than in the general question posed to deconstruction in its dialogue with Anglo–American philosophy of ordinary language. Moati's interests have ranged from Slavoj Žižek to Emmanuel Levinas,[13] and he approaches the discussion opposing Derrida and Searle as dispassionately as possible. He betrays no undue sentimentalism, he does not bring his personal testimony; in place of a disciple's piety he displays the candid probity of a philosophical investigator. This was a prerequisite, as the ground appeared mined given the fracas, the exchange of insults, and finally an excess of mutual incomprehension. One needs to have sympathy for both camps in order to avoid effects of transference and counter-transference. There is no adulation, adoration, detestation or denigration of any kind, here. Moati prefers to point out Derrida's blind spots and Searle's dead ends rather than make any blind endorsement. Moati insists on Derrida's dependence upon "metaphysical" models that he had been the first to debunk, while he sees in Searle a dangerous rejection of the unconscious. This is the condition for an impartial assessment of what can be learned from the debate today— and there is a lot to learn.

---

[11] Leonard Lawlor, *Derrida and Husserl: The Basic Problem of Phenomenology*. Bloomington: Indiana University Press, 2002.

[12] Raoul Moati, *Derrida/Searle: Déconstruction et langage ordinaire*. Paris: Presses Universitaires de France, 2009.

[13] See Raoul Moati (ed.), *Autour de Slavoj Žižek: psychanalyse, Marxisme, idéalisme allemande*. Paris: Presses Universitaires de France, 2010; and Raoul Moati, *Evénements nocturnes: essai sur totalité et infini*. Paris: Hermann, 2012.

What is at stake is the productivity of the concept of the performative as it was launched by Austin. Moati provides a useful genealogy for the concept, explaining why its contested legacy could be the object of a rivalry, a real tussle for appropriation, between Derrida and by Searle. Both use the term of "intentionality" systematically but with radically different meanings. As Derrida admits in the Afterword to *Limited Inc.*, he often felt closer to the speech act theory developed by Austin than to the phenomenological tradition he came from: ". . . I sometimes felt, paradoxically, closer to Austin than to a certain Continental tradition from which Searle, on the contrary, has inherited numerous gestures and a logic I try to deconstruct."[14] It was not absurd for Derrida to point to a Husserlian background in Searle, an unthought background of which the American philosopher would have been blissfully unaware. What Derrida gave us in the end was a more complex and subtle concept of the performative, a concept that could not be limited by reason and social regulation alone, a concept that would not dissolve itself in the aporias of impossible taxonomies, as seemed to be the case at the end of Austin's *How To Do Things With Words*. This new dynamism was not lost for innovative thinkers and activists like Judith Butler: she launched her reexamination of sexual difference by using a variation of Derrida's performative. For deconstruction, quite often, the performative tended to relay phenomenology or even to rescue it from its structural limits. I will focus on the strategic role played by the performative in Derrida's discussion of the "history of the lie."[15]

Derrida has been a master in the arts of division, and I will give one example of this activity. This should help us to limit the contours of new futures for Theory. My example is brought to me from the process that led to the writing of a book on lies,[16] published in French in 2005. The origin of this book was an invitation to discuss "Language, lies and ethics" at a conference at the American University of Paris. The conference took place on May 21, 2003 in Paris and Derrida was scheduled to be the main orator. Sadly, he had to cancel two days before—the conference's date overlapped with a series of biopsies that revealed to him the incurable pancreatic cancer from which he was to die a little more than a year later.

Thinking of the dialogue to come, I had reopened a difficult essay of his on the "History of the lie," which by then only existed in an English

---

[14] Jacques Derrida, "Afterword: toward an ethic of discussion", *Limited Inc.*, Samuel Weber (trans.). Evanston: Northwestern University Press, 1998, p. 130.
[15] Jean-Michel Rabaté, *The Ethics of the Lie*. New York: The Other Press, 2007, pp. 360–3.
[16] Jean-Michel Rabaté, *Tout dire ou ne rien dire: Logiques du Mensonge*. Paris: Stock, 2005.

version.[17] I had heard a first version of this talk as Derrida delivered it at the Tuscaloosa conference devoted to *Futures* in 1995. In that talk, Derrida attacked a sneering remark made by Tony Judt on French intellectuals who, he alleged, had never acknowledged the ethical hangover dating from the dark Vichy years. Derrida was included in the lot. Refuting this allegation in many ways, Derrida had begun by evoking two famous essays by Hannah Arendt, "Truth and politics" (1967) and "Lying in politics" (1972). Derrida set out to question some of her assumptions—and, to my dismay, I had to confess that these were my assumptions as well. As I had started gathering material on historical lies a few years earlier, I had read Arendt's essays and admired them for their wealth of details and capacious philosophical argument. It came to me as a surprise when I heard Derrida contradict Arendt on the topic of the political lie; my bafflement turned into an epistemological obstacle soon after.

Derrrida quotes a passage and inserts his queries within brackets. In order to give a sense of the discussion, I will first quote the paragraph on Arendt's sentence by itself. It comes from the second essay, triggered by the controversy around the publication of the Pentagon papers, and what they had revealed of official lies and state dissimulation about the Vietnam War. Arendt analyses the loss of credibility suffered by the American administration:

> The famous credibility gap, which has been with us for six long years, has suddenly opened up an abyss. The quicksand of lying statements of all sorts, deceptions as well as self-deceptions, is apt to engulf any reader who wishes to prove this material, which, unhappily, he must recognize as the infrastructure of nearly a decade of United States foreign and domestic policy.[18]

The relevance of this sentence to contemporary American politics has been emphasized by Eric Alterman in his attempt at reconstructing an American "history of the lie." His book, *When Presidents Lie: A History of Official Deception and Its Consequences*,[19] pays homage to Hannah Arendt's groundbreaking investigations. Alterman uses Arendt to point out the

---

[17] Jacques Derrida, "History of the Lie," *Futures of Jacques Derrida*, Richard Rand (ed.), Stanford: Stanford University Press, 2001, pp. 65–98. The French version, "Histoire du Mensonge: Prolégomènes," is to be found in *Cahier de L'Herne Jacques Derrida*, Marie-Louise Mallet and Ginette Michaud (eds). Paris: Éditions de L'Herne, 2004, pp. 405–520.

[18] Hannah Arendt, "Lying in politics", in *Crises of the Republic*. New York: Harcourt and Brace, 1972, pp. 3–4.

[19] Eric Alterman, *When Presidents Lie: A History of Official Deception and its Consequences*. Harmondsworth: Viking, 2004.

dangerous consequences of state lies and official deceptions.[20] He offers what I would call his "ethics of the lie" in a wonderfully astute and scathing conclusion entitled "George W. Bush and the Post-Truth Presidency."[21] I mention this so as to give a sense of today's debate. This seems to be what explicitly motivated Derrida's problematic: how can one write a "history of the lie"? Isn't lying an "eternal" factor of human life and, more pointedly, of political life? Could one witness an evolution in the old couple made up of lies and truth? Arendt is singled out because she is one of the most vocal defenders of the hypothesis that there has been such an evolution in the practice of lying. For her, the modern period has seen not only an increase in the production of lies but also the appearance of a different mode of lying.

Derrida aims at a foundational question; I will now quote the same passage with the remark that he inserted within brackets:

> The quicksand of lying statements of all sorts, deceptions as well as *self-deceptions* [I emphasize "self-deceptions", which will be one of our problems later on: Is "self-deception" possible? Is it a rigorous and pertinent concept for what interests us here, that is, the history of the lie? In strictest terms, does one ever lie to oneself? (J.D.)] is apt to engulf any reader who wishes to probe this material, which, unhappily, he must recognize as the infrastructure of nearly a decade of United States foreign and domestic policy.[22]

The question inserted between brackets points at a difficulty in the theory of lies: if a lie is defined by the fact that I know one thing and say another, how can I lie to myself? In other words, if a lie is defined by an intention to be deceitful and dishonest, how can there be an intention to betray oneself? This unassailable question leads to another aporia; if lying is to be understood as a purely inner process, how can one catch anybody lying?

Derrida is consistent when he asserts that one can never be caught lying: one can always say, "I was wrong but I did not mean to deceive; I am in good faith."[23] Thus, if the lie is restricted to an intention to deceive as it has been since Plato and Augustine, it may well be that a certain undecidability will prevent any possibility of verification. The only "proof" would have to come from the subject, especially when he or she falls under the category of

---

[20] Alterman, see footnote 19, p. 8.
[21] Alterman, see footnote 19, pp. 294–314.
[22] Derrida, see footnote 17, p. 71.
[23] Derrida, see footnote 17, p. 68.

"suspect"—which is why for centuries torture has been considered a logical way of extracting the confession, of forcibly breaking into the locked room prohibited to others in which the secret of perjury or deceit lay. Moreover, Derrida notes that the lie, in Greek *pseudos*, covers several meanings—and in Greek, the word means "lie" but also "falsehood," "cunning," or even "mistake." It also includes the senses of "deception" or "fraud" as well as "poetic invention." As Derrida wryly concludes this etymological review, this increases "the possible misunderstanding about what is meant by 'misunderstanding . . .'"[24]

In order to see what Derrida attacks or questions in Hannah Arendt's theory of the lie, it is worth summing up her thesis in the most developed essay, "Truth and politics." Her essay was a response—a very theoretical response, to be sure—to the controversy generated by Arendt's book on Eichmann, *Eichmann in Jerusalem: A Report on the Banality of Evil* (1963). What had infuriated many people, among them several friends of Arendt's, was less her decision to find in Eichmann a "banal" man and therefore not a monster, than her bitter accusations against the complicity of the Jewish authorities with the Reich's final solution. According to her, the truth that was being veiled by Eichmann's trial in Jerusalem had to do with the cooperative attitude of many Jews who deliberately helped the Nazis in their own extermination. I'll just quote a much debated passage since it throws a keener light on what Arendt and Derrida have in mind when they talk of the historicity of the lie. Arendt remarks that the prosecutor regularly asks witnesses: "Why did you not rebel?" and adds that this "served as a smokescreen for the question that was not asked."[25] She then adds this:

> And thus it came to pass that all answers to the unanswerable question Mr. Hausner put to his witnesses were considerably less than "the truth, the whole truth and nothing but the truth." True it was that the Jewish people as a whole had not been organized, that they had possessed no territory, no government, and no army, that, in the hour of their greatest need, they had no government-in-exile to represent them among the allies . . . no cache of weapons, no youth with military training. But the whole truth was that there existed Jewish community organizations on both the local and international level. Wherever Jews lived, there were recognized Jewish leaders, and this leadership, almost without exception, cooperated in one way or another, for one reason or another, with the

[24] Derrida, see footnote 17, p. 66.
[25] Hannah Arendt, *Eichmann in Jerusalem: A Report on the Banality of Evil.* New York: Penguin, 1992, p. 124.

Nazis. The whole truth is that if the Jewish people had really been unorganized and leaderless, there would have been chaos and plenty of misery but the total number of victims would have hardly been between four and half and six million people.[26]

This accusation culminated in Arendt's singling out Rabbi Baeck, who preferred not telling the Jewish inmates at Auschwitz that they were going to be gassed, and also had believed that it was "more humane" to have a Jewish police force who would arrest families and send them to the death camps; Arendt notes that they were in fact more brutal and less easily bought than regular German functionaries since they had too much to lose.[27] No doubt, the uproar was enormous, and Arendt had to fight against all sorts of accusations herself, including the reproach that she had made more than 600 factual mistakes in her book.[28] This is what motivated her long and thoughtful meditation on "Truth and politics." Her starting point is the ancient conflict between truth and politics; she had discovered for instance that Eichmann had been caught at that time first because the German government had finished paying war settlements, and also because Eichmann had been selected as emblematic, whereas a few other ex-Nazis would be allowed to escape. Where then was the "whole truth," wasn't it always corrupted, even by the "good side" as soon as one took into account the pragmatic and realistic aims of politics? Could one call upon the idea of the "whole truth" without being swayed by partisanship, allegiances determined by race or creed? Some of the worse insults had been directed at the fact that Arendt seemed to have forgotten her solidarity with her people. As some French journalists had asked provocatively, could one call her a pro-Nazi Jew? Now that the dust has settled, commentators notice much more the extraordinary moral and mental courage displayed by Arendt, especially in her demonstration that there is no "radical evil" and that the Shoah was not to be considered as an exception in the long history of genocides.

Her article, collected in a book entitled symptomatically *Between Past and Future*, begins with her recognition that lying seems inevitable or even necessary in politics. Is it always legitimate to tell the "whole truth"?[29] Quoting Plato, Kant and Spinoza, she wonders whether one can simply assume that

[26] Arendt, see footnote 25, pp. 124–5.

[27] Arendt, see footnote 25, p. 119.

[28] For a good account of the controversy, see Elisabeth Young-Bruehl's biography, *Hannah Arendt: For Love of the World*. New Haven: Yale University Press, 1982, pp. 328–78.

[29] This question is posed in the first footnote of Hannah Arendt, "Truth and Politics," *Between Past and Future*. New York: Penguin, 1993. Hereafter, BPF and page number.

even if the world may perish, the truth should be said wholly and totally—in other words, undividedly. Hobbes had remarked cynically that only abstract truths like mathematical truths were readily accepted by all, because they would threaten no-one (BPF, p. 230). What about factual truths, Arendt asks, like the role played by Leon Trotsky in the Russian revolution? She generalizes, and opposes the abstract truths of philosophy and the sciences to these facts, that for her are "infinitely more fragile things than axioms, discoveries, theories." (BPF, p. 231) The focus of her essay will then be on factual truth as opposed to philosophical truth—she observes that today the contrast seems to have disappeared as we think that everything is political, and therefore reducible to opinion. What matters all the more is the preservation of those small nuggets of truth that she calls historical facts. They create problems when they are unwelcome, and the new regime of the lie entails that they will have to be eliminated, as Trotsky's person had been all but erased from the Stalinist accounts of the Russian revolution.

Factual truths, unlike philosophical truths, are not self-evident, they have no power of coercion, they have no reason for being what they are, and they are not subject to debate. They represent only what they are, since they embody actuality as opposed to possibility in Aristotelian categories: "nothing could ever happen if reality did not kill, by definition, all the other potentialities originally inherent in any given situation." (BPF, p. 243) Unlike philosophical truth, whose power to inspire or persuade has been stressed by most authors, especially when it comes to describing better political regimes as in Plato's *Republic*, factual truth cannot inspire action, become exemplary, or generate ideals; yet it is essential to the political realm. This is the locus of the lie, at last caught red-handed: "The hallmark of factual truth is that its opposite is neither error nor illusion or opinion, no one of which reflects upon personal truthfulness, but the deliberate falsehood, the lie." (BPF, p. 249) Clémenceau famously stated that, no matter what lies would be told about the First World War, nobody would deny that Germany had invaded Belgium in 1914. Arendt comments by saying that he was still naïve and unacquainted with the "art of rewriting history" (BPF, p. 249), which tended to dominate in the second half of the century. It follows that the modern liar will do everything he can to blur the boundaries between factual truth and opinion.

This leads to a discussion of the fact that the liar is a man of action, he changes reality, he replaces it with something else, and paradoxically, one might even conclude that this action testifies to human freedom: "our ability to lie—but not necessarily our ability to tell the truth—belongs among the few obvious, demonstrable data that confirm human freedom." (BPF, p. 250) This, however, generates a specifically modern regime of the lie. The traditional political lie concerned secrets and hidden intentions, it was directed at an enemy and it lacked the element of self-deception. On the other hand, the modern political lie concerns things that are not secrets but are known more or less to everyone; they are directed at everyone and not just the adversary; and they fully include self-deception. This follows the old motto: "the more successful a liar is, the more likely it is that he will fall prey to his fabrications." (BPF, p. 254) The modern manipulation of facts ushers in a pure simulacrum, and image-making is the main concern. However, there is some hope for Arendt, since "no existing power is anywhere near great enough to make its intimate image 'foolproof.'" (BPF, p. 256) The consequence is that regimes that engage in this kind of manipulation must constantly invent new images.

Finally, what is created by this massive output of manipulated images is a general cynicism in the public. This is the worst consequence of political lying, the destruction of our sense of reality as being stable and also verifiable.

> . . . the result of a consistent and total substitution of lies for factual truth is not that the lies will now be accepted as truth, and the truth defamed as lies, but that the sense by which we take our bearings in the real world—and the category of truth vs. falsehood is among the mental means to this end—is being destroyed.
>
> (BPF, p. 257)

The only way of avoiding such a psychotic world is to trust certain institutions, in which observers can feel that they are outside the realm of the political (BPF, p. 259). Universities can play this role, especially when they recognize the need to write history truthfully. Important writers, when they are animated by a passion for truth that is so strong that it makes them stand above the conflicts of opinions, like Homer or Isak Dinesen, will also uphold these high standards. The conclusion of the essay takes on a Kantian or Heideggerian ring: "Conceptually, we may call truth what we cannot change; metaphorically, it is the ground on which we stand and the sky that stretches above us." (BPF, p. 264)

I have mentioned Heidegger on purpose: in many of her philosophical essays, one can sense that Arendt is in a critical dialogue with her former mentor, professor and lover. Has she has avoided the perversion systematically addressed by Heidegger, which is to reduce truth to an adequation between a statement and facts? Has she grasped the doctrine of ontological difference for which what matters is *aletheia*, or the un-concealment of Being? This is not so sure, and moreover we can note that she has had to split Truth conceptually into two different concepts: the Platonician or philosophical truth (the sum of the angles of a triangle) on the one hand; and facts coming from the world of men in action, like which side has started a World War. Besides, at a pragmatic level, it is curious to note that she leaves no room for the investigations of journalists, as if they were always tainted with partisanship, whereas in the past decades one can say that their role has been primordial in discovering and denouncing unwelcome factual truths. I will conclude on the provisional paradox that, in order to reach "the whole truth," she has been forced to divide Truth between irrefutable "philosophical" truths that have little to do with everyday concerns, and "factual truths" that have to be fought over for their own sake but in a dispassionate manner.

When he enters the fray in a belated way, Derrida does not hesitate to provide his own examples of factual truth. I have mentioned the skirmish with Judt, and he had no difficulty in showing that he, at last, had repeatedly called attention to the responsibility of the French state about the extermination of Jews during the Vichy years. He just needs to quote Kevin Anderson who mentions a 1992 petition signed by 200 French intellectuals, including himself.[30] Similarly, Derrida engages with recent controversies concerning President Chirac's official recognition of the responsibility of the French State in the deportation and assassination of Jews during the Nazi occupation. It is in this context that he mentions contested "truths" about boundaries and borders in the ex-Yugoslavia, in Israel and Chechnya. He notes wryly that there has been a performative violence of those who make the laws, who decide upon legitimacy and public consensus. He comments: "Who tells the truth and who lies in those areas? For the better and for the worse, this performative dimension *makes the truth*, as Augustine says. It therefore imprints its irreducibly historical dimension on both veracity and the lie."[31] Derrida adds that neither Kant nor Hannah Arendt have been able to take into account the performative dimension of the lie, just as they failed to pay attention to the unconscious dimension of the phenomenon.

Derrida outlines a program that comes very close to that of psychoanalysis, not, of course, without qualifications and reservations. When discussing the "performative violence of law-givers and the impossibility of knowing whose truth we face," we would need to approach them with the combination of a "logic of the unconscious" and a theory of the "performative."[32] This does not mean that the *current* and currently elaborated discourse of psychoanalysis or of speech-act theory is sufficient to the task. It means even less that there is a ready articulation between them—"or between them and a discourse on

[30] Derrida, see footnote 17, p. 85.
[31] Derrida, see footnote 17, p. 81.
[32] Derrida, see footnote 17, p. 82.

politics or the economy of the tele-technological knowledge and power."[33] Derrida's prudence is necessary and should warn us not to follow blindly either the post-Foucauldians or the neo-Marxists who assert that truth is only an outgrowth of political or ideological power.

How can we reconcile this pragmatic approach with the position I had mentioned at the beginning, in which Derrida seemed to stick to an entrenched version of lying as bound by intentionality? All this takes place in less than ten pages. I will try to retrace their logic. What makes such a summary more difficult is that Derrida provides us, like Hannah Arendt, with a compendium of major statements on lies by famous authors, from Plato to Nietzsche (without forgetting Augustine, Kant, Oscar Wilde, Fukuyama, Koyré, Marx and Austin) at the same time as he weaves his own argument. His point of departure is nevertheless more Nietzschean than Platonician (Arendt remains Platonician as long as she can), as he quotes a section of the *Twilight of the Idols* as a way to launch his problematic: there, Nietzsche offers to give his readers a clue as to how the "Real" world became a "Myth" and he calls this the "History of an error."[34] He sketches several, from Plato to the birth of Christianity, then via Kant, the rise of positivist science, a new assertive nihilism, finally culminating with Zarathustra's provocative teachings. Having surveyed the theses of Augustine, Kant and Plato, Derrida asserts firmly first that the lie is not an error, and then that the idea of a "history of the lie" would presuppose something like the history of the false witness and of perjury, a chronicle of "radical evil" which would have little to do with the history of truth or of error.

Finding his true ground more with Augustine, Derrida narrows the focus, and agrees with the Bishop of Hippo that one cannot lie to oneself. He then seems to take a phenomenological description as a valid starting point:

> Here, then, is a definition of the traditional definition of the lie, such as I believe I must formulate it here. In its prevalent and recognized form, the lie is not a fact or a state; it is an intentional act, a lying. There is not the lie, but rather this saying or this meaning-to-say that is called lying: to lie would be to address to another (for one lies only to the other; one cannot lie to oneself, unless it is to oneself as another) a statement or more than one statement, a series of statements (constative or performative) that the liar knows, consciously, in explicit, thematic, current consciousness,

---

[33] Derrida, see footnote 17, p. 82.
[34] Friedrich Nietzsche, *Twilight of the Idols and the Anti-Christ*. London: Penguin, 1990, p. 50.

from assertions that are totally or partially false; one must insist right
away on this plurality and on this complexity, even on this heterogeneity.[35]

Augustine was thus right to say that one could lie by uttering a true statement,
if this was done with the intention or desire of deceiving the other. I cannot
go at length here, but I will just remark that here is why I think that Derrida
is still today one of our best guides or "educators," as Nietzsche would say
of Schopenhauer. For even if Derrida sooner or late complicates the picture
and ends up leaving us torn, caught up in insurmountable paradoxes,
his point of departure is always rigorously simple, straightforward; it is
often easy to follow, step by step, since it always starts with phenomenological
analyses. Then there is almost always a moment of inner division, of
aporetic contradiction that leads to a jump away from the phenomenological
circularity founded upon a consciousness, a jump sending us toward a
globalized history, a history which can encompass the whole history of
philosophy and the evolution of material culture including a newer history of
technology.

Thus, we understand why Derrida needed the division between the big
Truths and smaller factual truths performed by Arendt's essay: by criticizing
not the division itself (which would be a critique that he could leave to
Heidegger, who would have no difficulty pointing out to Arendt that the
Truth has to be One or is not) but the absence of a reflection on the
performative dimension of the lie (a point which, as we have seen, is not so
obvious), Derrida can move forward and go beyond the limitations of his
phenomenological starting point so as to reach his pragmatic conclusion.
This is why, in conclusion, Derrida returns to a parallel between Heidegger's
and Arendt's theses.[36] He criticizes her "optimism" facing the ultimate victory
of truth over lies. One should take into account not only the possibility of a
radical perversion of truth, at least the new technologies that create "the
simulacrum of the iconic substitute" for the truth. However Derrida does not
despair of laying down the lineaments of a real history of the lie.

Having decided to write a book on lies that would analyze the historical
positivity of the lie, with chapters devoted to American presidents like
Clinton and Bush, but that would also engage with literature, film and popular
culture, I needed to accept the possibility of a "history of the lie" in the
modern world. At the same time, I wanted to analyze the paradoxes generated
by the logical and ethical undecidability lodged in the darkest recesses of the

[35] Derrida, see footnote 17, p. 68.
[36] Derrida, see footnote 17, pp. 93–8.

human psyche. Thus, to follow Derrida's suggestions, I had to work with the undecidability of the lie, and all its attendant legal or religious offshoots, like confession and perjury. Like him, I needed to use a phenomenological mode of analysis as a starting point, and then move beyond it. The most momentous consequence that this last movement entailed was that I had to allow room for the possibility of a self-lie or of self-deception, even though Derrida seemed to prohibit this.

Such phenomena have been analyzed by Pascal, Nietzsche, the French moralists, Schopenhauer and, of course, Freud. My wish was to cover all the ground from the "intention to deceive" (which condenses the essence of the lie for a long tradition going back to Plato and Augustine) to the performative loop that makes us forget that we lie when we do in order to be better liars, so that often we don't even know that we have lied. The unconscious circularity of lying derives no doubt from the "Machiavellian brain" that makes us lie to ourselves in order to be better liars. If one works with a "logic of the unconscious" and a theory of the performative, at some point one will have to confront the positions taken by Derrida and by Lacan as quite parallel. I could not develop this at length here, and can only lead you to the American version of the book.[37] There, I try to bridge the gap between Derrida and Lacan, showing that both understand that truth can have a "structure of fiction"—a point made earlier by Nietzsche, and also, perhaps more cogently even, by Freud.

Derrida would suggest the name of Heidegger so as to send us on a more foundational meditation. And he would be right, if we see in the later Heidegger a writer who constantly bridges the gap between the phenomenology of lying and the ontological promise brought about by the unconcealment of Being. It has to remain an "intention," understood not as the prison of a subjectivity limited to pure interiority, but a promise, that is to say a performative forever devoid of any constative value. He expresses this in a love poem to Hannah Arendt:

Our e-vent
It came to a close,
this mountain stroll
at the highest road
of your deepest advent . . .

---

[37] See my *Ethics of the Lie*. New York: The Other Press, 2007, especially pp. 264–381.

What is future—our e-vent?

Nothing then but this high
flood of pure fire
preserved inviolate,
intending, delicate.[38]

Following Heidegger's suggestion, we should try to see our future as an event, an event similar to that of falling in love. Armed with a concept of performativity that will not be "cleaned up" normatively of its constitutive ambiguities and inevitable infelicities, we will think and read better while letting important "events" happen to us. We will try to read texts slowly, patiently, and without ideological presuppositions (hence we will continue reading Heidegger even if we know that he was a Nazi for some time). We will not hesitate to blur the boundaries of genres, at least between the domains of philosophy and literature. In order to be attentive to the possibility of an event, we will have to take into consideration the long history of concepts underpinning contemporary debates. Such debates are tackled with more ethical urgency if we do not ignore quasi-immemorial philosophical genealogies—which does not mean that we will have to return endlessly to Plato, who was called by Derrida "the master of the perverformative."[39] Plato's perverse paternity over Greek philosophy cannot be denied even if we will want to expand the field so as to engage with other conceptual fields that have been excluded, whether they come from Asia, Africa or other hitherto invisible sources.

[38] Hannah Arendt and Martin Heidegger, *Letters 1925–1975*, edited by Ursula Ludz and translated by Andrew Shields. Orlando and New York: Harcourt, 2004, p. 80.
[39] Jacques Derrida, *The Postcard*, Alan Bass (trans.). Chicago: Chicago University Press, 1987, p. 136. I owe this to Charles Ramond's excellent *Le Vocabulaire de Jacques Derrida*. Paris: Ellipses, 2001, pp. 53–4.

5

Derrida's Anterior Futures

In *Of Grammatology* Derrida had announced forcibly "the end of the Book and the beginning of Writing,"[1] adding that, given his task of a radical undermining of logocentrism, the future could only present itself under the figure of absolute danger. The future appears as a monstrosity for which any epigraph is lacking. In a similar way, *Archive Fever* links the function of an archive to an experience of an unthinkable yet affirmative future; but first an important semantic distinction is needed:

> But it is the future which is at issue here, and the archive as an irreducible experience of the future.
>
> And if there is a single trait about which Yerushalmi remains intractable, if there is shielded from all discussion (psychoanalytic or talmudic), an unconditional affirmation, it is the affirmation of the future *to come* (in French, I prefer saying this with the to-come of the *avenir* rather than the *futur* so as to point toward the coming of an event rather than toward some future present).
>
> The affirmation of the future *to come*: this is not a positive thesis. It is nothing other than the affirmation itself, the "yes", insofar as it is the condition of all promises or of all hope, of all awaiting, of all performativity, of all opening toward the future, whatever it may be, for science or for religion. I am prepared to subscribe without reserve to this affirmation made by Yerushalmi.[2]

Just as Benjamin noted in the last "Thesis on the philosophy of history" that if the Torah prohibits any investigation of the future, the future has

---

[1] Jacques Derrida, *De la Grammatologie*. Paris, Éditions de Minuit, 1967, p. 14.
[2] Jacques Derrida, "Archive fever: a Freudian impression," Eric Prenowitz (trans.), *Diacritics*, Summer 1995, vol. 25, no. 2, p. 45. The French text is to be found in *Mal d'Archive*. Paris: Galilée, 1995, p. 109.

nevertheless to keep all its messianic potentialities.[3] Yerushalmi stresses the foundational function of Messianism. His "Judaism terminable and interminable" implies hope, a hope which is not just a "hope for the future" but "the anticipation of a specific hope for the future." Jewishness, which is not exactly the same as Judaism, appears indissociable from a valorization of the "to come" as a French term (*l'avenir*), which cannot be reduced to the futurity of *le futur*. The assertion of *l'avenir* is assertion itself, a pure *yes* in so far as it conditions all promises and hopes. How can the specifically French opposition between *avenir* and *futur* be translated into English? Will such an untranslatable trap us in the singularity of an idiom? Since one observes a bifurcation between Latin languages such as French, Spanish and Italian, that possess two terms for the future, and Germanic languages in which one finds only one term as in German and English (*Zukunft* and future), can we continue thinking beyond idiomatic difference?

The French semantic couple opposes *l'avenir* as the coming of any future event, and *le futur*, indicating the *being* of the future as hazard, risk, wager. For *futurus* derives from *esse*, the supine of the Latin verb "to be," when used to compose a future participle, *futurus*, which as a plural neuter, *futura*, would mean in classical Latin "things that are to come or to happen." *Futur* was current in the thirteenth century, whereas *avenir* is a later creation, appearing in the French language as a modification of the verb *advenir* in the fourteenth century when it signified "success in the future." A century later (around 1427), *avenir* would mean a "future time"—a time *à venir*, yet to come. And Littré's famous nineteenth-century dictionary opposes Pascal, as one who systematizes the finality of *l'avenir*, playing on means, ends and endings, when he writes: "The present is never our end. The past and the present are our means, the future alone our end." ("... *le seul avenir est notre fin*"),[4] to Gide who insists on the potentiality inherent in *futur* and asserts: "*Je confonds possible et futur.*" ("For me, possibility and futurity are identical.") However,

---

[3]   The passage is: "We know that the jews were prohibited from investigating the future. The Torah and the prayers instruct them in remembrance, however. This stripped the future of its magic, to which all those succumb who turn to the soothsayers for enlightenment. This does not imply, however, that for the Jews the future turned into homogeneous, empty time. For every second of time was the strait gate through which the Messiah might enter." Walter Benjamin, "Theses on the philosophy of history," in *Illuminations*, Harry Zohn (trans.). New York: Shocken Books, 1969, p. 264

[4]   Blaise Pascal, *Pensées*, A. J. Krailsheimer (trans.). London: Penguin, 1966, p. 43. There is no general agreement as to which French edition of the *Pensées* is the most reliable. For the sake of practicality, I have used Michel Le Guern's two-volume edition of Pascal, *Pensées*. Paris: Gallimard, Folio, 1977, p. 82: "*Le passé et le présent sont nos moyens, le seul avenir est notre fin.*"

Littré concludes etymologically but also a little enigmatically: "*Le futur est ce qui sera, l'avenir est ce qui adviendra.*" "Future is what will be, and the 'to come' is what will come"; one could add: *Comprenne qui pourra!*

In order not to be stuck in etymological quibbles, let us remember that it was Pascal's mathematical and metaphysical calculation of the future that introduced the new science of probability, while he kept deriding the Jesuits and attacking them for their reliance on theological "probability" in their casuistry. This was after he had invented the earliest prototypes of the computer with his "calculating machine." Pascal's overall strategy relies on the distinction between *avenir* and *futur*. For him, *avenir* supposes a distinction between stretches of time (it can be *proche* or *lointain*), which nevertheless supposes the possibility of programming the shift from one time to another: *prospective* is often implied. The French *futur* is both more ancient (with the overtones of *fut-fût* linking the preterite with a subjunctive) and more distant, opening up onto science fiction (and, why not, on futility, as we shall see with Mallarmé). An influential Science-Fiction series published by Denoël has been aptly titled: "*Présence du Futur*" (The presence of the future). This is also why the colloquial English phrase expressing despair and rejection of a hopeless current social situation—"No Future!"—can only be translated into French as "Pas d'avenir!" or "Aucun avenir!" A translation saying instead: "*pas de futur*" would indeed sound like an anglicism because, in French, it is usually understood that one has a *futur*, or several *futurs* (for instance in the sense of an always possible "future bride"), even if *l'avenir* looks bleak (it may be for the same reason or the same person!). Similarly, one would not really say "*je travaille pour le futur*" (while "*je travaille pour l'avenir*" is correct) since one is generally expected to toil for a directly foreseeable *avenir* yielding concrete results and not for a very hypothetical *futur*. Moreover, *futur* introduces a modalization of being through a grammar that defines a shift in tenses rather than calling up another time. Consequently, I will follow the future of *futur* for a while, at least in order to provide a heuristic vantage-point assessing the *avenir*'s posterity.

In all these analyses, I will have to trust chance, using the hazard as dice or dies of language to question the calculations of "generations." It seems that "posterity" is contained in *l'avenir* much more than in *le futur*. We will also have to pay attention to the commercial overtones: "futures" is used commonly in the sense of commercial "shares," which associate a degree of uncertainty with a radical bet on the positive posterity of capitalism. A *wager* implies a calculation combining the plural and the future: it yields a plural "futures" that has to do with debt and risk, all thrown in a balance whose equilibrium is dependent upon a measure capable of calculating the "times to come." Thus, before reaching Pascal's famous wager, I will exploit a Christian parable, the story of "The steward of iniquity." Then I will sketch some aspects of a fundamental structure linking futurity to writing.

The economy of the future

My attention was first attracted to Luke's parable when I saw how Joyce used it as the culmination of his satire on a perverted Catholicism in *Dubliners*.[5] At the end of the story titled "Grace," Father Purdon's sermon in the Jesuit church of Gardiner Street epitomizes the spiritual simony that Joyce associates with petty-bourgeois values. Dublin is the capital of simony: all values have been reduced to commodities, while commercial interest still needs a religous sponsor to disguise its cynicism. The preacher, whose name calls up a notorious street in the red-light district of Dublin while evoking a Jesuitical "pardon" easily granted to sinners, concludes his sermon with these words:

> "For the children of this world are wiser in their generation than the children of light. Wherefore make unto yourselves friends out of the mammon of iniquity so that when you die they may receive you into everlasting dwellings."
>
> Father Purdon developed the text with resonant assurance. It was one of the most difficult texts in all the Scriptures, he said, to interpret properly. It was a text which might seem to the casual observer at variance with the lofty morality elsewhere preached by Jesus Christ.[6]

The modernized text of Luke XVI used by Father Purdon is at variance with either the King James Version or the Catholic Bible where one does not find "when you die" but "when you fail" (this may be a deliberate distortion, by which Joyce points out the Jesuitic veil thrown over a purely commercial meaning). The basic story is well-known: a master, a lord, an *Adon*, who is also a "rich man," has heard rumors that his *oikonomos* has "wasted his goods" and tells him two things that are slightly contradictory: first that he has to "give an account of [his] stewardship," then that he will be dismissed ("for now thou canst be steward no longer"). The *oikonomos* is aware that he has very little time before being actually dismissed, and he does not attempt to "give an account" or to defend himself. Knowing that he has been denounced,

---

5   I have used this passage in a different context in my *James Joyce and the Politics of Egoism*. Cambridge: Cambridge University Press, 2001, pp. 210–14.

6   James Joyce, "Grace," *Dubliners*, R. Scholes and A. Walton Litz (eds). New York and London: Penguin and Viking, 1976, p. 173.

we may infer that the rumors were founded. Thus the *oikonomos* calls all the debtors of the master and finds a trick "so that they may receive (him) into their houses." When a debtor owes a hundred barrels of oil, he changes the debt to fifty barrels; another debtor owes a hundred quarters of wheat, he changes it to eighty quarters. This is a scene of forced writing and hurried dictation: "And he said to him: Take thy bill (*gramma*) and sit down quickly and write (*grapson*) fifty ... He said to him: Take thy bill and write eighty." (Luke XVI.6–7)

The story of the Steward of Iniquity (*Villicum iniquitatis*) is a parable linking debt and writing: the *oikonomos*'s model, insofar as it is a model (since its exemplarity is given by default, for want of a natural wisdom in religious matters, opposed to human ruse and cleverness in practical or financial matters) shows how to steal from a debt, which is after all a rather wise and exhilarating perspective on the future. Because the *oikonomos* has been asked to give an account of his stewardship, he suddenly—all too quickly—launches into a systematic anti-economy. The *oikonomos*, who has already mediated between a Lord who is a capitalist and a crowd of debtors, begins perverting this relationship. There is indeed a degree of anarchy in the rapid reductions he authorizes, from 100 to 50 in one case, from 100 to 80 in another, which may be ascribed to a lack of preparation, to pure and ingenious improvisation. Thus one can say that the *oikonomos* steals from the debt, and by doing so he takes away even more of his master's money; at the same time, he gives from the debt to the debtors who will profit marginally. Here is an instance in which stealing is exactly synonymous with giving. However, as a good *oikonomos*, he does not erase the debt, even if he could have been tempted to do so. Could he not simply cancel the debt, and destroy these accusing tablets altogether? No, this would exceed his power as *oikonomos* and would also diminish the paradoxical force of the parable. Its meaning is predicated upon a particular writing, a writing that keeps a trace of another trace which has nevertheless to be read through partial cancellation or obliteration.

One of the ironies of the parable's outcome is that the master, instead of being furious, praises his *oikonomos* ("And the lord commended the unjust steward, forasmuch as he had done wisely" Luke XVI.8). In fact, whether he knew it or not, this was the best plan to be hired again. However, his original strategy aimed at being invited by all or some of the debtors, who no doubt would then have shown some measure of gratitude. The *oikonomos* expects to be without money or job, and is above begging or working with his hands ("To dig I am not able; to beg I am ashamed"), therefore he will have to depend upon others. The context of this potentially scandalous commendation of an "unjust" man whose "iniquity" is praised is revealing: Luke, writing in the name of Jesus, means to attack the Pharisees who, as we know, were with the Scribes the staunchest defenders of the old dispensation, and the guardians of the Mosaic faith after the destruction of the Temple by the Romans. Luke's story questions the Pharisees' aristocratic and capitalistic self-righteousness, their denial of debt and ultimately blindness facing the impending catastrophe. The *oikonomos* who "gives" by reducing debts which are not his own, in the hope of a future charity, is aware that somehow his accounts, like those of everybody, will not tally. One cannot pay back fully: debt remains, one can never be free from it, it is far wiser to gain new accomplices than to bet on one's purity facing the Law. The righteous Pharisees are said to be "covetous": they are indeed misers above all because they feel secure. They labor under the delusion that they are the elect, the *ariston*, the chosen ones; their riches, in the economic and spiritual sense, that should prove their moral distinction, are in fact spurious—precisely because they believe mistakenly that they have no debt to pay for.

The predicament of the *oikonomos* can be universalized to all humanity: we are all going to account for our lives, and we are going to be found wanting. The catastrophe of death and judgment is impending. The only way we may postpone its terrible effects seems to be in a cunning calculation: if we cannot make our accounts look right, at least we can redirect a former prevarication into the direction of the others. Thus we shall partly atone for the misdemeanor. We shall add to our wrongdoing in one sense (instead of justifying the past— there is no time for that, this would be wasting one's time) and risk a faster dilapidation of the master's fortune. But this will gain for us the friendship of people whose complicity we try to buy in advance. Luke's wager is a human one, since it bets on the sense of a human reciprocity, not on a divine pardon. The direction is towards the community not towards a vertical or transcendent relationship.

This parable about economy supposes an economy of debt, in debt, always hinged around a sense of futurity but also underpinned by a reciprocal sociability. Real economy is based upon the accountants, debtors, IOUs, books of accounts that inscribe the names, and the quantities one owes. God is indeed the arch capitalist in this story: the *Adon* as master is pleased to have discovered that even if his steward steals a little, at least he is very clever. He will not find a better one (if he loses some money with him, it will only be a fraction of what his sound investments and astute transactions will bring him). If one accepts to allegorize the tale, then the *oikonomos* functions precisely as Jesus is supposed to act according to Christian doctrine. He takes away from our sins what appear as a sort of eternal debt, a debt which can be diminished, but he also takes away from the old Jewish Law. The *oikonomos* facing the Master is in the same position as Jesus the Son facing his divine

Father—or as Moses facing God. Both steal from the debt of sin, lessening it in order to reduce the burden of humanity. Jesus's conclusion—"for the children of this world are wiser in their generation than the children of light"—initiates a paradoxical economy: in order to be as wise on the spiritual level as on the practical, one must learn the basic rules of capitalism by playing on futures and shares, on proportions and fractions. It may be possible to calculate a reduction of 50 per cent or only 20 per cent in the debt that corresponds to sin.

The appeal of this parable was immense for Jesuit casuists. On top of this, Father Purdon significantly omits the counterpart provided by: "No servant can serve two masters ... You cannot serve God and Mammon." (Luke XVI.13) Here, money is seen less as a "general equivalent" measuring future exchange than as a measure of inequity. This point is essential to the parable, since it explains how it can be read as a sort of negative "wager" argument: it is better to bet on some future outcome of one's actions that to attempt to justify past deeds. Money cannot be mistaken for a sign or token of election. A rapid evaluation of chances with the others has to prepare a new start in life, since a half-clean slate looks more secure than the uncertain outcome of a real trial. It is not necessary to try and justify oneself in front of the Law. A prudential judgment—implying one's interest—is to be preferred to an evidential judgment—implying proofs, evidence, testimonies—because we are always in haste. There is no time for the endless deferral of a Kafkaian trial, that always abruptly ends in death. The *oikonomos*'s prudential grammatology in which a stroke of the pen reduces a debt culminates in a translation of death as a simple economic "failure." Thus the parable points to Christ as a Redeemer who buys humanity out of original sin. We learn that failure can be positive, and that we can live with an interminable debt, provided we have been wise enough to bet on the Future. This Future, however, is also a past event (the coming of Christ) which will be duplicated in a messianic moment (the second coming). All of which leads us to the Pascalian argument.

Pascal's wager

Pascal's famous argument entails a double series of calculations. The first level is deliberately simplistic: the decision between "Either God exists, or He does not" should be solved by a simple decision in favor of infinity against the finite stake ("if you win, you win everything; if you lose, you lose nothing"[7]).

---

[7] Pascal, see footnote 4, p. 151. I shall refer to the English translation as P. and the page number.

But this too-easy solution does not take into account the price to be paid: it soon appears as exorbitant if one has to "give everything" ("you must risk all"). Then really begins the complex calculation of chances:

> ...even though there were an infinite number of chances (*hasards*), of which only one were in your favour, you would still be right to wager one in order to win two; and you would be acting wrongly, being obliged to play, in refusing to stake one life against three in a game, where out of an infinite number of chances (*hasards*) there is one in your favour, if there were an infinity of infinitely happy life to win.
>
> (P, p. 151)

In fact, as most commentators agree, whether they think that the argument is directed at the Libertines only, or at all men, this wager could never convince or convert any one. Faith is not a matter of chance-taking, one cannot be with belief. What is Pascal's aim then? First, he shows very effectively that the "argument" describes in fact an ontological situation in which not betting is already a bet. Not choosing is already choosing against. The *pari* (wager) is also a demonstration of the *parti/partie*[8] axiom: a game is being played, and each player should know the stakes. "A bet must be laid. There is no option: You have joined the game (*Vous êtes embarqué*)."[9] The saying "Nothing ventured, nothing gained" cannot simply obtain here: one has to risk and venture.

But this ontological situation, which has been described as leading to modern Christian existentialism, to Kierkegaard for instance, displaces the issue of ontology. This is why Heidegger quotes Pascal approvingly in the first pages of *Being and Time*: just as God cannot be "proved" rationally, the concept of Being is undefinable (Pascal had written: "... in order to define *being* one must say 'It is ...' and hence employ the word to be defined in its definition."[10] If one cannot prove rationally the existence of God (as in Descartes's metaphysics, for instance) then what remains is a personal dilemma which might hopefully be solved by a rational calculation of risk. The wager replaces traditional proofs by a pragmatic assessment, stressing

---

[8] Le Guern refers to Pascal's "Treatise on the arithmetic triangle" for a definition of the word "*parti*" as "stakes" or "the money a player must be ready to lose as soon as he puts it on the table." The *parti* presupposes the notion of a *partie*, a game one is free to enter into or to leave at one's leisure. Le Guern (ed.), *Pensées*, I. Paris: Gallimard-Folio, 2004, pp. 290–1.

[9] In Le Guern (ed.), *Pensées*, II. Paris: Gallimard-Folio, p. 11. Krailsheimer translates weakly: "Yes, but you must wager. There is no choice, you are already committed." (P, p. 150)

[10] Heidegger quotes Pascal in paragraph 1 of *Being and Time*. See Heidegger, *Basic Writings*, David Farrell Krell (trans.). New York: Harper, 1993, p. 43.

decision and choice. Choosing implies a risk, but this risk can be calculated. As Nicholas Rescher writes: "... the level of the discussion is shifted from *establishing a fact* to *justifying an action*."[11] Pascal announces contemporary decision theory; the second level of the argument, that takes into account the cost of the wager, has recourse to preponderant expectations. But beyond the relatively complex mathematical structure of double bifurcations which I shall not reproduce here, what stands out self-evidently is that Pascal's conclusion is simply that it is not absurd to believe in God, even if this belief entails the "*abêtissement*" (humiliation) of reason. The calculation aims at establishing the rational rights of the heart's "reasons" over Reason. The "heart" is the locus of the undoing or auto-deconstruction of reason by itself. Thus, if one remains unconvinced at the end of the demonstration, Pascal suggests help from a community: "Follow the way by which they began" (P, p. 152) and join a community of believers.

However, there is a second level in Pascal's argumentation, which supposes another type of proof: the Bible. His main strategy has been in fact less to frighten the Libertine than to convince him to start reading the Book in a correct way. Writing offers a different type of proof, which supposes that one can learn to read—the way to man or God—between the two infinities, in the "mean" of meaning between extremes. Paul de Man's epigraph to *Allegories of Reading* ("When we read too fast or too slowly, we understand nothing")[12] could remind us of a good speed or indeed proportion necessary for the right kind of understanding. The principle of the "mean" applies to every domain: "First principles are too obvious for us; too much pleasure causes discomfort; too much harmony in music is displeasing; too much kindness annoys us: we want to pay back the debt with something over." (P, p. 92) Pascal then quotes Tacitus's cynical comment: "Kindness is welcome to the extent that it seems the debt can be paid back. When it goes too far gratitude turns into hatred." (P, p. 92) which may help us to understand why the Steward does not want to abolish his Lord's debts altogether ... The calculation of the exact reading focus similarly presupposes a good usage of time: "We never keep to the present. We recall the past; we anticipate the future as if we found it too slow in coming (*Nous anticipons l'avenir comme trop lent à venir*) and were trying to hurry it up, or we recall the past as if to stay its too rapid flight." (P, p. 43) The ontological vertigo created by the argument of the two infinites and the

---

[11] Nicholas Rescher, *Pascal's Wager: A Study of Practical Reasoning in Philosophical Theology.* Notre Dame: University of Notre Dame Press, 1985, p. 7.

[12] "*Quand on lit trop vite ou trop doucement on n'entend rien*", quoted in Paul de Man *Allegories of Reading.* New Haven: Yale University Press, 1979, p. v. See P, p. 38.

difficult "mean" also applies to the time (and the subjective poise or position) any reading activity presupposes.

The outcome of the "wager" has been to transform the hesitant Libertine into a literary critic whose main assumption is that nothing has been left to chance in a text.[13] The notion that we are all "embarked" in a game of decision-making plunges us radically in a hermeneutic situation. The text at hand is indeed the text of the Bible which may seem so obscure at first sight. Pascal's starting point is that the contradictions and ambiguities in the Bible all make sense. "Every author has a meaning which reconciles all contradictory passages, or else has no meaning at all; the last point cannot be said of the Scriptures and the prophets: they were certainly too sensible (*avaient trop de bon sens*). We must therefore look for a meaning which reconciles all contradictions."[14] One must find the plane of meaning on which all the surface contrarieties of the text are harmonized. This is why Pascal founds his hermeneutics on Augustine's symbolism, in which the model of meaning is prophetic discourse. It implies four elements: an enunciator who is supposed to be conscious of the double level of meaning; a tropologically coded message working through a mixture of figurative and plain statements; a key to the rhetorical tropes used, distinguishing between passages that keep a literal meaning and passages in need of a tropological interpretation; and a consideration of the inherent temporality of the text, distinguishing between events that have already taken place and events still to come in the future.

For instance, Adam is not to be understood as a "literal" character. Pascal quotes the Latin phrase (*Adam forma futuri*) from Rom. V.14 ("Adam is the figure of him that was to come"). (P, p. 228) In typically Augustinian fashion, Adam's sin and fall are necessary for the coming of Christ, and even for the fact that time exists, which immediately entails the coexistence of several times: "If Adam had not sinned and Christ had not come, there would have been only one covenant and one age of man, and creation would have been represented as accomplished at a single moment." (P, p. 228) Adam is not just the "figure of him that was to come, meaning Jesus, but also the figure of a distinct type of futurity, a futurity that is underpinned by a past and eternally future "felix culpa."

In a similar way, circumcision is shown to have been merely a sign (P, p. 173). It is from this point of view, for instance, that Pascal can deduce that the true Jews and the true Christians share the same religion (but the stubborn Jews are wrong in taking circumcision literally). The threat of

---

[13] I owe this point to Pierre Force's *Pascal et l'Herméneutique*. Paris: Vrin, 1989, p. 100 n. 2.
[14] I have modified P, p. 106, since the translation seems to say exactly the opposite of Pascal's original idea. See also Le Guern, footnote 8, p. 180.

absurdity or contradiction becomes a methodological weapon: "All these sacrifices and ceremonies were therefore either figurative or nonsense. Now some things are too clear and lofty to be considered nonsense." (P, p. 109) In his approach to the ambiguous figures of the Bible, Pascal relies heavily on Raymond Martin's *Pugio Fidei adversus Mauros et Judaeos*, the exposition by an obscure thirteenth-century Spanish divine of rabbinical hermeneutics, recently republished in Pascal's time. From Martin's *Pugio*, Pascal learned the use of techniques of interpretation invented by the Rabbis but, of course, often fought against their conclusions. One of the main ideas Pascal has found there is that the prophets of the Old Testament clearly announce Jesus as the Messiah and God's son (this is based on complex numerological issues). The role of the unbelieving Jews then acquires a crucial function: they are both witnesses to the sacred nature of their religion and blind readers, misguided readers whose blindness forces one to interpret better. Their relationship to a division of time (*templum*) is thus crucial: "Anathema of the [Greeks] against those who compute the periods of time." (P, p. 130) Le Guern's edition replaces "Greeks" with "Jews", since he supposes that "Greeks" is a slip of the pen for "Jews": Jews, not Greeks, hate those who distinguish "before the Law, during the Law, under Grace."[15] As Pascal keeps repeating, Jewish prophecy has stopped after the coming of Christ, sending us back to the need to read the doubleness of the Law. "Double law, double table of the law, double temple, double captivity." (P, p. 133) This confirms the link between hermeneutics and prophecy: the "proof" of religion lies in the already inscribed futurity of the event in Scripture.

The demonstration of existential hazard throwing us between couples of infinities should lead one to conversion, a conversion less to religious fervor than to textual rigor. The uncertainty in man's lot as *l'avenir*—which has to be transcended or sublimated into the order of faith or the heart—nevertheless permits the certainty of a knowledge of a *futur*: there is a futurity already inscribed in the text of the Bible, which converges upon the Event of the Incarnation. For Pascal, indeed, the Messiah's futurity has already happened, Christ has come at the right time as the announced Messiah: without this, no reading is possible, no textuality can be defined. The Event alone provides the keystone of textual hermeneutics. The more uncertain our *avenir* looks, the more certain and convincing will the textual proofs of religion appear. This is why, indeed, "To have no time for philosophy is to be a true philosopher." (P, p. 212) Krailsheimer's translation distorts in an interesting and creative fashion the original statement (*Se moquer de la philosophie, c'est vraiment philosopher*).

---

[15] Le Guern, see footnote 8, pp. 216 and 325 for the endnote.

To deride philosophy, to mock philosophers is also to have "no patience" with a certain type of discourse, as Nietzsche knew too well. Pascal's hermeneutics, just like Luke's parable, never leave us enough time to think and consider: we are all hurried and bullied so as to realize that we have always already been "embarked" in a wager acquiring universal and ontological dimensions.

Wagering the Wagnis: Pascal, Rilke, Heidegger

Another philosopher who was rather impatient with all other philosophers, including a Nietzsche who had believed too early that he had put an end to metaphysics, Heidegger alludes often to Pascal's "heart," albeit with a certain ambivalence. Pascal figured very early in *Being and Time,* and he reappears in a significant context—a reading of Rilke's poetry—in Heidegger's essay "*Wozu Dichter?*" There, Heidegger glosses Rilke's notion of "*das Offene*" (the Open) and develops the idea of "unshieldedness" associated with it, or rather converted into the "sphere of consciousness."[16] Heidegger then opposes as two complementary versions of the "invisible interior" Descartes's *cogito* and Pascal's heart:

> At nearly the same time as Descartes, Pascal discovers the logic of the heart as over against the logic of calculating reason. ... Only in the invisible innermost of the heart is man inclined toward what there is for him to love: the forefathers, the dead, the children, those who are to come.
>
> (WAPF, pp. 127–8)

"Those who are to come" (*die Kommenden*) is a phrase that quotes a passage from a letter by Rilke in which Rilke speaks of "the dead" and "those who are to come" (*die Künftige*) as in need of a refuge, of an abode. This, for Heidegger, circumscribes a typically metaphysical attempt aimed at converting consciousness into an expanding sphere, until it becomes "the widest orbit" capable of containing the whole world. But the specific feature of the "heart" is that it is free from "the arithmetic of calculation," and becomes the "supernumerary" existence praised by Rilke in the majestic conclusion of his ninth Duino Elegy:

---

[16] Martin Heidegger, "What are poets for?" in *Poetry, Language, Thought,* A. Hofstadter (trans.). New York: Harper, 1971, p. 127. Hereafter WAPF. See *Wozu Dichter?* (1946) in *Holzwege,* Frankfurt: Klostermann, 1950, p. 302.

Siehe, ich lebe. Woraus? Weder Kindheit noch Zukunft
werden weniger ... Ueberzähliges Dasein
entspringt mir im Herzen.[17]

From this point, Heidegger then returns to a previous analysis of an
"improvised" poem by Rilke, in which Rilke expands the notion of a Nature
actively "risking" the creatures that are in it and born from it whenever they
find themselves "in the Open. The keyword glossed at length here is that of
Wagnis, that calls up both risk *and* balance (since Heidegger links them
etymologically: *wiegen* means to weigh, a balance is *Waage*—in old German
a *Wage*), all of which is close to *wägen*, to open paths in a forest such as these
Holzwege that provide a neat title to the collection of essays. This is the
improvised poem written by Rilke in a letter:

As Nature gives the other creatures over
to the venture (*Wagnis*) of their dim delight ...
so too our being's pristine ground (*Urgrund*) settles our plight;
we are no dearer to it; it ventures us (*es wagt uns*).
Except that we, more eager than plant or beast,
go with this venture, will it, adventurous
more sometimes than Life itself, more daring (*wagender*)
by a breath (and not in the least
from selfishness).[18]

Heidegger pounces on the verb "to will" to conflate Rilke's position with
Nietzsche's will-to-power: according to him, both Rilke and Nietzsche thus
complete Western metaphysics. Heidegger concludes that "Being is the
venture pure and simple.... The Being of beings is the venture" (*Das Sein ist
das Wagnis schlechthin.... Das Sein des Seienden ist das Wagnis*).[19]

The exercise in poetic close reading which takes a good 20 pages brings
Heidegger back to questions about the essence of this "venture"—a wager as
much as a risk. It seems at first that Rilke follows in the steps of Pascal more
than of Nietzsche—until we realize that all three affirm the same thing.

[17] "Look, I am living. On what? Neither childhood nor future / Are growing less ...
Supernumerous existence / wells up in my heart." One could also translate "*überzähliges
Dasein*" by: "existence beyond number, uncountable, infinite, endlessly open." Rainer
Maria Rilke, *Duino Elegies*, J. B. Leishman and S. Spender (trans). New York: Norton,
1963, p. 77, for the translation and p. 113 for remarks on the word "*überzählig*."
[18] Rilke quoted in Heidegger, see footnote 16, p. 99.
[19] *Wozu Dichter?* in *Holzwege*, see footnote 16, p. 275.

Heidegger asks: "What do they dare, those who are more daring?"[20] Since Being cannot transcend itself to reach into something else, for Being is the *transcendens* pure and simple, then one has to come to the conclusion that the only "venture" more daring than Life itself is a risk which takes poetic language—hence all language—as its stake. Heidegger has already situated the heart's space as the only inwardness that can meet the Open: "The interiority of the world's inner space unbars the Open for us. Only what we thus retain in our heart (*par coeur*), only that do we truly know by heart." (WAPF, p. 130) After having posited Being as presence and absence via language—"Being, as itself, spans its own province, which is marked off (*temnein, tempus*) by Being's being present in the world. Language is the precinct (*templum*), that is, the house of Being." (WAPF, p. 132)—Heidegger meditates upon the fact that when we go through the woods, we already go through the word "wood" even if we do not speak or think the word. He then describes the object of the "dare," of the *Wagnis* as language: "... we have an intimation of what they dare who are sometimes more daring than the Being of beings. They dare the precinct of Being. They dare language." (WAPF, p. 132) The Being capable of accomplishing the dare is called an "Angel," an Angel identical with Zarathustra: "... the creature which is Rilke's angel, despite all difference in content, is *metaphysically the same* as the figure of Nietzsche's Zarathustra." (WAPF, p. 134) Like Zarathustra, the poet, because he is more "willing" than modern men who believe in self-assertion, can will a pure Nothing (WAPF, p. 140). Thus Being can echo through poetic song. For Heidegger, it was Hölderlin more than Rilke who would rise up to the lofty expectations of this risky wager with language. Yet a little before, Mallarmé understood, half a century after Hölderlin and half a century before Rilke, the true nature of this risk.

Mallarmé's die

To link Mallarmé's and Rilke's wagers, I shall start from a curious historical coincidence: as his letters show, Mallarmé discovered the esthetics of Nothingness and the pleasure of the Casino at about the same time. In April 1866, in a letter he sent to his wife after a three-day trip to Nice and Monaco with his friend Lefébure, he mentions that the "Monaco excursion has been delicious" and that he has won "some money at the roulette" with which he has bought a surprise gift for Maria.[21] He enthusiastically comments on the

---

[20] See footnote 16: WAPF, p. 131; and *Holzwege*, p. 293.
[21] Stéphane Mallarmé, *Correspondance*, B. Marchal (ed.). Paris: Gallimard-Folio, 1994, 291. Hereafter, C. The translations are all mine.

experience a little later, explaining that he "resuscitates": "Lefébure has lifted the veil that had been hiding for ever the Nice setting, and I was deliriously drunk with the Mediterranean. Ah, my friend, how divine is this terrestrial sky!" (C, p. 300) The almost Nietzschean overtones coming from a landscape that had similarly inspired the German thinker acquire only retrospectively the dimension of an existential and intellectual crisis. Two years after the fact, in April 1868, Mallarmé commemorates the fecund "stay in Cannes", which had allowed him to "dig down into verse" (*creuser le vers*) and reach a major artistic breakthrough after the dismal encounter with utter nothingness.

A letter to Villiers de l'Isle-Adam comments upon the famous crisis: "For the Future (*pour l'avenir*), at least for the next future, my soul is destroyed. My thought has reached the point where it could think itself and has no strength at its disposal to evoke in a unique Nothingness the void dissminated in its porosity." (C, p. 366) Mallarmé nevertheless announces the "interior dream" of two parallel books, one on "Beauty," the other on "the sumptuous allegories of Nothingness," books he feels impotent to produce: "Really, I am afraid to *begin* (although, it is true *Eternity* has scintillated in me and devoured any surviving notion of time) where our poor and sacred Baudelaire ended." (C, p. 367). But the same letter concludes on a more optimistic note, begging forgiveness for a silence "ancient about *Morgane* . . . and future (*futur*) about the riches the *Journal* will bring me." (C, p. 367) The mention of Villiers's drama *Morgane* suggests a "martingale" with which the poet hopes to win some money, if not at the roulette, at least as a journalist. Throughout the correspondence, one observes a systematic bifurcation between *l'avenir* which describes the time of the future work whose "vague plans" he cannot make more precise and has to postpone (C, p. 369) and *le futur* or *futur* used as an adjective. The latter is reserved for a potentiality of writing as a gamble still determined by past calculations: "You would save from Nothingness very divine pieces of work that suffer from being half-immersed in the future (*navrées d'être à moitié plongées dans le futur*)." (C, p. 373)

In 1869, we find an extraordinary series of letters to various addressees, all dictated by Mallarmé to his wife. The poet was suffering from a strange writer's hysteria, and his doctor had forbidden him to touch a pen. In the first of these, Maria's errratic spelling (her native language was German) transforms *futur* into *fûtur*: ". . . the simple fact of writing installs hysteria into my head, which I want to avoid for you, dear friends to whom I owe a Book and future years (*des années fûtures*)." (C, p. 425) The submerged pun on "*fût-il?*" suggests a creative futurity quite aware of its risky status, and still in need of specific studies, among which one would find what Mallarmé calls his "egyptology." This is how he describes his situation through his wife's pen:

The first phase of my life is over. Consciousness, overburdened with shadows, wakes up slowly to shape a new man, and has to find back my dream after its creation. This will last a number of years during which I must relive the life of humanity since its childhood as it becomes conscious of itself.

(C, p. 425)

This second—and last—"crisis" of 1869 relegates to the past of the work everything that preceded it, including the text whose title "The future phenomenon" points in the direction of Hegel's phenomenology.

The poet's correspondence keeps promising a work to come, even when the metaphysical encounter with absolute Nothingness commemorated by *Igitur* is over and the poet has accepted that he is a simple *littérateur* and not a philosopher or a hero of the spirit. In 1871, he again postpones the essential writing: "But to begin immediately, no. First, I must get the needed talent, and my thing has to become ripe, immutable, instinctive; almost anterior, and not of yesterday." (C, p. 509) Mallarmé's future creation is founded upon a sense of the unpredictable lines of chance. In order to document the evolution, one would have to follow thematic links between the prose-poem entitled "*Le Phénomène Futur*" and the "last" realization of a project such a *A Throw of the Dice Will Never Abolish Chance*. I will limit myself to a few hints gleaned from the poems, which all testify to a similar sense of a paradoxical futurity:

"A Fan" (of Madame Mallarmé)
With nothing else for speech
Than a pulsing in the skies
Our future verse shall rise (*Le futur vers se dégage*)
From a precious lodging . . .[22]

Or again in "Funereal Toast":

. . . We are nothing, then,
Save for the sad opaqueness of the future ghosts we bear.
(*Nous sommes / La triste opacité de nos spectres futurs*)
Is there, of this destiny, nothing that will remain?
. . . A solemn agitation of language in the air,
In commemoration of a calm catastrophe . . .

(CP, pp. 44–5)

---

[22] Stéphane Mallarmé, *Collected Poems*, Henry Weinfeld (trans.). Berkeley: University of California Press, 1994, p. 49. Hereafter CP.

The even more momentous last stanza in "The Tomb of Edgar Poe" states:

Calm block here fallen from obscure disaster,
Let his granite at least mark the boundaries evermore
To the dark flights of Blasphemy hurled to the future.
(*Aux noirs vols du Blasphème épars dans le futur*)

(CP, p. 71)

while a lighter Sonnet dedicated to Méry Laurent plays on similar tensions:

You know always, since years ago
Your dazzling smile has prolonged for me
The rose that plunges with its fair sea-
Son
into the past and the future also.
(*Dans autrefois et puis dans le futur aussi*)

(CP, p. 55)

There are huge affinities and convergences between Mallarmé's letters, his rare published poems, and the numerous notes for an unfinished "Book."[23] Blanchot has demonstrated in his *Livre à venir* that Mallarmé's absolute "Book" was in an essential sense always future in the sense of always "to come," against Scherer's short-sighted optimism (Scherer edited the notes as if they were the actual book).[24] However, more recently, another thesis on the lost or vanishing "Book" has been proposed, a thesis that would stress the past and "future perfect" realization of the "Book," closer to the sense of *le futur* than to Blanchot's *à venir*. Dragonetti, in *Un fantôme dans le kiosque*, starts from the idea that Mallarmé's meditation on the absolute Book implies also, as a dialectical counterpart, the contingent inscription of the vanishing author in a futile everyday life, from which at least a few postcards or sonnets are occasionally sent to contemporaries. A rigorous reflection on the interaction between the theory of modernity and its social locus of production can lead to a radical thesis: this is why Dragonetti, in his study of Mallarmé and the ghost of the "quotidian," claims that the perfect (and only possible) realization of Mallarmé's *Livre* was his

---

[23] I have developed these insights in *Ghosts of Modernity*, Gainesville: University Press of Florida, 1996, pp. 84–121.
[24] See Maurice Blanchot, *Le Livre à Venir*. Paris: Gallimard, 1959, pp. 270–97. Blanchot discusses *Le "Livre" de Mallarmé*, edited by Jacques Schérer. Paris: Gallimard, 1957.

own correspondence.[25] Mallarmé worked more with a view to the social inscription of his writings, especially toward the end of his life, when he busied himself with countless poems for anniversaries, banquets, commemorations, burials, and all the rituals surrounding the busy but empty life of a literary *Maître* than with the neo-Hegelian agenda presupposed by Blanchot. With the *"loisirs de la poste,"* Mallarmé invented a new genre in which futility and ingenuity triumph: the address of his correspondent became the pretext for a brief poem, almost always a quatrain which the mailman must decipher in order to forward the message. His poems were thus indistinguishable from gifts for friends, as they were written on fans, fruits, packages of candies, tobacco or coffee. For lack of the absolute "Book," poetry seemed condemned to fulfilling the function of miniature decorations: ornamentation appeared as the bourgeois rewriting of an ontological futility, a systematic Pascalian *divertissement*.

Mallarmé's ghost was less the real ghost of his dead son Anatole than the impossible, tyrannical, and totalitarian *bouquin*. Just as he was describing to his disciples the absolute task of a "Supreme Fiction," his main poetic activity consisted in rhyming addresses. The death of the Hero, for which the notes for the Book elaborate several scenarios, was a demise that Mallarmé reserved for himself in a self-fulfilling prophecy; by this, he would confirm his inability to create a Work to which he had devoted his entire life. Is it accidental, then, that he died of a laryngeal spasm while struggling with the fantastic creation of the Book? It is not so much that physical demise serves as an indication of the "elocutionary disappearance" of a poet who disappears with a vengeance into a pure but inaudible language, but rather, that the crisis which seized him is called in French by a name derived from English, *faux croup* (spasmodic croup): a *"faux coup"* or "false throw of the dice" grabbing you in the throat, leading to death throes that parody the final dice throw of Death as a dishonest croupier. Caught in this fatal spastic throw, Mallarmé seems to have literally died from the discrepancy between his sublime aspirations to the *Livre* and the awareness that he would never fulfill them.

Like Rilke's *Orpheus*, the poet identifies with a pure trace, his exile becomes writing, in a last metamorphosis which is not devoid of pathos. Mallarmé's lifelong effort at combining Hegel's ghostly phenomenology of negativity and Poe's gothic specters and apparitions needed an added help from the *Geist* of History. Trapped between the Ghost of all Ghosts, the absolute but impossible "Book" embodying his solution to a radically new poetical language in

---

[25] Roger Dragonetti, *Un fantôme dans le kiosque: Mallarmé et l'esthétique du quotidien.* Paris: Seuil, 1992.

French, and the *Angelus Novus* of a pure language, a "new angel" similar to the figure which Walter Benjamin saw in Klee's painting, an angel who sees the chain of historical events as "one single catastrophe which keeps piling wreckage upon wreckage,"[26] leaves Mallarmé stranded, voiceless, deprived of a future. He can only wait for the last fit of his fateful "croup" to meet his own ghost, a specter speaking all the languages at once, but without him.

Toward a ghostlier futurity

When he died, Mallarmé thought that he left "no legacy." He had no son (since Anatole had died), and doubted that his daughter would take up the poetic project. The last letter written for his family, between two horrible seizures, stresses the desperate character of this past futurity. Alluding to the "half-centenarian heap of notes" that he alone could have deciphered or used, Mallarmé advocates utter destruction: "Burn, therefore; there is no literary heritage there, my poor children ... Believe that it was to be very beautiful." (C, p. 642) Nevertheless, the gesture leaves us with the task of rethinking his poetics of chance: *Un Coup de Dés jamais n'abolira le Hasard*. The grammatical link between "never" and the future points toward an impossible calculation of chance. So much depends upon the chance echoes or the rhymes provided by a given language, rhymes yoked together in a new type of ideality by a text. Such an ideality supposes that one forgets the time it takes to read or write the "Book." Or the task has to be left to Joyce's "ideal reader" suffering from an "ideal insomnia," a reader expected to devote an entire life to the reading of the Book.

Joyce, Rilke and Pascal meet upon one crucial point: there exists not just a "good" reader but an "ideal" reader—to be constructed—and that the concept is intimately bound with the text's specific futurity. Pascal's ideal player or ideal hermeneute confirms the ideality of the reader, a reader functioning as the "faithful steward" of textual economy. However, with Mallarmé, and perhaps Derrida, such a perfect adequation of speed with writing becomes all but impossible. We cannot help reading too fast or too slowly, and have to resort to the hospitality of friends, just like Luke's steward, to find a true balance. Hospitality allows us to bypass the limited economy of textuality, and forces us, in a daring wager, to venture the future of language. Is this an illusion, just a Wagnerian "*Zukunftsmusik*"? Such a conceptual crux is evoked

---

[26] Walter Benjamin, "Theses on the philosophy of history," in *Illuminations*. London: Pimlico, 1999, p. 257.

by a question posed by a character of *Finnegans Wake*: "The mujic of the footure on the barbarihams of the bashed?"[27] Is this, once more, the anthem of a "music of the future"—a *Zukunftsmusik*, which means in German empty promises, wilful delusions, illusions created by deception or wishful thinking? Yet these are played with barbaric means, or on the barrel organs (*orgues de barbarie*) of the past. Are the new men created by the Soviet revolution an avatar of the Barbarians of the past? No matter what the answer may be, Joyce never questioned the prophetic nature of his book. He mentioned in February 1940 the Russian invasion of Finland: "The most curious comment I have received on the book is a symbolical one from Helsinki, where, as foretold by the prophet, the Finn again wake, and volunteer Buckleys are running from all sides to shoot that Russian general."[28]

---

[27] James Joyce, *Finnegans Wake*. London: Faber, 1939, p. 518, line 28.
[28] James Joyce, *Letters I*. New York: Viking, 1957, p. 408; the idea is reiterated in a letter to Jacques Mercanton, see Joyce, *Selected Letters*. London: Faber, 1975, p. 403.

6

A Future without Death?

When in 1966 Foucault published *The Order of Things* and concluded with a few ominous sentences announcing the "end of man," the apocalyptic tone of his final predictions was greeted with dismay and incomprehension. Half a century later, Arakawa's and Gins's strenuous efforts to rethink concretely and dynamically the foundations of what makes us "human beings" have endowed Foucault's words with a new relevance. They are worth quoting once more:

> In fact, among all the mutations that have affected the knowledge of things and their order, the knowledge of identities, differences, characters, equivalences, words ... only one, that which began a century and a half ago and is now perhaps drawing to a close, has made it possible for the figure of man to appear. And that appearance was not the liberation of an old anxiety, the transition into luminous consciousness of an age-old concern, the entry into objectivity of something that had long remained trapped within beliefs and philosophies: it was the effect of a change in fundamental arrangements of knowledge. As the archaeology of our thought easily shows, man is an invention of recent date. And one perhaps nearing its end.
>
> If those arrangements were to disappear as they appeared, if some event of which we can at the moment do no more than sense the possibility—without knowing either what its form will be or what it promises—were to cause them to crumble, as the ground of Classical thought did at the end of the eighteenth century, then one can certainly wager that man would be erased, like a face drawn in sand at the edge of the sea.[1]

Arakawa and Gins have acted upon Foucault's admonitions by investigating the conditions of possibility of a new episteme that would take stock of the

---

[1] Michel Foucault, *The Order of Things: An Archaeology of Human Sciences.* New York: Random House, 1970, pp. 386–7.

exhaustion of the humanistic paradigm, a paradigm defined by the promotion of "man" as an object of action and knowledge. This was not limited to an old humanism: in Heidegger's anti-humanist philosophy, man as Dasein was taken to be a mortal being whose authenticity was determined and conditioned by a singular relation to death, a point to which I will return with Adorno. Since the beginning of Aristotelian logics, we have been taught to reason on the various ways in which we may be concerned by the fact that Socrates is mortal. Precisely by starting at the root and negating the "major" of such an apparent truism, Arakawa and Gins immediately launch a complex re-arrangement of knowledge that is capable of taking in technological advances that have marked our new century. Their revisionist re-definition of man in this post-human state is tantamount to launching a scientific revolution.

Such a gesture entails moving back and forth between different disciplines that are endlessly re-combined, connected and articulated, taken as they are in the nets of a scientific idiom that needs new terms so as to de-familiarize old notions weighed down by centuries of use and abuse (thus the importance of specific coinings such as "landing site," "biocleave," "architectural surround" and so on). But this linguistic creativity does not remain purely semantic, of course, since the new language it produces is born out of real problems and experiments, and thus entails more than rethinking an *episteme* but working concretely on the creation of objects, from poems, novels, films and paintings to installations, houses, temples, parks, museums and even whole cities.

As we have seen earlier with Agamben and Derrida, Foucault's last project was devoted to an exploration of "bio-power," a regime that "brought life and its mechanisms into the realm of explicit calculations and made knowledge-power an agent of the transformation of human life."[2] Bio-power originally described a set of "procedures" and "technologies" that aimed at controlling the body; but as Foucault discovered as he was examining the history of sexuality and the way Ancient thinkers in Athens and Rome would talk about the "care of the self," the same procedures could also be used to free the body, to teach it "how to live" better. Foucault sums up this type of "classical" and pre-Christian problem as the fundamental question: "Which *techne* do I have to use in order to live as well as I ought to live?"[3]

These pre-classical problems have also concerned a non-Western thinking about the "good life," to which Arakawa and Gins also refer. This was the problem

---

[2] Quoted by Paul Rabinow in the "Introduction" to the *Foucault Reader*, Paul Rabinow (ed.). New York: Pantheon Books, 1984, p. 17.

[3] Rabinow, see footnote 3, p. 348.

faced by a blind and deaf girl like Helen Keller when she tried to live a normal life. Arakawa and Gins take Helen Keller as a model: each day upon awakening she had to make the world anew, thus exemplifying what a real artist will wish to do.[4] Her example makes us go deeper into ourselves and test the limits of our perception, analyze how we construct our world. We can then apply new hypotheses to the building of large-scale structures. The vast array of discourses mobilized by Arakawa and Gins, from Deleuzian or Heideggerian philosophy and linguistic analysis to art criticism, from phenomenology to urban studies, poetry, design, sociology, neuro-sciences, biotechnologies, neuro-physiology, cognitive sciences, Buddhist logics of the blank meaning, contemporary physics, embryology, evolution theory, ecology and, of course, architecture, attests to the vitality of a procedural thinking that traverses all categories.

Inter-connectedness is a keyword here, and it has been deployed in several domains: first in the buildings realized by Arakawa and Gins; then in the art-work, poems and books. Art leads to a reflexive process combining the theory of its own genesis and procedures with a view of a possible, but unheard of, future, for instance a future in which death will be abolished. Art leads to a recognition of the preeminence of architecture: both are activities that should be called "poetic" in the strictest sense of the word. Looking for predecessors in this slow emergence of a multiple concern for life, ethics and architecture, some help comes from Hermann Broch. In his trilogy, *The Sleepwalkers* (1931), we find a theory that is very similar. In the third installment of the theoretical digressions on the "Disintegration of values" that are interspersed throughout the narrative of the "Realist," Broch addresses issues of architecture and the abolition of death:

> The primacy of architectural style among the things that characterize an epoch is a very curious phenomenon. But, in general, so is the uniquely privileged position that plastic art has maintained in history. It is after all only a very small excerpt of the totality of human activities with which an age is filled, and certainly not even a particularly spiritual excerpt, and yet in power of characterization it surpasses every other province of the spirit, surpasses even science, surpasses even religion.[5]

The character at the origin of these meditations is a philosopher walking through the streets of Berlin in the late twenties, a critical thinker appalled as

---

[4] From a note by Madeline Gins on her book *Helen Keller or Arakawa*. New York: Burning Books, 1994.
[5] Hermann Broch, *The Sleepwalkers*, Willa and Edwin Muir (trans). New York: Random House, 1st edn, 1945 [1996], p. 397.

much by the coldness of modernist architecture as by the weakness of the new decorative *Kitsch*. In his musings on contemporary architecture, he echoes one of Broch's most systematic assertions, the idea that whatever man does, it is in order to annihilate death:

> And perhaps all the disquietude which bad architecture evokes, forcing me to hide in my house, is nothing else than dread. For whatever a man may do, he does it in order to annihilate time, in order to revoke it, and that revocation is called space. Even music, which exists only in time and fills time, transmutes time into space, and it is absolutely probable that all thought represents a combination of indescribably complicated many-dimensional logically extended spaces.[6]

The mention of Broch's name is not random: like the poets-painters-architects Arakawa and Gins, he was a gifted novelist and poet allied with a capable mathematician who had studied Husserl and Brentano; like Arakawa and Gins, he was a practical utopian who had been a successful industrialist besides studying the philosophy of sciences and history, political theory and critically observing mass psychosis.[7] His theoretical thought never reached its full exposition as Nazi persecution forced him into exile, and it was first Hannah Arendt who kept the impact of his ideas alive (she wrote a glowing introduction to his essays in the collected works published by Rhein-Verlag in 1955 in which she stressed his concept of an "earthly absolute" in which death is abolished). Arendt has been followed since by the novelist Milan Kundera who claimed Broch as a model in the effort to write novels that leave room for knowledge, at least under the form of epistemological questions.[8] At the end of his life, Broch hesitated between writing novels and short stories after his acclaimed *Death of Virgil*, drafting literary essays on Austrian compatriots like von Hoffmannsthal, and disseminating political tracts on the "earthly absolute," "the city of man" and "total democracy." The theme of the "abolition of death" led him to the idea of a strong democracy capable of borrowing some weapons from totalitarian regimes but able to preserve inalienable human rights, which includes for instance the suppression of the death penalty.

---

[6] Broch, see footnote 5, p. 398, transl. modified.

[7] A systematic exposition of his philosophy can be found in Ernestine Schlant, *Die Philosophie Hermann Brochs*. Bern: Francke Verlag, 1971, especially pp. 155–80 for an analysis of the concept of the "Earthly absolute" and its political and psychological consequences.

[8] See Milan Kundera "Notes inspired by the sleepwalkers," in *The Art of the Novel*, Linda Asher (trans.). New York: HarperCollins, 1993, pp. 47–67.

In that context, one can think of another precursor of the anti-death utopia, the Russian thinker Nicolai Fyodorotich Fyodorov. Fyodorov is perhaps the first philosopher who wanted to "Make death illegal," allowing us to think of a utopia without being blinded by jargon. Fyodorov,[9] a philosopher, teacher and librarian, founded an immortalist philosophy that had few precedents. His main concern was human brotherhood but his first theme was the scientific elimination of death. He thought that the solution to all of humanity's problems lay in the attempt to resurrect all the dead. This he called the "common task" and his works were collected under the title of *The Philosophy of the Common Task*.[10] His doctrine is based upon the program of a "common task" that consists in resurrecting all the dead of all ages through scientific means. If, he argued, men and women could unite to achieve this, all the other problems of political organization would fade away as insignificant in comparison. But since the earth would become too crowded once the dead are resurrected, another task is to conquer space in order to be able, later, to provide new planets for these multitudes. In spite of the apparently delirious nature of these theories, Fyodorov had a strong impact on Fyodor Dostoevsky, Leo Tolstoy, and above all Konstantin Tsiolkovsky, the father of the Russian Sputnik program.

In the 2003 Québecois film, *The Other Side of the Moon* (*La Face cachée de la lune*), the director Robert Lepage pays a humorous and moving homage to Tsiolkovsky. Since the end of last century, Fyodorov's thought has received new interest and advocacy in connection with cryonics, cryonic hibernation, and all the doctrines and schools promoting prolongevity. For all these, Fyodorov had been a precursor since he advocated the ethical priority of a research and development project. By the common task, he meant communal work on the physical resurrection of the dead, anticipating future advances in medical technology. Fyodorov was the illegitimate son of Prince Pavel Ivanovich Gagarin and Elisaveta Ivanova, a woman of lower-class nobility.

---

[9] See N. F. Fyodorov, "The question of brotherhood or kinship, of the reasons for the unbrotherly, unkindred, or unpeaceful state of the world, and of the means for the restoration of kinship," in J. M. Edie, J. P. Scanlan, M. Zeldin, and G. L. Kline (eds), *Russian Philosophy*. Chicago: Quadrangle Books, 1965, pp. 16–54. I have used here N. F. Fyodorov, *What Was Man Created For? The Philosophy of the Common Task: Selected Works*; E. Koutiassov, and M. Minto (eds), *L'Age d'homme*. Lausanne: Honeyglen, 1990; M. Soloviov, "The 'Russian trace' in the history of cryonics," *Cryonics*, vol. 16, no. 4, 1995, pp. 20–3; G. M. Young and F. Nikolai, *Fedorov: An Introduction*. Belmont, MA: Nordland Publishing Co., 1979; and T. D. N. F. Zakydalsky, *Fyodorov's Philosophy of Physical Resurrection*. Ann Arbor, MI: UMI, 1976.

[10] See above all, the texts translated by James M. Edie, James P. Scanlan and Mary-Barbara Zeldin, with the collaboration of George L. Kline, in *Russian Philosophy*, Vol. III. Chicago: Quadrangle, 1969, pp. 11–54.

One of his first disciples, Dmitri Karakozov, became an anarchist who tried to shoot the Tsar in 1866. It is no accident that this name sounds similar to that of a famous character invented by Dostoevsky. Indeed, for some critics, Dostoevsky wrote the *Brothers Karamazov* as an attempt to come to terms with problems posed to him by Fyodorov. This is more visible in the first version in which the sons talk about their "common task," which will be the resurrection of their father. However, Dostoevsky later rewrote the novel, finding that the idea was too bizarre and that it would not do in the plot.

Fyodorov was obliged to leave his father's home at age four after Prince Gagarin's death. His fascination for the "dear departed" has something to do with the attachment he kept for a father too soon departed. He spent most of his life as a librarian at the Rumiantsev Museum in Moscow, a library he knew intimately, having read most of the books it contained. There, he became a mentor for the young Konstantin Tsiolkovsky. Until his death, he worked in the Archives of the Ministry of Foreign Affairs, advising scholars in the most varied disciplines. All his life, Fyodorov was known to lead an almost ascetic life. As his reputation grew and as he grew older, friends advised him to spare himself, which led to his end. During a severe Moscow winter, he was persuaded to take a cab instead of walking in the snow—he died of the pneumonia that he caught in the cab. The philosophy of the common task was also called "projectivism," as it was based upon a series of scientific projects; this laid the foundations for a typically Russian pragmatism. His style is often strange, and I will quote a passage whose involved sentences call up Beckett's word litanies in the novel *Watt*:

> With each new person resurrected knowledge will be growing; it will reach the height of the task just when the human race arrives at the first person who died. Moreover, for our great-great-greatgrandfathers resurrection should be even easier, incomparably easier, i.e. for our great-great-greatgrandchildren it will be incomparably more difficult to resurrect their fathers than for us and for our great-great-greatgrandfathers; for in the resurrection of our fathers we shall make use not only of all previous experiences in the task, but shall even have the collaboration of our resurrectors; in this way it will be easiest of all for the first son of man to resurrect his father, the father of all people.[11]

Obviously, the resurrection of the dead can only be a gradual if not interminable process. First, one should work just with recently deceased

[11] Quoted by George M. Young, Jr, *Nikolai F. Fedorov: An Introduction*. Houston: Nordland Publishing International, Incorporated, p. 105.

people, since they are fresher and easier to treat, and then find the traces of those who died long ago and whose bodies have entirely disappeared. And in the end, all the revived dead will be provided with synthetic bodies. The immense efforts needed, the huge sums of money required, the need to gather information over all continents and for long periods of time will entail a concentration of knowledge. This concentration in its turn requires a vast confederacy of humanity. They should all live in peace, if not in a single republic, possibly under the enlightened leadership of a Russian statesman— an idea that had pleased Stalin himself.

The love for one's forefathers corresponds to an interminable mourning, a mourning devoid of any trace of Freudian melancholia: its logic is based upon an ethical and scientific attitude, the literal raising of the dead. Politics should be replaced by a general scientific effort in which all mankind will be united. Physics, physiology, medical science, biology, and aeronautics will have to be studied together if one wants to solve the innumerable technical problems generated by the task of reviving the dead. But when the common task is launched, it is valid for all men. Fyodorov evinces an egalitarian universalism, and he states that salvation has to be for the brotherhood of all men and women. He believed that matter was made up of the dust left by our ancestors; this myriad of infinitesimal particles would soon be accessible to microscopic technology. Such a science poses technical problems, but this is nothing in comparison with the vision of the future it promises. In the end, men will become immortal through rational efforts, and even if this remains a dream, what matters urgently is a moral obligation to work toward the creation of space inhabited by all who ever lived. In the twenties, Fyodorov's generous theories had convinced Maiakovsky. There is an anecdote reported by Roman Jakobson. Maiakovsky exclaimed: "But I am absolutely convinced that there will be no death. They will resurrect the dead!" Jakobson expressed only the faintest surprise when he discovered that the futurist poet had been swayed by Fyodorov's materialistic mysticism.[12] For Fyodorov as for Broch, Arakawa and Gins, a future revolution should be peaceful because it rests on the alliance of technology and ethics, leading ultimately to a revolution in thought. It will ineluctably be brought about by the creation of a new logic of sense and the senses. Broch expresses this as a "digression":

> Now it may be asserted with some confidence that a sweeping revolution
> in the style of thinking—and the revolutionary aspect of all these

---

[12] See Roman Jakobson, "On a generation that squandered its poets," translated by Ed Brow, in *Twentieth Century Russian Literary Criticism*, Victor Ehrlich (ed.). New Haven: Yale University Press, 1975, p. 139.

phenomena entitles us to infer such a complete revolution in thinking—
invariably results from the fact that thought has reached its provisional
limit of infinity, that it is no longer able to resolve the antinomies of
infinity by the old methods, and so is compelled to revise its own basic
principles.[13]

This leads to the claim made by Arakawa and Gins with their famous "We
have decided not to die." Their statement entailed that death had to be viewed
differently, not just like a factor in human biology over which we have no
control, but as standing for the objectivity of the human body: its being
"natural" and not our own, the very emblem of a "given" that we cannot shape
or retake. Can this given, death as the "datum" of life, be in its turn historicized?
Is our biological existence the last refuge of natural given-ness beyond the
scope of any socio-historical factor?

In the *Jargon of Authenticity*, Adorno attacks Heidegger's absolutism of
death, and mentions in passing (as he did in a conversation with Ernst Bloch
in 1964) that any utopian thought should not feel bounded or constrained by
death seen as ineluctable fate—almost a divine Law. He writes: "It is also the
possibility of thinking about the elimination (*Abschaffung*) of death that
would be blasphemous (for him)."[14] Adorno reproaches Heidegger for having
substituted death to God. Death is the key to the concept of "authenticity"
that Adorno rejects. In a curious proximity to Freud's remarks at the end of
Beyond the Pleasure Principle, Adorno asserts that if the "abolition of death"
by science is "highly unlikely,"[15] nonetheless, it should remain thinkable. Such
a utopian thought is felt to be either ridiculous or blasphemous by Heidegger.
His "jargon of authenticity" sacralizes and eternalizes the blind acceptance of
the naturally given:

> The jargon goes hand in hand with a conception of man from which
> every memory of natural rights has been expunged, even though man
> himself is elevated into something like a category of nature. Theology
> held out the hope of eternal life to mankind caught up in the intolerable
> transience of a false and unfulfilled life. This vanishes in the celebration
> of transience as an absolute.[16]

---

[13] Broch, see footnote 5, p. 481.

[14] T. W. Adorno, *Jargon der Eigentlichkeit, Zur deutschen Ideologie*. Frankfurt: Suhrkamp,
1970, p. 115. The translation is mine. I would like to thank Adrian Daub for pointing out
these texts to me.

[15] Adorno, see footnote 14, p. 130.

[16] T. W. Adorno, from *Jargon of Authenticity*, translated by Rodney Livingstone, in *Can One
Live after Auschwitz? A Philosophical Reader*, Rolf Tiedemann (ed.). Stanford: Stanford
University Press, 2003, p. 180.

Adorno insists, this immediacy of life should never be "absolutized," and what Heidegger calls "being-towards-death" consists in such an absolutization. Adorno insists on the mediation of the immediate, and refuses to mystify or mythify life. Adorno's staunch insistence that one should consider the mere possibility of the abolition of death does not mean, as it did with Fyodorov, a radical transformation of the atoms and the substances that maintain bodies in life. He calls for a more dialectical awareness of the interpenetration of the subjective and objective poles in life. Finally, what he attacks in Heidegger is a mythical (or religious) mode of thinking. Already in the *Dialectic of Enlightenment*, Adorno and Horkheimer had defined the abolition of death as the main impetus behind the anti-mythological thinking represented by the cunning of Odysseus. This is most visible in the *nekuia*, the hero's descent into the underworld: "Indeed, the motif of forcing the gates of hell, of abolishing death, is the innermost cell of all antimythological thought."[17] The world of myth is characterized by ritualistic repetition, and thus death condenses the repetition compulsion, as Freud will assert (we will return to this theme in the next chapter).

In the *Dialectic of Enlightenment*, Odysseus figures as the representative of enlightenment science curbing the power of myth. Science can trick the mythic forces of tradition. If the *Dialectic of Enlightenment* leaves room for a utopian "abolition of death," which would be associated with Odysseus' release from Hades, there is also a false abolition of death, always associated with the ludicrous repetition that we see in Kafka's story of the hunter Gracchus. His hearse has taken a wrong turn, and he has to continue his journey through a planet transformed into a secular limbo. Gracchus will not die, but his eternal life is empty. His survival is nothing but a compulsion to repeat, the eternal return of present moments. Adorno's characterization of the "false" abolition nevertheless implies that he believes in the possibility of a true "abolition of death." I will return to this theme via Freud soon. Close to Adorno, there is an artist who was important for Arakawa and Gins, Marcel Duchamp, and Duchamp exemplifies both Adorno's critical function required of art, and the passion for scientific speculation that animated the thought of Fyodorov. To these two legitimate postulations, he would add his disabused note, perhaps as an echo of Gracchus's fate. In 1962, Duchamp told Katharine Kuh that he had avoided artistic narcissism by inventing games: "I was never interested in looking at myself in an aesthetic mirror. My intention was always to get away from myself, though. I know perfectly well that I was using

---

[17] Max Horkheimer and T. W. Adorno, *Dialectic of Englightenment*, Edmund Jephcott (trans.). Stanford: Stanford University Press, 2002, p. 60.

myself. Call it a little game between 'I' and 'me.'"[18] This is of course imbued
with the touch of sardonic humor that became Duchamp's signature. It is
nowhere more apparent than in the epitaph he had chosen for himself:
"*D'ailleurs, c'est toujours les autres qui meurent*." The off-hand motto inscribed
on his tombstone, meaning "Besides, it is always the others who die," quoted
his "writings," a simple collection of puns. The first text reads: "Epitaphe . . . et
d'ailleurs c'est toujours les autres qui meurent // dernier." (p. 145)[19]

This becomes:

EPITAPHE:
. . . ET D'AILLEURS
C'EST TOUJOURS LES AUTRES QUI MEURENT.

(p. 147)

The Note is consistent with Duchamp's belief that one never "knows" one's
death. When his former lover Mary Reynolds was dying of cancer, he wrote:
"The main thing is to die without knowing anything about it, which is in any
case what always happens."[20] Such an insight has been food for metaphysical
consolations since Seneca at least, and has been expressed in syllogistic manner
by Nabokov. Confirming Duchamp's effort to deny death, his motto functions
like an enthymeme, that is an incomplete syllogism or a creative paralogism. Its
formulation sums up John Shade's intimations of immortality in *Pale Fire*:

A syllogism: other men die; but I
Am not another; therefore I'll not die.[21]

One needs to pay attention to the precise syntax of Duchamp's epitaph. In
formal French, one would expect: "*D'ailleurs, ce sont toujours les autres qui
meurent*." The choice of a spoken style with the contraction "*c'est*" contradicts
the solemnity of the occasion, although it is marked by the capitals in the
second text. One senses a joke concealed by Duchamp's dying words. His
"*c'est toujours . . .*" echoes moreover the signature of his *alter ego*, Rrose Sélavy,
a rose blossoming as Rose. *C'est la vie*, the French phrase one often says in
English when someone dies, provides another twist to Gertrude Stein's

[18] Calvin Tompkins, *Duchamp, A Biography*. New York: Henry Holt, 1996, p. 251
[19] Marcel Duchamp, *Notes*. Paris: Flammarion, 1999, pp. 145 and 147.
[20] Letter to Henri-Pierre Roché (17 July 1950), in *Affectionately, Marcel. The Selected
    Correspondence of Marcel Duchamp*, Francis M. Naumann and Hector Obalk Ludion
    (eds). Ghent/Amsterdam: Ludion Press, 2000, p. 290 (French text) and p. 291 (translation).
[21] Vladimir Nabokov, *Pale Fire*. New York: Random House, 1977, p. 40.

famous "Rose is a rose is rose." We should just delete the accent of Sélavy as a last name, thus cutting off the rose's thorns. Man Ray had translated the phrase as: "*Rose, cela vit!*" or: "Rose, it lives!" In this "*vit*" an obscene pun is hidden ("*vit*" is "dick" in French), which means, as we will see in the next chapter, that the Freudian drive or the Freudian Id are with us forever . . .

Yet death has not (yet) been abolished. As Derrida has stated, each time a person dies, the whole world dies: each death is the end of the world. When Arakawa died, it was even more difficult to talk about the death of an artist who has decided not to die. At the time, I happened to teach a book that I had always loved, Sōseki Natsume's novel from 1905, *I am a Cat*. In the middle of the novel narrated by a hilariously spunky and cynical cat, a cat who has never been named by his owner, a stray cat barely accepted in a household, I found these words: "I've decided not to die."[22] It is not the cat who speaks here, but his owner, a hypochondriac teacher of English literature who looks very much like the author.

The context is simple—the statement is reported by the cat's owner's wife to a cousin, and it concerns an insurance salesman. In spite of all the entreaties and logical demonstrations of the salesman, the owner of the cat refuses to be insured. "The insurance man makes sense to me," the cousin says. "I certainly agree. But your uncle cannot see it. He swears he'll never die. "I've made a vow," he told that salesman with all the pride of a nincompoop, "never, never to die."[23] We need all the obliquity of the reported statement to make better sense of the statement "I have decided not to die": in other words, it has to be quoted.

However, at the end of the novel, quite surprisingly and shockingly, it is the cat who dies; he drowns trapped in a jar after having drunk beer for the first time. Perhaps he has been punished for his frankness, and tricked into getting drunk . . .[24] His death is a liberation, a coming to peace with the universe. Indeed, this was the only way for Sōseki Natsume to finish his endless novel, a sort of Japanese *Tristram Shandy*. While in Sterne's masterpiece, the hero can never bring back the narrative to the moment of his birth, here the death of the narrator as a cat ensures the immortality of the author. The novel is still today one of Japan's best known and most loved narratives. There not enough room to discuss the novel, replete as it is with

---

[22] The novel's title is *Wagahai wa neko dearu* ("I am a cat"). I am quoting the excellent translation by Aiko Ito and Graeme Wilson of *I am a cat*. Tokyo: Tuttle Publishing, and Singapore: Rutland, 2002, p. 369.

[23] See footnote 22, p. 370.

[24] See Sari Kawana, "A narrative game of cat and mouse: Parody, deception, and fictional whodunit in Natsume Soseki's *Wagahai wa neko dearu*," *Journal of Modern Literature*, vol. 33, number 4, Summer 2010, pp. 1–20.

echoes of Zen Buddhism, hilarious parodies of a Western culture seen through the eyes of a Japanese cat. In all this, one perceives that death is nothing, and that personal illumination is all.

When I discovered that Arakawa's statement, "I have decided not to die," hence "We have decided not to die," was a quote from a famous Japanese novel, my discovery brought something that I found liberating. It unlocked a store of fond memories of the artist, memories of him as a witty speaker came back along with images of him as a dreamy observer when Madeline Gins read her obituary for Jacques Derrida in New York for instance. For me, Arakawa, a wonderful artist who had become a militant for a change in human consciousness, had just turned into a cat. Cats have nine lives, whereas their owners have only one—or perhaps more? If one's life is productive, charged with multiple intensities, then one can forget one's grief and find in this death that is also a non-death an immense source of courage for the future.

7

The No Future of an Illusion

CLOV: Do you believe in the life to come?
HAMM: Mine was always like that. (Exit Clov.) Got him that time![1]

Beckett's quote echoes with the discussions of "futures" in Chapter 5. My chapter on the futures was given at a conference organized around Jacques Derrida's concept of the future as "what is to come," and was published in *Futures: Of Jacques Derrida*.[2] The conference took place in the fall of 1995, and I still have the program, with FUTURES in a bold font recalling Mallarmé's *Un Coup de dés*. The titles of the presentations were listed and no time assigned to them; we were supposed to let chance decide. Each of us threw dice, and the numbers were supposed to say in which order we were going to speak. Inevitably, as soon as luck assigned our turns, we started swapping our respective slots. As we have seen earlier, I highlighted the difficulty of translating into English the nuances brought by the use of two words in French, *"l'avenir"* and *"le futur."* Had I attempted to circumvent my worry facing a key Derridian idea, that of a radical openness to the future that he called "messianicity without a Messiah"? My commonsense reaction was that, even if we can agree with Kafka that there is hope, an infinity of hope, although not for us, the question soon boils down to whether one believes in the Messiah or one doesn't. This seemed to raise the issue of a "turn to religion" that many readers had seen looming in Derrida's later works, especially in *Acts of Religion*. Thus I felt hugely relieved when I discovered the work of Martin Hägglund, whose first book, *Radical Atheism*,[3] attacks Christian or neo-Christian recuperations of the later Derrida by using Derrida's own concept of survival, a direct application of a Levinassian analysis of the trace, but without the religious vocabulary of Levinas. I had loved this book, but found myself in disagreement with his second book. There, Hägglund moves into the field of modernist literature by discussing Proust, Woolf and Nabokov. The new book,

---

[1] Samuel Beckett, *Endgame*. New York: Grove Press, 1958, p. 49.
[2] Richard Rand (ed.), *Futures: Of Jacques Derrida*. Stanford: Stanford University Press, 2001. See Chapter 4 here.
[3] Martin Hägglund, *Radical Atheism: Derrida and the Time of Life*. Stanford: Stanford University Press, 2008.

Dying for Time,[4] provides important readings of the works of Proust, Woolf and Nabokov, who are all three envisaged from the point of view of temporality. Once more, Hägglund operates with the concept of "survival," an angle or vantage point that allows him to tackle difficult and central issues in the corpus of these authors, such as the question of "immortality" that is often presented as the Platonism of Proust, a Platonism condensed in "eternity" reached via the illumination of "Time regained." This timelessness discovered through time would be the goal of the narrator's quest in *La Recherche*.

My misgivings over the strategy used by Hägglund became more acute when I reached his last chapter, which is a critical analysis of Freud's meta-psychology. The argument follows a reading of Plato. In both cases, the thesis is the same: any desire for immortality will be interpreted as being in fact a desire for endless survival. Since survival implies a concept of time and duration, this very concept of time destroys from within any notion of eternity. Thus, when Hägglund revisits Plato's Symposium, it is to argue that "The survival of a mortal being is thus quite different from the immortality of an eternal being." (DFT, p. 7) Again and again, he plunges us into the ineluctable modality of temporality as defined by the structure of traces and survival:

> To be sure, Diotima holds that the desire to survive ultimately is driven by the desire to be immortal." According to her own analysis, however, proper immortality would require a state of being that is "always the same in every respect" (Plato 208a) and "neither comes into being nor passes away, neither flowers nor fades" (Plato 211a). As is clear from this definition, the timeless state of immortality would eliminate the very condition of survival. In a state where nothing comes into being or passes away, *nothing survives*. Thus, we will see that the desire for survival … cannot be driven by the desire for immortality. The desire to perpetuate a temporal being is incompatible with the desire to be immortal", since immortality would not allow anything to live on in time.
>
> (DFT, p. 7)

What if Socrates, Diotima, or the participants in the banquet in this context, happen to believe in gods? Would they be convinced by the argument that temporality and finitude are the only terms through which we must think philosophically? What if there are gods, gods in whom we may not fully believe but whose function is to reconcile the fact of living eternally with the enjoyment of time-bound objects, not to speak of women and men? This is,

---

[4]   Martin Hägglund, *Dying For Time*. Cambridge, MA: Harvard University Press, 2012. Subsequently abbreviated as DFT.

of course, not to say that I believe in the Greek gods, but that I find in this case, since we are with Plato, the demonstration to be hurried, simplified and reductive. Heidegger takes much more caution and uses up many more pages when he argues for the radical finitude of the human condition. Derrida too has begun there, as we know. What is missed here is a systematic phenomenological analysis of the desire for immortality, and of the role played by gods in our unconscious. Even if we do recognize the inevitable limitations provided by temporality, this structural condition should not be brought upon every human decision, fantasy or cultural production indiscriminately. The positioning of something like immortality or immortal gods is akin to a desire for the future. This desire ought to be taken into account if we do not want to drop the problematics of time and finitude as a heavy philosophical brick upon the banquet table laid by Plato.

The same table has been laid, albeit not so richly, by Freud. In his final chapter, Hägglund discusses Freud and categorically denies that there should be anything like the "death drive." The notion seems a pure contradiction to him. Hägglund also rejects the Freudian idea that the unconscious is unaware of time and mortality. This, he argues, is purely speculative and not based upon clinical evidence. He presses further by reiterating his main thesis:

> "The most important move here is to distinguish between immortality and survival. Freud argues that because we cannot imagine our own death, we unconsciously believe that we are immortal. Freud is certainly right that we cannot imagine the state of being dead ... since in order to do so we have to imagine ourselves as surviving to witness our own death and thus necessarily fail to imagine ourselves as dead. It does not follow from this argument, however, that we are unconsciously convinced that we are immortal. Rather, what follows from Freud's argument is that even in our own relation to death we fantasize about survival. To fantasize about *living on* after death is not to fantasize about being immortal, since to live on is to remain subjected to temporal finitude."
>
> (DFT, p. 2012: 114)

This highlights what worries me in this rehearsal of the idea of survival. Shouldn't we leave aside the logical inference deriving from the concept of time and take the timelessness of the unconscious as part of an equation that should function at an imaginary level? We might avoid being censorious, as if we had to fault Plato and Freud for having missed a crucial distinction, not realizing that this notion of survival introduces a new terminology linked with different concepts? Moreover, does it matter "at the end of the day"—

a current cliché that we will have to question—if we call "survival" what was called "immortality" by Plato or Freud? The difference may not amount to much since, on Hägglund's analysis, the issue of survival always entails a balance of chronophobia and chronophilia, which leaves us radically undecided, to quote Leslie Hill's hermeneutics of hesitation.[5]

It is inevitable to reopen the discussion with Freud, and to understand why his concept of the future is predicated upon the death drive. Such a coupling of the future and the death drive was an idea shared by three thinkers who saw the decadence of psychoanalysis after Freud had passed away in 1939: Adorno, Herbert Marcuse and Jacques Lacan. Adorno had reacted to the "Californization" of psychoanalysis that he had experienced during his American stay from 1938 to 1949. In a lecture given in English in 1946 in San Francisco, Adorno debunked Freudian revisionism. The theoreticians he chose for his attack were Erich Fromm and Karen Horney. Both tried to erase what they considered to be Freud's "pessimism" and his "pansexualism." But they replaced Freud's complex meta-psychology with a weak culturalism. "Revised psychoanalysis,"[6] a text based on a 1946 lecture, takes issue with the way in which Karen Horney aimed at getting rid of Freud's theory of the drive. Horney meant to transform it into a theory of character and of human environment, and ultimately into strategies of social adaptation. Horney's *The Neurotic Personality of Our Times* (1937) alleged that the root of neurosis was not sexual but social, in a context marked by intense competition. Such culturalist optimism clashed with the "darker" side of Freud, whose philosophy should be placed, according to Adorno (Lacan would agree) next to that of Mandeville or Sade. Freud's grandeur, Adorno concludes, lies in his radical ambivalence facing culture and civilization. Indeed, Freud always insisted that social harmony could not be postulated as a norm but had to be questioned, at least in so far as it had to be seen as the product of a social process of repression. We will explore this theme more systematically.

Lacan followed the same path when he tackled what Herbert Marcuse in a notorious pamphlet had called the "obsolescence of psychoanalysis."[7] For Lacan, this was caused when psychoanalysis was caught up between incompatible claims, biological neuro-scientism or adaptive psychological meliorism. Lacan refused to modernize psychoanalysis by adapting it or updating it via medical treatments based on psychotropic drugs. Instead, he

[5] Leslie Hill, *Radical Indecision: Barthes, Blanchot, Derrida, and the Future of Criticism*. South Bend, IN: University of Notre Dame Press, 2010.
[6] Theodor W. Adorno, "Die revidierte Psychoanalyse," *Soziologische Schriften*, Vol. I. Frankfurt: Suhrkamp Verlag, 1997, pp. 20–41
[7] Herbert Marcuse, *The Obsolescence of Psychoanalysis*. Chicago: Black Swan Press, 1967.

raised the stakes, and posited psychoanalysis as a therapy based on the use of language. The analyst's measured silence belongs to language, since its role is to embody radical otherness. Psychoanalysis should open itself to scientific advances in domains like linguistics, mathematics or symbolic logics. Lacan and Adorno shared an insight that, at first sight, sounds like a paradox: it is the concept of the death drive that prevents obsolescence. In other words, the obsolescence of psychoanalysis became evident as soon as it refused to look death in the face.

Thus, in his readings of Freud's texts from the fifties onwards, Lacan argued that one should not talk of a "death instinct" but of a "death drive." His philological precision differentiating Freud's *Trieb* from his lingering Darwinism had a critical agenda. It attacked the second generation Freudians who had dropped the idea of a "death drive," who had blamed it on what they took as Freud's innate pessimism, his tragic view of life. Accepting fully this tragic sense of life, Lacan was to say that the death drive offered the most basic figure for all drives. It illustrated the way in which drives operated blindly, as it were, using objects and aims that they discarded in favor of a pure ͏   ͏cific goal. For Adorno, one finds a similar idea in his gr͏   of the Kafkaian parable of Hunter Gracchus that I ha͏   ͏͏. Gracchus was a man who had missed his own death by͏   ͏ugh he had died, he was condemned to roam the earth. He ͏   ͏ortal in spite of himself. For Adorno, Gracchus is the bo͏   ͏ to die in a Marxian scheme, while exemplifying the͏   ͏eaning of "between life and death" that the death camps of the͏   ͏   ͏ with a vengeance.[9]

͏   ds its crucial place in Adorno's groundbreaking reading of Beckett. Adorno states that the drama staged by Beckett's major plays (*Endgame*, above all) is not death as in classical tragedy but the "abortion of death." In *Endgame*, the pathos of the play comes from a sense that even after all is over, one has to go on. This corresponds to our post-holocaust situation, when the mechanization of death in the camps has generated a new level of the unspeakable. The idea, therefore, is that the best denunciation of a post-apocalyptic post-Holocaust situation, a predicament in which we are still caught, can be achieved by a dramatization of the non-death of the subject.

---

[8] Franz Kafka, "The Hunter Gracchus," Stanley Corngold (trans.), in *Kafka's Selected Stories*. New York: Norton, 2007, pp. 109–13; and "The Huntsman Gracchus," Joyce Crick (trans.), in *A Hunger Artist and Other Stories*. Oxford: Oxford University Press, 2012, pp. 113–20.

[9] T. W. Adorno, "Trying to understand *Endgame*," in *Can One Live after Auschwitz? A Philosophical Reader*, Rolf Tiedmann (ed.). Stanford: Stanford University Press, 2003, p. 227. Hereafter, TUE and page number.

Hamm's actions and speeches in *Endgame* do not betray a fear of death but a wholesale fear that "death could miscarry." (TUE, p. 289) What is crucial for me at any rate is that this analysis does not lead us in the direction of spectrality, of the ghosts or all sorts of uncanny *revenants*—no Derridean "hauntology" here; on the contrary, what stands out is that "mourning has become impossible." (TUE, p. 267) Mourning has been replaced by parody and by the mute faces of despair. The libidinal investment on new objects will never take place.

Adorno attacks "modernism": like futurism, modernism is "what has become obsolete in modernity." (TUE, pp. 259–60) What is obsolete corresponds to the utopia of modernity: the discourse of idealist philosophy of consciousness and freedom represented by phenomenology and existentialism (say from Sartre to Heidegger), and the discourse of well-meaning liberal humanism, or a Marxist rationalism *à la* Lukacs. Indeed, here Lacan and Adorno converge: facing the obsolescence of psychoanalysis, the best way out is to traverse death and tarry with the negative of the Law. In other words, we need to struggle with a thinking of death that will not be identical to Heidegger's "jargon of authenticity." In other words, one has to assert: "No Future" as pre-condition for the assertion of the possibility of a future, and this will be a theme that I will pursue through Freud, Kant and Beckett.

This idea is shared by Lacan when he discusses Freud's *Todestrieb*, the death drive, as necessary to the consistency of psychoanalytical discourse. "Position of the unconscious" presents the death drive as a key-stone of psychoanalytical theory in the context of a discussion of mythological aspects of Freud's meta-psychology. Following Adorno's famous statement that in psychoanalysis, nothing is true but is exaggerations, Lacan plays on these allegories in a self-conscious and baroque manner. In a discussion of the mythic Libido, Lacan accepts Freud's sweeping biologism, to the point that he asserts that drives are shared by animals. Drives are the effects of a limit in humans and animals alike. Here, as with Hägglund, Lacan's analysis of death follows from a discussion of Plato's *Symposium*:

> *Libido* is this lamella that the organism's being takes to its true limit, which goes further than the body's limit ... Thus lamella is an organ, since it is the instrument of an organism. It is sometimes almost palpable, as when a hysteric plays at testing its elasticity to the hilt.
>
> Speaking subjects have the privilege of revealing the deadly meaning of this organ, and thereby its relation to sexuality. This is because the signifier as such, whose first purpose is to bar the subject, has brought into him the meaning of death. [*Ceci parce que le significant comme tel a, en barrant le sujet par première intention, fait entrer en lui le sens de la*

mort.] (The letter kills, but we learn this from the letter itself.) This is why every drive is virtually a death drive.[10]

The "intention" or "purpose" of language in its most material aspect, its being made up of signifiers, is to teach us about death. Language entails a pedagogy of death, an unconscious pedagogy that impacts us when we struggle to learn words and syntax. Lacan sees the death drive as part of the symbolic order of culture (it is concerned with keeping a record of death for further generations), but it is also concretely anchored in the body, via the flesh of mothers. This sends us back to the idea of a radical finitude introduced by the concepts of reproduction, generation and bodily succession in time. Yet, far from insisting on mere "survival," Lacan insists that one needs a myth connected with the pantheon of the Greek gods. Only a myth, like that of Aristophanes in *The Symposium*, can allow us to visualize the architecture of the drives. We are also reading texts, Plato's text and Freud's text, in order to reactivate the energy of Freudian insights on the drive. This requires that we grasp concretely the function of writing as a layering of traces, all of which somehow point to death in one form or the other. We all learn death from language, which entails that we keep a link to the death drive as brought to us by language in that it both kills and preserves the sense of life as mortal. This neo-Hegelian idea is in Freud too (it is operative in the earliest formulations of the unconscious presented as a differential layering of traces and signs in the letter 52 to Fliess) in the *Project*, etc. This reappears in the later formulation of the *Todestrieb*, which, we need to remember, is not yet called "Thanatos" in *Beyond The Pleasure Principle*, since this was a term later coined by Paul Federn.

On the way to this discovery, we will have to grapple with the illusions brought by any consideration of the future. This is why we need now to turn to Freud's book *The Future of an Illusion*.[11] I will begin by offering a rapid breakdown of its theses. Freud states at the outset that we are limited in our predictions of the future: first we have to understand the present, and for that we need to know the past. After this rapid preface, the term "future" never reappears as such in the text. Freud distinguishes two key features in a *Kultur*. I'll leave the word in German since the term is half-way between Culture and Civilization. There are first the material techniques to subdue and control the forces of nature for our benefit through the development of economy and technology. Then, there is the management of the relations between

---

[10] Jacques Lacan, "Position de l'inconscient," in *Ecrits*. Paris: Seuil, 1966, p. 848; and in *Ecrits*, Bruce Fink (trans.). New York: Norton, 2006, p. 719.

[11] Sigmund Freud, *The Future of an Illusion* (1927). London, Penguin, 2008. Hereafter, FI and page number.

individuals, especially for the distribution of wealth, which corresponds to social institutions and globally to politics.

In rethinking these functions, one must not forget that, for Freud, humans resent *Kultur* more than they love it: they are soon aware of the fact that *Kultur* limits their drives via *Versagung* (frustration), *Verbot* (interdiction) and *Entbehrung* (deprivation)[12]—an ancient trinity of negative affect and prohibition that makes up the Law (I'll return to the capitalized Law with Kant at the end of this essay). Thus, most social regulations imply prohibition, and often on the pain of death. No matter what its negative aspects may be, Freud argues that *Kultur* should nevertheless be defended against individual anarchy. Leaders cannot avoid using coercion of some sort to curb anarchic drives. If exploited workers are not in love with their work, they will learn to find an outlet in their sexual or political passions. It is here that childhood experiences crucially shape us since they train us to love our *Kultur*. Fundamentally, *Kultur* is kept together not by economics or politics, but by mass psychology.

Hostility to another *Kultur* occurs regularly when nations interact because of the narcissistic investment in one's culture. A way to prevent a state of war of all is by having people share common cultural ideals like the arts, science, or sports. Cultural ideals can generate an identification with *Kultur* that will be valid even for the underprivileged. The proletariat shares in such sublimation that allows it to belong to a *Kultur*. Yet, *Kultur* has one drawback: most people feel that it has been imposed on the masses by the privileged few. In several passages of the book, Freud responds to the situation created in Soviet Russia. It is mentioned strikingly as a "great experiment in *Kultur* (*Kulturexperiment*) in the vast country that stretches between Europe and Asia." (FI, p. 8) What follows is a remark about the links between politics and ideology: Freud notes the astonishing agreement given by subjected classes to their own alienation: "This identification of the oppressed classes (*der Unterdrückten*) with the classes who rule and exploit them is, however, only part of a larger whole. For, on the other hand, the oppressed classes can be emotionally attached to their masters; in spite of their hostility to them, they may see in them their ideals; unless such relations of a fundamentally satisfying kind subsisted, it would be impossible to understand how a number of civilizations (*Kulturen*) have survived so long in spite of the justifiable hostility of large human masses." (FI, p. 17)

The political and ideological context makes it very important to be able to distinguish between ideals and illusions. A *Kultur*'s collective formation of

[12] See Sigmund Freud, "Die Zukunft einer Illusion," in *Fragen der Gesellschaft, Ursprünge der Religion, Studienausgabe*. Frankfurt: Fischer, 1974, p. 144.

values entails some illusions, mostly found in religious ideas. Why should they be called illusions? For Freud, nothing in nature can prove them, and they correspond too exactly to the projections of wish-fulfillment. Therefore they must be suspected. There is a certain logic in the elaboration of these illusions. Without *Kultur*, we would be in a state of nature, and nature is marked by destruction, natural disasters, pandemics or personal deaths. In order to ease our anxiety, we ascribe human characteristics to a nature that we cannot control. Thus, humans created gods, first animals, then female gods, followed by the anthropomorphic gods of the Greek pantheon. Finally, we fashioned a paternal god with the single God of monotheism.

The religious illusions needed by a *Kultur* lend credibility to the Law. It is easier to follow commandments like the interdiction to kill one's neighbor if such a law is ascribed to God's will. Whoever participates in a *Kultur* limits his or her murderous and libidinal desires in order to please God. However, if the problem posed by a *Kultur*'s illusions is condensed in religion, the historical basis of religions rests on "facts" that can never be proved scientifically. On the other hand, any critical investigation into their nature will be accused of impiety. However, since the age of Enlightenment, science has begun to dispel religious illusions. Religion can thus be equated with neurosis, a mild neurosis experienced by children when they are taught to suppress their libido for their own good. The true stage of adulthood is reached when one can investigate the world by using science and reason. The leitmotiv of the last pages is that "science is not an illusion."

Given that this book bridges the gap between *Totem and Taboo* from 1913 and *Civilization and its Discontents* from 1930, one may wonder about the choice of the title. By calling this "the future" of an illusion, is Freud implying that illusion has a future, even if he insists that science alone should define our future? He has seen that religious illusions come from our fear of the future, since the role of religion is to provide a consolation for the after-life. He also notes that science is not likely to give any kind of consolation for the future. Is he also suggesting that any discourse about the future partakes of an illusion? Are we all the victims of a universal illusion, which would be that it is possible to talk about the future?

When T. S. Eliot reviewed the book, which he did as soon as the English translation was published, he was severe. He began by criticizing the lack of a thorough consideration of the future: "We can hardly qualify it by anything but negatives; it has little to do with the past or the present of religion, and nothing, so far as I can see, with its future."[13] He went on ruthlessly: "It is

---

13   T. S. Eliot, "*The Future of an Illusion*, by Sigmund Freud," *Criterion*, VIII, Vol. 3, 1929, pp. 350–53.

shrewd and yet stupid; the stupidity appears not so much in historical ignorance or lack of sympathy with the religious attitude, as in the verbal vagueness and inability to reason."[14] Freud is taken to task for a circular mode of reasoning that describes the task of *Kultur* as to defend it against its enemies. Obviously, Eliot is baffled by the concept of *Kultur*. Above all, he cannot see why an illusion should be distinguished from an error, which is crucial for Freud's reasoning. He quotes disapprovingly a passage in which Freud opposes Aristotle's errors on the generation of vermin to productive illusions like those of the Columbus: "... it was an illusion on the part of Columbus that he had discovered a new sea-route to India."[15]

In fact, Freud establishes a rigorous distinction between error (*Irrtum*), illusion (*Illusion*) and delusion (*Wahnidee*). The last category belongs to psychiatry and the first to epistemology:

> Illusions need not necessarily be false—that is to say, unrealizable or in contradiction to reality. For instance, a middle-class girl may have the illusion that a prince will come and marry her. This is possible; and a few such cases have occurred. That the Messiah will come and found a golden age is much less likely ... Thus we call a belief an illusion when a wish-fulfilment is a prominent factor in its motivation, and in doing so we disregard its relation to reality, just as the illusion itself sets no store by verification.
>
> (FI, p. 49)

Here again, there can be no principle of verification, except for the statement that at times "miracles happen." Freud may have conceded too much: why not indeed, wait for the Messiah or for the Prince? He needs to introduce the term of "ignorance" (*Unwissenheit*) to sound more categorical: "Ignorance is ignorance; no right to believe anything can be derived from it." (FI, p. 51) In other words, this *Unwissenheit* has little to do with the unconscious, the *Unbewusst*. Ignorance is not the unconscious, even if it may derive from it. Rationalism seems to dominate in Freud's text, which is why Eliot can deride Freud's scientism. Eliot compares his "parvenu science," all too eager to assert a belief in positivism, with the "real scientists of real sciences" who are often less assured of their "truths" than Freud. What he misses nevertheless is that Freud denounces here what Lacan later called man's "passion for ignorance" as a huge motivation among believers of all sorts.

---

[14] Eliot, see footnote 13, p. 351.
[15] Eliot, see footnote 13, p. 353. See FI, p. 48.

A less negative critic of Freud was his friend, the Pastor Oskar Pfister. He wrote to Freud about *The Future of an Illusion* from the point of view of a religious man who was in sympathy with psychoanalysis, at a time when Freud had told him that his book was merely reflecting his own views and not to be taken as the official doctrine of psychoanalysis. Pfister saw clearly the roots of Freud's atheistic rationalism in the Enlightenment:

> Your substitute for religion is basically the idea of the eighteenth-century Enlightenment in proud modern guise. I must confess that, with all my pleasure in the advance of science and technique, I do not believe in the adequacy and sufficiency of that solution of the problem of life. It is very doubtful whether, taking everything into account, scientific progress has made men happier or better. According to the statistics, there are more criminals among scholars than in the intellectual middle class, and the hopes that were set on universal education have turned out to be illusory. Nietzsche summed up your position in the words: "The reader will have realized my purport; namely that there is always a metaphysical belief on which our belief in science rests—that we observers of to-day, atheists and anti-metaphysicians as we are, still draw our fire from the blaze lit by a belief thousands of years old, the Christian belief, which was also that of Plato, that God is truth and that truth is divine . . ." But supposing that this grew less and less believable and nothing divine was left, save error, blindness, lies? . . .[16]

Pfister asks whether Freud would agree to publish his antithetical views in *Imago*, and Freud granted this wish in the next letter. This was the origin of a spirited response by Pfister, which was entitled "The illusion of a future."[17] Pfister's essay is everything that Freud's book is not: it is witty and philosophical, and moreover it is well written, whereas Freud's book is couched in a style which is, quite uncharacteristically, often dull. Pfister's references are multiple, he has read Nietzsche, as the previous quote shows, and he knows Kant and Feuerbach—he even generously supposes that Freud repeats Feuerbach's critique of religion: "For his idea that all religions represent only wishful constructs, Freud rightfully does not claim precedence

---

[16] Sigmund Freud and Oskar Pfister, *Psychoanalysis and Faith: Dialogues with the Reverend Oskar Pfister*, E. Mosbacher (trans.). New York: Basic Books, 1963, p. 115.

[17] Oskar Pfister, "The Illusion of a Future: A friendly disagreement with Prof. Sigmund Freud," Susan Abrams and Paul Taylor (trans), *International Journal of Psychoanalysis*, no. 74, 1993, pp. 559–78. The essay was first published in *Imago* in 1928, with Freud's benediction. Hereafter, IF and page number.

... With unsurpassable consistency, Feuerbach, almost ninety years ago, developed his thesis of theology as disguised anthropology and of religion as a dream." (IF, p. 563) Pfister debunks Freud's unsophisticated scientism, showing convincingly that there is room for more than one position facing religious faith in psychoanalysis. He argues that the vision of religion as an obsessional neurosis is a caricature. Pfister's essay concludes on a note of reconciliation: "And thus *The Future of an Illusion* and 'The illusion of a future' unite in the strong belief whose credo is: 'The truth shall make you free!'" (IF, p. 578)

Pfister does not believe in the replacement of religion by science, which is Freud's main tenet. And he refuses the view that the only role of religion is to help the police by buttressing morality. He states that he has met as many patients turned atheists because they reacted aggressively to the faith of a father whom they wanted to "kill" or reject, as neurotics turning to religion because they projected a father image onto a powerful god. As to anthropomorphic projections, science is as often guilty of these as religion. And many scientists owe their discoveries to wish-fulfillments. He calls for more Dionysian spirit in a Protestantism that he also criticizes for its excessive complacency. Like Nietzsche, he calls our *Kultur* an "un-civilization" that is no better than a "thin apple-peel over a blazing chaos." (IF, p. 570) Thus the "reality" that he wants to promote in this Christian "realism" should be open to all aspects of life, and not just the taming of animals and the domination of nature. Finally, he justifies his own title in this way: "How should we imagine the future of the illusion that Freud has raised objections to? It is also my view that it must fall and disappear if only an illusion." (IF, p. 577) He calls for a new metaphysics that can complement and not contradict science—as with the Texans who had condemned a teacher for having taught Darwin in 1925, an obscurantist incident condemned both by Freud and by Pfister—a harmonious combination of knowledge and belief. On this view, there is a future for religion only if it stops being an illusion. Conversely, the illusion of a future corresponds to Freud's positivistic belief in progress marked by science.

When Pfister thanked Freud for his open-mindedness in allowing him this open discussion of divergences, Freud replied that this was natural. As he wrote, his aim was less theoretical than pragmatic: just as in "Lay analysis" he had wanted to protect psychoanalysis from doctors, with *The Future of an Illusion* he had tried to protect it from the priests. This was his true "fantasy of the future."[18] "My remarks that the analysts of my phantasy of the future

---

[18] Freud and Pfister, see footnote 16, p. 126.

should not be priests does not sound very tolerant, I admit. But you must consider that I was referring to a very distant future. For the present I put up with doctors, so why not priests too?"[19] This testifies to Freud's obdurate belief in the future of psychoanalysis, a future that he saw threatened by several dangers, the worst of which were religious high-jacking and medical straight-jacketing. What Pfister had perceived accurately was the proximity of psychoanalysis to the ethos of the Enlightenment; for Freud, indeed, the Enlightenment was an "unfinished program," as Habermas stated, that is a program that had to be complemented and perpetuated.

This explains why in the end Freud was not convinced by Pfister, to whom he wrote: "You are right to point out that analysis leads to no new philosophy of life, but it has no need to, for it rests on the general scientific outlook, with which the religious outlook is incompatible."[20] When he expanded his views on faith in *Civilization and its Discontents*, a more worthy interlocutor would be Romain Rolland, not Pfister. Similarly, Pfister was not convinced either by Freud; this went further than a difference of opinion about religious faith since, more fundamentally, the one theoretical concept that he could not accept was the death drive. He wrote to Freud: "I regard the 'death instinct,' not as a real instinct, but only as a slackening of the 'life force,' and even the death of the individual cannot hold up the advance of the universal will, but only help it forward."[21] Pfister's romantic Protestantism never crossed the line to become Jungian, but its "progressive" optimism could not accept Freud's view of the drives as following the paradigm offered by the death drive.

We have seen that in *The Future of an Illusion*, a book that Eliot had called a "strange book,"[22] Freud used the term of "future" only twice, each time in fact on the first page. Later in the text he analyzes the religious belief in "life after death." Thus death looms larger and becomes a key issue. This sends us back to a more systematic confrontation with death that had taken place earlier, in 1920. This was when Freud wrote *Beyond the Pleasure Principle*, a book in which he reopens the discussion of death. Freud begins by exploring notions of repetition, of pleasure and of reality taken as three fundamental principles. It is thus only in Chapter 5 that Freud generalizes from the compulsion to repeat to a "natural" tendency to return to a previous state of things. Life would just be a detour, a "circuitous path" along a return to inorganic matter from which it has come. This could then be rephrased as the

---

[19] Freud and Pfister, see footnote 16, p. 128.
[20] Freud and Pfister, see footnote 16, p. 129.
[21] Freud and Pfister, see footnote 16, p. 131.
[22] Freud, see footnote 11, p. 353.

old motto: "The aim of all life is death."[23] A whole page develops this idea, with the striking image of the "guardians of life" who helped the organism strive for survival then, transformed into the "myrmidons of death."[24]

When Derrida comments on Freud's text in the *Postcard*, he makes at this point a detour via Heidegger, arguing that *Beyond the Pleasure Principle* and *Sein und Zeit* have a similar program:

> When Freud speaks of *Todestrieb, Todesziel, Umwege zum Tode,* and even of an "*eigenen Todesweg des Organismus,*" he is indeed pronouncing the law of life-death as the law of the proper. Life *and* death are opposed only in order to serve it. Beyond all oppositions, without any possible identification or synthesis, it is indeed a question of an *economy* of death, of a law of the proper (*oikos, oikonomia*) which governs the detour and indefatigably seeks the proper event, its own, proper propriation (*Ereignis*) rather than life *and* death.[25]

Derrida has perceived something crucial here, although I believe that this conflation of Heidegger and Freud is misleading. Moreover, he is not paying attention to the text's rhetorical progression. Above all, he bypasses the fact that those pages state a thesis that Freud will then reject.

Indeed, once Freud has reached this point in his argument, he turns around and exclaims: "It cannot be so." (BPP, p. 47) This is the very complex movement that leads from the end of Chapter V to Chapter VI, in which Freud multiplies detours, aporias and counter-examples. Finally, he introduces the death drive surreptitiously almost, in a parenthesis in the original text: "The opposition between the ego or death instincts and the sexual or life instincts would then cease to hold," (BPP, p. 53) and: "*Der Gegensatz von Ich(Todes-)trieben und Sexual(Lebens)trieben würde dann entfallen*" (*Jenseits*, p. 253). But this collapsing of the two sides is not allowed any longer. Hence this surprising assertion: "Let us turn back, then, to one of the assumptions that we have already made, with the exception that we shall be able to give it a categorical denial." (BPP, p. 53; *Jenseits*, p. 253) The assumption that he is attacking from now on is the theme of life and nature moving inexorably to death. We tend to think that we are all destined to die from internal causes

---

[23] Sigmund Freud, *Beyond the Pleasure Principle*, James Strachey (trans.). New York: Norton, 1989, p. 46. Hereafter, BPP and page number.

[24] Sigmund Freud, *Jenseits des Lustprinzips, Studienausgabe III, Psychologie des Unbewussten.* Frankfurt: Fischer, 1982, p. 249; and BPP, p. 47.

[25] Jacques Derrida, *The Postcard: from Socrates to Freud and Beyond,* Alan Bass (trans.). Chicago: University of Chicago Press, 1987, p. 359. Hereafter, P and page number.

and that there is nothing to do about it. I have already discussed the logic of
"*c'est la vie*" proffered when we hear of someone's sad but anticipated death.
Such a thought is debunked by Freud who reasons by saying that this idea,
illustrated by countless poets, is in fact a simple comfort: "Perhaps we have
adopted the belief because there is some comfort in it. If we are to die
ourselves, and first to lose in death those who are dearest to us, it is easier to
submit to a remorseless law of nature" (Freud, 1989, p. 53). In short, Freud is
telling us in no uncertain terms that if universal entropy can be construed as
a "law of Nature," there is no reason to believe that we have voted it, to
paraphrase Joyce's quip in *Exiles*.[26]

In an effort to test the validity of this widespread belief about the
inescapability of death, Freud finally comes to another conclusion. Following
Weissmann, Freud reopens the biological debate and contrasts the dying
cells of any organism with an undying germ-plasm. Death has therefore
become less "natural" since it is a late acquisition of organisms; Freud quotes
the findings of Woodruff who had shown that infusorians can, if placed
in a refreshed environment that nourishes them, reproduce themselves by
fission for more than 30,000 generations (BPP, p. 57). The focus of the
discussion then becomes that of "senescence" versus "rejuvenation." Besides,
in cases when the solution has not been renewed and a certain degeneration
can be observed, this process can be reversed when two animalculae blend
together; then they achieve an instant regeneration and avoid the degeneration
that leads to death. It is in the context of such speculations that Freud
asserts forcibly that he believes in a dualism of the drives, a principle that
is constructive (*aufbauend*) and a principle that is "de-structive" or
"deconstructive" (*abbauend*) (BPP, p. 59; *Jenseits*, p. 258).

In an earlier passage, Derrida objected to such a translation; he criticizes
the eagerness of those who retroactively import "deconstructive" themes in
translations of Marx and Nietzsche. Nevertheless, he grudgingly accepts that
one engages in such a project, albeit with some ambivalence:

> If one were to translate *abbauen* as "to deconstruct" in *Beyond* . . . perhaps
> one would get a glimpse of a necessary place of articulation between
> what is involved in the form of an asthetic writing and what has interested
> me up to now under the heading of deconstruction.

(P, p. 268)

---

[26] "Robert (*impatiently*): No man ever lived on this earth who did not long to possess—I
mean to possess in the flesh—the woman whom he loves. It is nature's law.
Richard (*contemptuously*): What is that to me? Did I vote it?"
James Joyce, *Exiles* in *Poem and Exiles*. London: Penguin, 1992, p. 190.

In these introductory pages to a very long and detailed reading of Freud's *Beyond the Pleasure Principle* (Freud's text has less than 80 pages, Derrida's commentary is more than 150 pages long), Derrida discusses Freud's debts to philosophy, and his denial of a debt. He lists Schopenhauer and Nietzsche above all. He notes that when Freud seems to agree fully with Schopenhauer, he decides to take a "bold step forward" and quotes the text in German (P, p. 268). Derrida then describes Freud's strategy in startling terms: first it does not come back to itself in a Hegelian manner, it does not follow a hermeneutic circle, it simply progresses according to a series of detours: "It constructs-deconstructs itself according to an interminable detour (*Umweg*): that it describes 'itself', writes and unwrites." (P, p. 269) This entails that theses such as "death is the result or end of life" cannot be ascribed to Freud just like that. Neither can the Nietzschean tag of the "eternal recurrence of the same" apply to Freudian metapsychology. Freud even turns into the devil, or at least he is the "devil's advocate," and this devilish turn explains his constant shifting between theory and autobiographical writing (P, p. 271).

However, a hundred pages later, Derrida seems to have forgotten his earlier methodological precaution when he reaches the same passage at the end of his commentary. All too quickly, he identifies Freud both with Schopenhauer and with Heidegger. Perhaps because he was afraid that the equation between a Freudian deconstruction (*Abbau*) and the death drive would carry negative connotations, perhaps because he is simply too eager to superpose Freud and Heidegger. However, an equation between "deconstruction" and death would not bother Freud in the least.

Indeed, at this point of his "speculation," Freud realizes that he may have come too close to the dualistic theory of Schopenhauer, whose philosophy, before that of Heidegger, presents death as the purpose of human life. The concept of the "will" embodies an unconscious sexual instinct that is on the side of life (BPP, pp. 59–60). We have to read Freud with great care: "We have unwittingly (*unversehens*, which means both 'unexpectedly' and 'without being fully aware') steered our course into the harbour of Schopenhauer's philosophy." (BPP, p. 59; *Jenseits*, p. 259) This suggests that one should not want to remain in this safe but dead end: "Let us make a bold attempt at another step forward." (BPP, p. 60) This "bolder" step is to assume that libido or love can "rejuvenate" certain cells, while noting that too much narcissism (seen here as the opposite of love for another being) will lead to death in some cases, as witnessed by the uncontrolled reduplication of cells we find in cancer: cancer offers the paradox of a disease brought about by a refusal to die, which thus destroys the organism. We now understand better why the ego drive can be equated with death, while the sexual drive can be equated with a life-giving force. This is clearer in the original: "*Wir sind ja vielmehr*

von einer scharfen Scheidung zwischen Ichtrieben = Todestrieben und
Sexualtrieben = Lebenstrieben ausgegangen."[27] (*Jenseits*, p. 261) In the analysis
that follows, Freud is not saying that more love could cure cancer, but he is
not that far from such a thought. The couple of ego drive and death drive is
opposed to the second couple of sexual drive and life. If we can identify here
the seeds of the dualism of Eros versus Thanatos, we may note—a point that
will not be lost on Lacan—that it is the Ego that is placed on the side of
Thanatos.

Following Lacan's central intuitions about the death drive, Slavoj Žižek
has expressed clearly the paradoxical nature of Freud's thought. He returns to
Lacan's thesis that we encountered first, namely that the death drive provides
the general form for all drives. He uses the example of Wagner's Flying
Dutchman to make a point that rings very close to the position taken by
Adorno:

> Where is the death drive here? It precisely does not lie in their longing to
> die, to find peace in death: the death drive, on the contrary, is *the very*
> *opposite of dying*, it is a name for the "undead" eternal life itself, for the
> horrible fate of being caught in the endless repetitive cycle of wandering
> around in guilt and pain.[28]

Another Wagnerian hero, Tristan, is seen in the same structure: in Act III, he
does not despair because of his fear of dying but because of his fear of losing
Isolde:

> . . . what makes him so desperate is the fact that, without Isolde, he *cannot*
> *die* and is condemned to eternal longing—he anxiously awaits her arrival
> so that he can die. The prospect he dreads is not that of dying without
> Isolde (the standard complaint of a lover) but, rather, that of endless life
> without her . . .[29]

We are back to the paradigm offered by Hunter Gracchus in Kafka's tale that
so impressed Adorno. Is this exactly what Freud has in mind in his
speculations on death in *Beyond the Pleasure Principle*? His thinking has

---

[27] "Our argument had as its point of departure a sharp distinction between ego-instincts,
which we equated with death-instincts, and sexual instincts, which we equated with life-
instincts." (BPP, p. 63)
[28] Slavoj Žižek, *The Ticklish Subject: The Absent Centre of Political Ontology*. London: Verso,
1999, p. 352.
[29] Žižek, see footnote 28.

become so tentative and paradoxical at the end of the essay that it is hard to assume a linear development of a thesis, but while agreeing with Žižek's forceful reading, I would add here that Freud posits on top of his metapsychology geared to enhance the power of love another level in the dialectics by opposing "obsolescence" and "juvenescence." He trusts "juvenescence" fully, even though he may still look to Derrida as a "granddaddy," and in this sense agrees with Adorno's refusal to admit that the fate of individuals is bounded by an absolute Death that has replaced an absolute God.

The word "juvenescence" had been creatively renewed when abbreviated as "juvescence" by T. S. Eliot in his poem "Gerontion": "In the juvescence of the year / Came Christ the tiger."[30] Freud might not have allowed himself to be devoured whole by such a tiger. Undoubtedly, he would have preferred the ending of another poem: "I should be glad of another death" ("The Magi"), but he would have formulated it as: "I would be glad of another theory of death." This is what he has attempted to do with *Beyond the Pleasure Principle*. A good illustration of the lasting impact of his speculative forays of the twenties is given by a letter that Freud wrote in December 1938 to the novelist Rachel Berdach who had just sent him a novel. Freud thanked her and wrote:

> Your mysterious and beautiful book [*The Emperor, the Sages and Death*] has pleased me to an extent that makes me unsure of my judgment. I wonder whether it is the transformation of Jewish suffering or surprise that so much psychoanalytical insight should have existed at the court of the brilliant and despotic Staufer which makes me say that I haven't read anything so substantial and poetically accomplished for a long time ... Who are you? Where did you acquire all the knowledge expressed in your book? Judging by the priority you grant to death, one is led to conclude that you are very young.[31]

How could Freud deduce that Rachel Berdach was young just because she saw death everywhere? We tend to see young people totally oblivious of death and mortality. Not Freud. This baffles Max Schur when he mentions this letter.[32] In fact, we know that Berdach was not so young at the time, but she confessed that she had written this historical novel when she was quite young

---

[30] T. S. Eliot, "Gerontion," in *The Waste Land and Other Poems*. London: Faber, 1988, p. 18.

[31] Sigmund Freud, *The Letters of Sigmund Freud*. London: Dover, 1992, p. 1192.

[32] Max Schur, *Freud: Living and Dying*. Boston: International Universities Press, 1972, p. 516.

and had just lost a dear friend. However, the answer to the question is given by the conclusions of *Beyond the Pleasure Principle*. According to Freud, very early on, we need to give ourselves the comforting thought that death is due to a sad but common fate, an *anangke* against which nothing can be done. A young person will emphasize death as the ultimate truth of life, preferring to steel her heart in advance against future losses. An older person who has less to lose and everything to gain by betting on science and sexuality held firmly together will be less tempted to take death as an absolute end.

It is in this context that one can understand Freud's decision to be treated for a Steinach operation that would "rejuvenate" him. In November 1924, Freud had a vasectomy performed that would leave him "rejuvenated," which was the term used by Steinach who promoted this as a male enhancement surgery. What would make older people younger was an infusion of home-grown male hormones. This same simple vasoligation was performed on Yeats in 1936, after which he reported an increased vitality in his sexual life and poetic creativity. Freud was less enthusiastic, although he felt that the operation had brought about a respite from his cancer. Harry Benjamin, a disciple of Steinach, asserted that he had heard from Freud that the operation had achieved its aim.[33] This would tend to show, first, that Freud trusted the then budding science of endocrinology, and also that he saw in the new interventionist medicine tools for a possible reversal of the ageing process. It is quite likely that this belief had informed his attitude facing the "future" when discussing religion in 1927.

There would be a future to be thought of as a categorical imperative, but curiously such a transcendental can only be reached via death. Death is a *via negativa* leading to this *a priori* of the future. By saying "No Future," we can be truly ready for the future. We cannot give any content to the future: it should remain a pure form. Here we see a curious alliance between Freud and Kant. Freud had mentioned Kant in his 1913 Introduction to *Totem and Taboo*: ". . . taboo still exists in our midst. To be sure, it is negatively conceived and directed to different contents, but according to its psychological nature, it is still nothing else than Kant's 'Categorical Imperative' which tends to act compulsively and rejects all conscious motivation."[34] In 1920, Freud adds a decisive complement to Kant's theory that time and space are "necessary forms of thought" when he includes the timelessness of the Unconscious into the process (BPP, p. 31). And we know that the latest notes that Freud took

---

[33] See "Freud got Steinached," in Patricia Gherovici, *Please Select Your Gender*. New York: Routledge, 2010, pp. 79–80.
[34] Sigmund Freud, *Totem and Taboo*. New York: Random House, 1946, p. x.

contained an attempt at distinguishing his metapsychology from Kant's system: "Space may be the projection of the extension of the psychical apparatus. No other derivation is probable. Instead of Kant's *a priori* determinants of our psychical apparatus. Psyche is extended; knows nothing of it."[35] In the same way that it does not know that it exists in space, our psychical apparatus knows nothing about death, since it steadily but mistakenly believes in its own immortality. A consideration of death is thus a good spot to try and think both *a priori* conditions of human psyches and the general question of the future.

I will use this bridge towards Kantian philosophy to move on to Kant's considerations of the future. I'll start from a text written, not by Kant but by a disciple who spoke in Kant's name as he was responding to an attack on his system, in Kraus's review of Ulrich's *Eleutheriology*.[36] Johann August Heinrich Ulrich's *Eleutheriology, or On Freedom and Necessity* (Jena, 1788) was a total refutation of Kant's main tenets. Ulrich, a professor of philosophy at Jena and a disciple of Leibnitz, was a proponent of a determinist, rationalist and scientific philosophy. He denounced what he took to be Kant's contradictions. Kant, he argued, believed in determinism facing an intellectual reason but postulated an absolute freedom facing practical reason, for which freedom is an absolute principle. Ulrich refused the idea that morality should require an absolute freedom for its deployment. What he attacked in Kant were timeless and abstract categories like the "categorical imperative." If freedom remained an ideal, the question should be: how to mediate between absolute categories and the banal demands of experience, in which chance plays a certain role. Kant took some notes and gave them to Kraus, an old friend from Königsberg. Kraus discussed this *Eleuthériologie* and showed that Kant had not bypassed the link between the practical and the theoretical. The question was to reconcile an insight into natural necessity, by nature determined, with the "unconditional spontaneity" of understanding that alone can lead us to the world of morality. Both Kant and Kraus assert that nothing can be known of freedom: it is not an object in the world, but a principle. This enhances the need for principles that are valid for all time. A principle will by definition include the future. Thus freedom and its future have to be defined as absolutely constitutive, exactly as time and space are constitutive of our perception of the empirical world. They reject scientific determinism that finds an ultimate

---

[35] Sigmund Freud, "Findings, Ideas, Problems" (June 1938), in *Standard Edition of the Collected Works of Freud*, vol. 23, p. 299.
[36] Immanuel Kant, *Practical Philosophy*, M. Gregor (trans.). Cambridge: Cambridge University Press, 1996, pp. 125–31.

foundation in a vague providence. A future of the future will be Kant's fine line drawn between the unpredictable and the unconditional.

One finds a similar transcendental move in Kant's famous essay on "Perpetual peace," an essay whose title sounds more like "Eternal peace" than "Perpetual peace," the phrase used by the philosophers who discussed it from Bernardin de Saint Pierre to Rousseau. As Kant reminds us, if we take the expression literally, "perpetual peace" refers to death, which is why the sign appeared, as a joke, in front of a cemetery.[37] The joke soon generates a paradox: while peace is close to entropy and death, any real theory about peace needs to opt for perpetuity or "perennity." The very concept of peace entails a certain idea of sustainability.

We all dream of seeing the world being one day, at last, in peace. Kant's philosophy tries to think the conditions for a lasting peace, a peace not for the next generations, but for all the foreseeable future. He proves that "peace" equals "perpetual peace" by establishing a maxim: "No Treaty of Peace Shall Be Held Valid in Which There Is Tacitly Reserved Matter for a Future War."[38] True peace is not a truce; a peace treaty that would be a truce, the temporary suspension of hostilities while each side is busy re-arming, is the opposite of peace. If therefore "peace" and "perpetual peace" are synonymous, a transcendental futurity has to be built in the handling of all peace-negotiations, in any effort at creating international tribunals, guidelines for adequate treaty-signing, etc. Kant believed that a representative democracy would establish a state of law among the nations, while entertaining no illusions about man's true nature: human nature is "depraved." Only a rule of law can mitigate the original sin of human propensity to murder. Thus, one should promote hospitality and cosmopolitanism.

The recurrent objection is that all this remains pure theory that can never be applied. The divorce between theory and practice may be the consequence of his attribution to any system of international relations and the imperative to assert perpetual peace. Kant has foreseen the objection and deals with it in the essay that attacks the "common saying": "This May be True in Theory, but it does not Apply in Practice." If doctors and lawyers fail because they are good in theory but ignorant of their theories' applications, any amelioration will come from more theory, not less.[39] Kant is here replying to Moses Mendelssohn who denied the idea that humanity could be seen as progressing

---

[37] Immanuel Kant, "Toward perpetual peace," (1795), in *Practical Philosophy*, Mary J. Gregor (trans.). Cambridge: Cambridge University Press, 1996, p. 317.

[38] Kant, see footnote 37, p. 317.

[39] Kant, see footnote 37, p. 279.

toward a greater good. Anticipating Walter Benjamin's skepticism facing the myth of progress, Mendelssohn multiplied reasons why humanity seems to be constantly lapsing into barbarism. Kant refuses this thesis, arguing that without a minimal belief in progress, all we have is a world reduced to a bad play. History turns into an old farce, not even a tragedy:

> To watch this tragedy for a while might be moving and instructive, but the curtain must eventually fall. For in the long run, it turns into a farce; and even if actors do not tire of it, because they are fools, the spectator does, when one or another act gives him sufficient grounds for gathering that the never-ending play is forever the same.[40]

Not blind to the endless succession of wars that have marked the march of humanity, Kant decides to hope for better times. His optimism is not devoid of stoicism or skepticism, yet it ushers in an anthropology that furthers the program of the Enlightenment. It offers hope in spite of all: we have to hope even if it is without any ground for hope, a position that recalls that of Beckett.

If our present can be thought absolutely, it has to be thought from the point of view of the law, and the law inherently contains a future—perhaps not a historical future, but at least the conditions for a future. The law's "No"s, its very prohibitions, its very "death threats" are factors that keep open a future for the future. If the law's main function is to say "No," saying "No" even as in "No Future," this is to provide a transcendental structure that can give access to a future. We are condemned to the future, in other words. Beckett had seen this and presents the idea in a condensed manner in "The calmative." Here is the passage in French: "*A moi maintenant le départ, la lutte et le retour peut-être, à ce viellard qui est moi ce soir, plus vieux que je ne le serai jamais. Me voici acculé à des futurs.*"[41] But when I looked for the translation of the last sentence, I was surprised to see that the English version skips it: "For me now the setting forth, the struggle and perhaps the return, for the old man I am this evening, older than my father was, older than I shall ever be."[42] Could Beckett find no equivalent for what may variously be glossed as "I was driven back against futures" or "I was cornered, had my back against futures"? To have one's back against the future reminds us, as did Walter Benjamin in his

[40] Kant, see footnote 37, pp. 305–6.
[41] Samuel Beckett, "Le calmant," in *Nouvelles et textes pour rien*. Paris: Minuit, 1958, p. 45.
[42] Samuel Beckett, "The calmative," in *Complete Short Prose, 1929–1989*. New York: Grove, 1997, p. 64.

Theses on the Philosophy of History, that we are prohibited from investigating the future. When the storm coming from Paradise propels the angel of history into the future, it blows him backwards. Like him, we may enter the future with our arses first, but we will enter it, I promise you.

8

The Styles of Theory

Crimes against fecundity

The human embryo in the womb passes through all
the evolutionary stages of the animal kingdom ...
Every age had its style, is our age alone to be refused a style?
Adolf Loos, *Ornament and Crime: Selected Essays.*
Riverside, CA: Ariadne Press (1908)

Le style, c'est l'homme même

Wittgenstein revisited a well-known motto in a fragment from *Culture and Value* dated from 1949 when he jotted down twice: "'Le style c'est l'homme,' 'Le style c'est l'homme même.' The first expression has cheap epigrammatic brevity. The second, correct version opens up quite a different perspective. It says that a man's style is a picture of him."[1] The notion of "description" might send us back to an older discussion opposing Bertrand Russell to the younger Wittgenstein, but this is not the route I want to follow here. I would like first to pay attention to the redoubling of a "selfsame self" that finds a corroboration, a proof or a clue in an "x" that confirms it is indeed "himself" or "herself." Quite often, Wittgenstein takes "style" in a dismissive sense, as evinced by an earlier statement from 1939–1940: "Even a work of supreme art has something that can be called 'style' (*Stil*), something too that can even be called 'mannerism' (*Manier*). They have less style than the first speech of a child." (CV, p. 37 e). Who is this "they"? A note tells us that it refers to mannerist artists, whose imitative mode fits the comparison with a child's speech. Such negativity does not spare his own philosophical works and includes Wittgenstein's own style, as judged by himself: "My style is like bad musical composition." (CV, p. 39 e) This stresses the particular musicality of his philosophical language, revealing moreover a disparaging modesty. These tensions find a resolution in the often quoted paragraph:

[1] Ludwig Wittgenstein, *Culture and Value*, Peter Winch (trans.). Chicago: University of Chicago Press, 1980, p. 78 e. Hereafter CV and page number.

I think I summed up my attitude to philosophy when I said: philosophy ought really to be written only as a poetic composition. It must, as it seems to me, be possible to gather from this how far my thinking belongs to the present, future or past. For I was thereby revealing myself as someone who cannot quite do what he would like to be able to do ...

(CV, p. 24 e)

What is often quoted out of context—"*Philosophie dürfte man eigentlich nur dichten*", it could be translated as "Philosophy should be written only as poetry"—takes on a nostalgic ring if we understand it as the regret of a "stylist" who seems aware that he has fallen short of his higher expectations. Indeed, there is a latent contradiction between the philosophy of everyday language in which so many plural language games are to be observed and the perfect epigrammatic quality of the statements of the Tractatus: "*Die Welt is alles, was der Fall ist...*"[2]

Theory often appears caught up in this dilemma: we face either an endless exploratory discourse that unfolds in the hope of acquiring new insights and new concepts, or the cryptic and arresting grandeur of philosophemes that can be quoted and commented, but fail to reveal their meaning immediately. What do I mean by "philosopheme" here? It could be defined as any little phrase similar to those mentioned by Samuel Beckett's character Malone ("I know these little phrases that seem so innocuous and once you let them in, pollute the whole of speech").[3] They function as theoretical tags, quotable one-liners from famous authors, mottos and aphorisms that can be mentioned independently of their original context. They are characterized by character-istics of form: they tend to be dense, paradoxical, oxymoronic even. In their best shapes, they are arresting "sentences" avoiding mere "sententiousness."

Their brevity and notable structural parallels are two additional features. They are closer to maxims or to lines of poetry that one can memorize easily than to "concepts." I'll provide a short list to exemplify this: *Die Sprache spricht* (Heidegger), *Tout autre est tout autre* (Derrida), *Cogito ergo sum* (Descartes), *Le coeur a des raisons que la raison ne connaît pas* (Pascal), *Rose is a rose is a rose* (Stein), *Je est un autre* (Rimbaud), *Les non-dupes errent* (Lacan), *Verum Ipsum Factum* (Vico), *Rien n' aura eu lieu que le lieu* (Mallarmé), *O my friends, there are no friends* (Aristotle, translated by Derrida), *Wo Es war, soll Ich werden* (Freud), *D'ailleurs c'est toujours les autres qui meurent* (Duchamp),

---

[2]   Ludwig Wittgenstein, *Tractatus Logico-Philosophicus*. London and New York: Routledge, 1990, p. 30.
[3]   Samuel Beckett, *Malone Dies, in Three Novels: Molloy, Malone Dies, The Unnamable*. New York: Grove Press, 1991, p. 193.

Ubi nihil vales, ibi nihil velis (Geulincx) and, finally, *Le style c'est l'homme même* (Buffon). One could multiply examples, but the number of these sentences, potentially great, is not infinite. They all evince several characteristics: a notable syntactic compression,[4] a high dependence on a language's amphibologies that renders literal translation quasi impossible (which is why they are often memorized in the original), and a tantalizing ambiguity attracting commentaries that proliferate given the impossibility of a direct translation, as we saw in Chapter 1.

If we agree that these sentences, by condensing styles of thinking and styles of expression mummify for eternity the monumental cadavers of their authors, it is because they function above all else as clues. As clues, they call up a whole context, which has to be rethought through and through as a process; it is a process of thought, no doubt, but at times, a whole life-style is implied (can we quote Heidegger without evoking the snowy slopes of the Feldberg, the Spartan but cozy hut in Todtnau, the inspiring trees of the Black Forest?). This follows from Wittgenstein's main insight when he revisits Buffon's famous saying. Since "Style is the man himself"—individuality is captured in a description. Style provides a link between a rational level and the "musical" aspect of a way of thinking depending from the author's body. Therefore, style is what affects an audience most, because it is a marker of extreme singularity, while leading to a whole system, like an ethics of language. Style triggers an infinite investigation if we stress less the formal qualities than the process at work. It is to this aspect that I want to turn now. Moving from Joyce to Poe, I will try to use a certain type of detection via clues that send the literary sleuth or the "stylistician" turned detective on the right track. In the end, one might have to pose the question of an essence of style. And when I will suggest that it has something to do with crime, this will be an allegorical and hyperbolic way of speaking about death, negativity and destruction.

I will deal with style suspiciously by posing questions that any detective would ask a suspect, which will make me negotiate between the literary and the forensic. I will begin by examining the "Oxen of the sun" episode of *Ulysses*, a difficult episode in which we see Joyce romping through the various histories of English style. It is a good episode to tackle if one really means to understand what style is. When I taught this episode in the seventies, I would use Wolfgang Iser's groundbreaking *The Implied Reader* (1972).[5] Now I add to Iser's approach concepts found in Jacques Rancière's work. It is possible that their approaches

---

[4] See Virginia Tufte's *Artful Sentences: Syntax as Style*. Cheshire: Graphics Press, 2006.
[5] Wolgang Iser, *The Implied Reader*. Baltimore: Johns Hopkins Press, 1974.

to style are complementary. In 1972, Iser defined style as the imposition of a cultural "form" on reality, which led him to affirm that Joyce's play with styles had a strong ethical component. For Iser, Joyce's ultimate meaning was a critique of the illusion that language and reality will ever coincide. His language games with constantly varying styles would alert readers to the constructed nature of reality. More recently, Rancière links the aesthetics of style with ethics and politics, which entails a different emphasis. In *Mute Speech* (2005),[6] Rancière starts from the contradictions that he sees in formalist approaches so as to connect a new aesthetic regime defined by the autonomy of style and its domination over all other concerns, to efforts towards a democratic liberation that frees one from all constraints. For him, then, style will be defined by a new rapport between subjectivity and the power to express, which in the end brings us back to issues of ethics and politics.

Since my focus is on the "Oxen of the sun" episode, I will pay attention to Joyce's conceit in elaborating this episode within Homeric parallels. I would like to combine Iser's and Rancière's approaches while keeping in mind the equation posited by Joyce between the art of stylistic variation, an art that he pursues systematically throughout "Oxen of the sun," with what he calls "crimes against fecundity." This last phrase refers to the fact that the scene takes place in a maternity hospital where Mrs Purefoy is giving birth to a baby. Meanwhile, Stephen Dedalus, Leopold Bloom, and several other medical students chat irreverently about conception, coition, contraception, and other themes pertaining to sexuality and obstetrics. Joyce famously said that his main idea was the "crime against fecundity" when we use birth-control. I found myself asking: what are we slaughtering with Joyce when we play games with style? Did Joyce want to kill literary clichés only, or was he launching a more ambitious program such as a new view of language, caught both in its evolutionary function and as leading back to universal history? This led me to broaden the issue of style, since style is always a synecdoche revealing a whole vision. And finally this brought me to a more delicate question: I had to assess whether Joyce's novel, not the author himself, with all we can learn on his life, beliefs, prejudices, and foibles, could be called "pro-life," that is, opposed to abortion, or pro-choice? Had he remained a Catholic at heart, or did he allow free play to unleash styles that would assert the domination of writing—Derrida's "dead letters" hidden inside a French letter, as it were—in its urge to conquer everything? Since I had almost reached an

---

6   Jacques Rancière, *Mute Speech*, James Swenson (trans.). New York: Columbia University Press, 2011. I owe a lot to friendly discussions with Gabriel Rockhill who wrote an excellent "Introduction" to this translation, "Through the looking glass: The Subversion of the modernist doxa", pp. 1–28.

impasse, I had to move around Joyce and look at other models, and in order to leave room for a less anxious and more spacious problematization, I found myself moving back and forth between Joyce and Poe. I decided to insert my Joycean musings into Benjaminian analyses of Poe's famous tale of "Marie Roget," a move I justified by paying closer attention to the gothic qualities of Joyce's style in "Oxen of the sun."

To make better sense of these peculiar combinations, I will begin with two anecdotes. The first one dates from the mid-nineties, from a time when I had just moved to Philadelphia. One evening, I accompanied two female friends to a demonstration supporting a local family-planning facility that had been threatened by anti-abortion activists. We marched for a while in the streets of downtown Philadelphia with a crowd of people chanting slogans. After an hour or so, there was a lull in the chanting and a tired silence followed songs and slogans. A sudden inspiration seized me, and I shouted: "James Joyce, Pro Choice!" To my astonishment, the entire group repeated it. For a while, we were all walking around City Hall chanting "James Joyce, Pro Choice." This was my only moment of political triumph in North America. Even if I was proud of my contribution at the time, doubts came creeping in soon after. Hadn't Joyce described the argument of "Oxen of the sun" as being underpinned by the idea of "the crime committed against fecundity by sterilizing the act of coition"? Was James Joyce really or simply "pro choice"? Should one have to choose in this case, or could one leave the issue undecided, as most scholars who have worked on "Oxen of the sun" tend to do?

The second anecdote comes from my experience as a pedagogue teaching *Ulysses*. A few years ago, I had reached "Oxen of the sun" and was discussing a passage that I always find hilarious, the mock-epic evocation of food and drink displayed in the waiting room of the maternity hospital. Here is the passage:

> And there were vessels that are wrought by magic of Mahound out of seasand and the air by a warlock with his breath that he blases in to them like to bubbles. And full fair cheer and rich was on the board that no wight could devise a fuller ne richer. And there was a vat of silver that was moved by craft to open in the which lay strange fishes withouten heads though misbelieving men nie that this be possible thing without they see it natheless they are so. And these fishes lie in an oily water brought there from Portugal because of the fatness that therein is like to the juices of the olivepress.
>
> (U., ch. 14: ll. 146–53)[7]

---

[7] James Joyce, *Ulysses*, H. W. Gabler (ed.). New York: Vintage, 1986. I refer to quotes by U., chapter number and line number.

I asked my students what this evoked for them. They seemed embarrassed, and then one asked: "Are they in a bathroom? Flushing floating turds?" I shook my head. Another: "Are they squashing olives in a printing press?" A third one: "Frying fish for dinner?" None of them was able to understand the literal meaning of the passage. I tried to help them: "Think of sardines in a can." "Sardines in a can?" What was that? They were not sure. Not only had they not been able to recognize what Joyce had obliquely depicted (glass bottles and headless sardines in oil) but they claimed that the notion of a sardine can was outlandish. Their grandparents might have eaten that, a long time ago. It dawned on me that a sardine can was as archaic for them as telephones with wires, those tangled "strandentwining cables" mentioned by Stephen. Their story was confirmed when I heard that in April 2010 the last American cannery had closed: no sardine can would ever be produced in the US. And then I didn't make things easier when I told my students that sardines had to be headless not only because that was the way they were prepared, but because Joyce was establishing a correspondence with the earlier stages in the development of the embryo. Headless sardines refer to the period when the foetus is a blob floating in amniotic fluid. The discussion made me aware not only of my age but also of the hermeneutic difficulties facing "Oxen of the sun." Styles as they are fore-grounded in this episode are only perceived as such when recognition patterns implying some competence are set in motion. Without this minimal competence, the succession of styles is not recognized. There is a learning curve entailed by stylistic recognition, and it begs the reader's participation; even more, a whole education. In fact, as I hope to show, the topics of style, obstetrics, and forensic science, and beyond that, scientific or neo-scientific discourses on generation(s) are intimately connected.

Indeed, the scholarship on the "Oxen of the sun" episode is divided between two types of approaches. One is concerned with debates on sexuality (Richard Brown) or birth control (Mary Lowe-Evans). In *James Joyce and Sexuality*[8] and *Crimes Against Fecundity: Joyce and Population Control*,[9] we do learn a lot about the material that Joyce had read, about his position in the debates of the times, but no mention is made of the stylistic devices used to present these problems. The other approach is more textual or genetic. In Robert Janusko's canonical *The Sources and Structures of James Joyce's Oxen*,[10] we discover Joyce's literary sources and his reliance on compilations—George

---

[8]   Richard Brown, *James Joyce and Sexuality*. Cambridge: Cambridge University Press, 1989.
[9]   Mary Lowe-Evans, *Crimes Against Fecundity: Joyce and Population Control*. Syracuse: Syracuse University Press, 1989.
[10] Robert Janusko, *The Sources and Structures of James Joyce's Oxen*. Ann Arbor, UMI Research Press, 1983.

Saintsbury's *A History of English Prose Rhythm* (1912) above all—but the political or ideological problem is all but avoided.

This is the time to go back to Wolfgang Iser's exemplary reading of "Oxen of the sun." It is to be found in *Der Implizite Leser* (1972). The English version provided by the author is called *The Implied Reader: Patterns of Communication in Prose Fiction from Bunyan to Beckett.*[11] With this book, Iser launched a phenomenological approach to literature in English. It was founded upon a central claim, that the act of reading is implied by any literary work. This led him to argue that it is this implied reader who discovers how a text signifies, how it presupposes and programs its reception. Any reader will thus learn to read herself or himself via an interactive hermeneutic process. Joyce's episode provided an important example in this phenomenological approach: here was a text that seemed to need the participation of the reader, even if it could not be taken for granted.

In the chapter devoted to Joyce, Iser began by quoting Eliot's "Ulysses, order and myth" essay so as to examine the problems posed by the idea of a continuous parallel between myth and the present time. He concluded that myth could not provide ready-made solutions, only new potentialities, and that the process of interpretation must be engaged with each time by new readers. This corresponded to the fact, observed by most commentators, that every chapter of *Ulysses* tends to be written in a different style. The relation between the world and literary language has become more complex since Einstein; important critics like T. S. Eliot and Hermann Broch had emphasized this. Thus, it is style that emerges as the central topic, as the hero even, in "Oxen of the sun." This is the episode in which Joyce forces his readers to be aware of the shaping function of art by foregrounding his linguistic manipulations.

Following insights provided by Goldberg's *Classical Temper*, Iser began his reading with a critique of Stuart Gilbert's canonical introduction to *Ulysses*. Gilbert had stated that Joyce wished to create a parallel between the sequence of period styles and the development of the embryo. For one thing, this reading was too serious and missed the comedy running through the chapter, defined by a great sense of fun when we see the degree of deformation brought about by each style (IR, p. 187). Iser analyzed a few examples, including the sardines in olive oil and concluded: "This incongruity between style and object is apparent all through the series of imitation from one century to the other." (IR, p. 189) Incongruity is the key-word in his careful readings. It leads to another principle: given this constant stylistic variation,

---

[11] Wolfgang Iser, *The Implied Reader: Patterns of Communication in Prose Fiction from Bunyan to Beckett.* Baltimore: Johns Hopkins University Press, 1974, subsequently abbreviated as IR.

one could perceive that "each style reveals a latent ideology, constantly reducing the reality to the scope of individual principles." (IR, p. 190) For Dickens, love is seen as peace and bliss, for Bunyan it ushers in a moral or Christian allegory, while for Carlyle a consideration of love is pretext for a quasi-Nietzschean affirmation of life, life overcoming everything. We have thus reached a perspectivist ethos since each style defines a point of view: "... the predetermined, predetermining nature of all style is demonstrated quite unmistakably through the individual variations. The judgment inherent in each style create a uniform picture of the subject presented, choosing these elements of the given reality that correspond to the frame of reference essential to the observation." (IR, p. 191)

A second conclusion can be drawn: if style reproduces only one aspect of reality and not reality itself, then style is closer to a distortion of reality. Joyce uses parodies, that is stylistic caricatures of the major writers of English literature, to highlight that we'll never know, for example, what love really is, but only what it was for Malory, Bunyan, Addison, Carlyle ... It would be idle to try to assign a truth-value to all the statements of the characters who voice such widely divergent theories about sexuality, reproduction, and contraception. Style would thus be shown to have failed in its attempt to provide a truthful picture of life. This is linked with a major principle that the essential characteristic of style is that it imposes a grid on an essentially formless reality (we are back to Eliot's contention here). Here, there is no objectivity since, ultimately, all styles are determined by the historical conditions that shape them.

However, this is not a nihilistic position either. Here is how Iser concludes:

> While the theme of this one chapter is love, the theme of Ulysses itself is everyday human life, and the stylistic presentation of this varies from chapter to chapter, because it can never be grasped as a whole by any one individual style. Only by constantly varying the angle of approach is it possible to convey the potential range of the "real-life" world, but in literature the "approach" is what gives rise to the style. By constantly changing the style, Joyce not only conveys the preconditioned, one-sided nature of each approach but also seems to set both object and observer in motion, thus accumulating an assembly of mobile views that show the essential expansiveness of reality. In this sense, "The Oxen of the sun" epitomizes the technique of the whole novel. The sequence of styles brings out the one-sidedness of each and the constant expansion of the object.
>
> (IR, p. 194)

Indeed, we know from Joyce's various schemata that the "organ" for the episode is the "womb," while its technique is "embryonic development." One can apply the four-fold type of reading launched by Dante about his own *Commedia* in his letter to Can Grande. Here we would have, at the first level, a literal level that could be explicated as follows. This is the first time Bloom and Stephen actually sit together and engage in some social rapport. Bloom visits the maternity hospital of Holles Street to see how Mrs Purefoy is doing. After three days of labor, she will finally give birth to a son (one of the rare "events" of *Ulysses*). Meanwhile Dixon, Lynch, Madden, Crotthers, Stephen, Lenehan, and Costello are drinking and Bloom sits there with them for a while. Then Buck Mulligan and Bannon appear. Finally, after a thunderstorm, the baby is born, and Stephen suggests they all leave to go to a pub.

This would be followed by a moral level, corresponding to the following point of view, as exposed by Joyce: "the idea [is] the crime committed against fecundity by sterilizing the act of coition."[12] This would be enacted by the cynical banter of the young men who variously deride the idea of reproduction and also engage in a series of pseudo-scientific discussions about embryology and heredity. Doctor Horne is Helios, whose oxen are slaughtered by the medical students' witty barbs.

Then there would be the allegorical level. The text embodies the growth of the foetus by progressing through nine months (Joyce's drawings). The first is represented by alliterative Anglo-Saxon prose; the second by Middle-English prose; the third by medieval prose like that in *Le Morte d'Arthur*. The fourth by Elizabethan prose; the fifth by Milton's Latinate prose; the sixth goes from Burton and Browne to Pepys via Bunyan. The seventh month is illustrated by eighteenth-century wits and the birth of realism, Defoe, Swift, Sterne and Burke; the eighth by Gothic novels, Dickens and Newman, and the ninth extends from Thomas Carlyle to modern slang.

And finally, there is the anagogical level. The series of English styles is either giving birth to the language of the future, a new prophetic tone in an American idiom, or destroying the very concept of style as such (much as "music" is destroyed—for Joyce and Bloom—if not necessarily for the reader at the end of "Sirens") and leading to a "writing degree zero," such as was announced by Roland Barthes—the utopia of being able to write without style, Beckett's own post-Joycean dream.

It is when addressing the fourth level that *Mute Speech*, Rancière's study of the evolution of nineteenth-century literary styles, from Balzac to Flaubert, Mallarmé and Proust, is most helpful. In his fast-paced survey, Rancière implicitly criticizes current accounts of modernism by looking at a longer

---

12 Joyce's letter to Frank Budgen, in James Joyce, *Letters*, I. New York: Viking, 1967, pp. 138–9.

history of genres and of the rules that govern representation. In the classical poetics of representation since Aristotle, fables, understood as the arrangement of an action, belonged to genres defined by conformity with the subject represented. These rules would de determined by the nature of the action and defined the regime of representation. Rancière stresses that the literary productions of the representative system are not necessarily conservative. The same sets of rules can express the hierarchical structures of monarchy, but also help the promulgation of a new republic, or even allow for the emergence of socialist aspirations in the middle of the nineteenth century, when workers attempted to give voice to their longings and frustrations.[13] However, the ancient hierarchy of *inventio* over *dispositio* and *elocutio* is destroyed once the modern principle of equality, the famous "indifference" of style to its topic or subject that come to the fore with Flaubert, becomes the norm.

The main issue is the way in which these categories impact on what Rancière calls the "distribution of the sensible" proper to the poetics of expressivity. The change happened in the middle of the nineteenth century. The representative system was founded on the subordination of the material side of the arts (*elocutio*) to the intellectual side (*inventio*). Victor Hugo's *Notre-Dame de Paris* (1831) provides an example of the collapse of the poem as it was understood within the representative order. In a series of superb analyses,[14] Rancière shows that Hugo's novel becomes a prose poem; by a process of contamination, Hugo's style petrifies when it expresses the stones of the cathedral. The hierarchical relationship between the intellectual and the material is undercut when Hugo's material language overthrows the stable hierarchy of earlier poetics. Hugo leads to Flaubert who leads to Joyce, and such a progression correponds to an evolution towards modernity: hierarchical fiction yields to language as such, and "style" is caught up in a material mode of functioning of language. When *elocutio* frees itself from *inventio*, it ushers in a new power of expression which animates objects in a new performativity. Hugo's inspired prosopopeia returns style to the matter of linguistic expression.

I cannot rehearse the minute close readings provided by *Mute Speech* and will only summarize some of its conclusions. One main conclusion is that the old regime controlling the distribution of genres will be overthrown with the rise to power of the novel. The novel contains in seed the principle of the equality of represented objects and subjects. The novel is a genre-less genre

---

[13] This is the main theme of Rancière's remarkable historical study, *The Nights of Labor: The Workers' Dream in 19th Century France*, John Drury (trans.). Philadelphia: Temple University Press, 1991.

[14] Rancière, see footnote 6, pp. 52–61.

capable of freely circulating through diverse publics and mediums. Such an all-encompassing genre refuses to be restricted to specific domains or privileged locations. Thus the principle of decorum is negated by a purely expressive language that abolishes "styles" in a total indifference of literature to the subjects represented. With the abolition of genres, "style" becomes "pure style" or, as Flaubert would say, it becomes an absolute manner of seeing things. There are no more beautiful or ugly topics, and Joyce, in that matter, appears truly as Flaubert's direct disciple.[15]

This model of writing leads to the modernist freeing of style as an absolute. Given this new anarchic freedom, one cannot distinguish between style as elevated speech and the plurality of spoken idioms. This changes the very notion of performative speech: the performative escapes from the space of the theatre, which had been previously reserved to persuasive rhetoric, and encroaches upon the space of the novel. The novel will be the site of a democratic letter endlessly wandering in the world without having any privileged place, exactly like Levinas's Kantian dog. This disturbing nomad roaming in the fields of meaning reconstitutes its place in the world of letters by a parody of an ideal genealogy. For Joyce, this genealogy entails the entire rewriting, albeit mocking and systematically parodic, of the tradition of English prose styles. The pastiches usher in a new poetics in which silent things and hitherto disenfranchised subjects take on a language of their own. This creates a new system of signs through which the expressive regime holds sway. Hence, at last, the general lability or translatability of all the arts into other arts or mediums.

Flaubert blended two principles of romantic poetry: the principle of the indifference of style before subject matter, and the principle of generalized linguistic performativity. The danger was that the principle of indifference risked destroying poetic difference. A little like Bouvard and Pécuchet at the end of the eponymous novel, the writer seems condemned to undo art as a principle of distinction in the world. In the end, he risks disappearing in the meaningless verbiage of the alienated masses and the humming chatter of freed objects. This drama is re-enacted at the end of "Oxen of the sun," when we hear only gibberish and, what is more, an American-inflected medley of slangs.

According to *Mute Speech*, the tension between the hierarchy of literary language and the principle of the indifference of style underpinned the literary disputes that took place from the end of the nineteenth century to the present. For Rancière, literature is fundamentally torn between the spirit and the letter.[16]

---

[15] For an excellent treatment of this derivation, see Scarlett Baron, *Strandentwining Cable: Joyce, Flaubert, and Intertexuality*. Oxford: Oxford University press, 2012.

[16] Rancière, see footnote 6, Rockhill's "Introduction" pp. 16–19, for a relatively critical account of this thesis. I am indebted to Rockhill's excellent summaries.

However, the tension between spirit and letter is productive, since it generates original attempts to deal with incompatible principles. Fundamentally, literature thrives on its effort to come to terms with the clash between the hierarchical writing of the spirit and the egalitarian words of letters. While noting that this problematic owes much more to the thought of Derrida than is acknowledged, it is in this productive tension that I would want to situate Joyce's hesitation between fecundity and sterility, a tension allegorically replayed in Joyce's spin on the politics of birth-control in Ireland and the world.

One important consequence of Rancière's work is that he forces us to abandon for good Walter Benjamin's opposition between an "aestheticization of politics" typical of fascism and a "politicization of aesthetics" provided by leftist programs, as in Brecht's political plays. For Rancière, the aesthetic realm is directly political because it creates a new organization of the sensible (*partage du sensible*). Are we so far from Iser with Rancière's categories? In a sense, yes, since what has changed is the way in which we articulate together literature, aesthetics and politics. Rancière sees in the distribution of the sensible the result of an aesthetico-political operation. Moreover, what he calls the "*partage du sensible*" should also be, in the context of Joyce's "Oxen of the sun," gendered, or even feminized. One is tempted to rephrase the concept of *partage* (sharing) with that of parturition, a real or metaphorical giving birth to presence and the world as represented and expressed, a "parturition of the sensible." In other words, Joyce would be suggesting in this episode (as well as in all of *Ulysses*, but more radically so obviously here) that the distribution of the sensible depends less from a male or phallic gesture of cutting, dividing and then sharing out to all, than from a feminine process that ends up by giving birth to reality as we know it. This is why, for Joyce, and also for Flaubert before him, literary creation had to be understood as a parturition of style. There would be a direct link between Stephen's amateurish villanelle in *A Portrait of the Artist as a Young Man* ("O! In the virgin womb of the imagination the word was made flesh" and the no less virgin poet of "Oxen of the sun": "In woman's womb word is made flesh but in the spirit of the maker all flesh that passes becomes the word that shall not pass away"). (U., ch. 14: ll. 292–3)

Le style c'est la femme même

This evolution has been well summed up by Genevieve Abravanel when she wonders why Joyce's gestation in "Oxen of the sun" had to lead us to a present idiom dominated by American-English slang. She notes that what Jennifer Levine has called one of "the most obviously subversive episodes" in *Ulysses* is a "linguistic prank" in its parodies of the evolution of literary styles from Anglo-Saxon to the present day. She continues:

> Set in a maternity hospital and riddled with images of gestation and development, the episode serves as an allegory for the organic, changeable character of the English language. Joyce's use of a gestation model is particularly powerful here because it implies that the chapter will end with birth and thus with something greater than the developmental stages that have come before. It is therefore especially striking that this episode should end with American English. Yet why does Joyce's gestating English language ultimately deliver up American slang?[17]

Her answer is simple but I believe irrefutable: it is a "conceit that undermines the structures of value that privilege Ben Johnson and Shakespeare over bawdy American curse words," since Joyce may be seen "turning even more starkly to American content to reflect upon the globalism and imperialism of the modern age." Thus, even though Joyce ascribed to Bloom the function of a "spermatozoon" in "Oxen of the sun," this role should be seen in the context of the general scheme of the organs in *Ulysses*.

By providing an organ for each chapter, Joyce places the narration within the body, but nowhere is this body seen so clearly as made up of language. In this case, it looks as if Leopold Bloom's diegetic role as an empathetic observer of the feminine body was meant to present him embodied in the text through a schematic "womb." Bloom's rare and cautious statements in the midst of carousing students is his way of experiencing his participation in a birth process. He approximates the interiority of a female perspective. In "Oxen of the sun," Bloom's *logos spermatikos* transcends its diegetic function and becomes united with Stephen presented as an "embryo philosopher." (U., ch. 14: l. 1295) Their convergence of males fascinated by the feminine process of parturition allegorizes the body of the text and merges into the fluid component in this embryonic sequence. The physical birth and the birth of language allegorize the process of writing. When Joyce unfolds and parodies the history of literary styles, Bloom and Stephen blend in the nine sections that follow Joyce's womb-schema. Finally, a new language is born, the language of the present and even the future. It entails also the new American

---

[17] Genevieve Abranavel, "American encounters in *Dubliners* and *Ulysses*," *Journal of Modern Literature*, vol. 33, no. 4, Summer 2010, p. 165. See her *Americanizing Britain: The Rise of Modernism in the Age of the Entertainment Empire*. Oxford: Oxford University Press, 2012.

idiom spoken by Poe—Poe forces us to look at the site of literature not only as that of a new parturition but also as that of a crime. Could it be that the two notions are intimately connected?

We now need to return to the quandary of a "pro-life Joyce" and a "pro-choice Joyce." We will be armed with what we have gained from the theoretical discussion. We can reformulate the question in this way: was Joyce trying to kill literary clichés in order to give birth to a new language, or was he demonstrating his mastery over language and being playful, telling a story in a highly stylized manner, via the conceit that the evolution of literary language is similar to the evolution of a human foetus? Or was he suggesting, twisting the old motto, that "*Le style, c'est la femme même*"? If the conflation of literary style and femininity had to be made, why did he need the idea of a "crime"? Who was the object of the murder, who perpetrated it?

Rancière exhibits through a typically—almost parochially—French cultural history the evolution leading to the principle of "indifference"; this shift had also been thought by the Victorians, albeit with a different stress. What they invented was the treatment of murder stories as a species of documentary drama that can be enjoyed for the thrills they offer without paying heed to moral issues. In this bracketing off of ethics lies the root of "esthetics." We may remember that the term of "aesthetics" was introduced into English for the first time as a translation from the German of Kant and Schiller by Thomas de Quincey in his famous essay "Murder considered as one of the fine arts."[18] The first of the two essays that established de Quincey's name among British humorists, and even gained for him a place in André Breton's *Anthology of Black Humor*, states that murder has two handles. It can be seized by the moral handle (which we can leave to priests and judges) or by the aesthetic handle (used by everyone else). That aesthetic handle turns murder into a spectacle and allows us to treat it purely "esthetically." The victim has been killed and cannot be resuscitated: let's just see whether this can make a good or a bad show. De Quincey's narrator considers at some length the murderer Williams, who had slaughtered two entire households, as a genius, an inimitable "artist" of murder. His crimes have to be assessed as works of art, and have set higher standards for forthcoming murderers. They all have been "signed" with his own personal stamp for posterity.

Thus, de Quincey tells us, via Kant, that murder is not a crime when it is art. The autonomy of esthetics means that the work of art simply turns into its own reality. The point is less that art will "kill" reality in order to assert its own laws than that it becomes self-reflexive; its significance is bounded by the

18 Thomas de Quincey, *On Murder*. Oxford: Oxford World's Classics, 2006, pp. 8–34.

deployment of its formal procedures, an active bracketing out of other worldly concerns that acknowledges the legislation of no human or divine tribunal. De Quincey attempts to found this articulation of ethics and esthetics on a distinction between action and contemplation. His central argument is that as long as we can do something to prevent a murder or help a potential victim, we must act—this is the realm of ethics. Should we happen to come too late when the murder has been committed, then we must be allowed to enjoy the crime scene as pure spectacle. However, such a clear-cut distinction between a "before" and an "after" moment simplifies the issue or misleads us. What makes murder stories thrilling is that there is a style in murder—an amusing passage of "Of murder" consists in having the members of the "Society for the Encouragement of Murder" assess certain criminals' styles and compare them with those of Dürer and Fuseli. A detective will use a similar stylistic expertise to find the perpetrator. He will also add an intellectual element of ratiocination that is lacking in de Quincey's sadistic hedonism.

Le style, c'est le crime même

We have seen in the Introduction how Poe's faith in the powers of ratiocination facing riddles and mysteries launched the genre of the detective fiction; Dupin's "supputations" are the intellectual opposite of the gothic clichés and romantic necrophilia displayed in "The raven." Poe's equivalence of love and death is grafted onto the popular coupling of madness and genius, the productive interaction between feminine irrationalism and male intellect, all of which intertwined in a conflict between subjective chaos and an artificially imposed social order.[19]

Poe was a sentimentalist in love with melodrama. Like Freud, he wished to be rational about his own enjoyment, especially when real life suddenly provided an equivalent to his thesis that "The death of a beautiful woman is, unquestionably, the most poetical topic in the world." Poe recognized a productive scandal when he saw one, as he did in the newspapers of 1841, with the tantalizing *fait divers* provided by the demise of young and beautiful Mary Rogers in New York. Walter Benjamin summed it up thus:

> The original social content of the detective story was the obliteration of the individual's traces in the big-city crowd. Poe concerns himself with

---

[19] I am condensing analyses of Poe and Benjamin that I have developed in *Given: 1° Art, 2° Crime—Modernity, Murder and Mass Culture*. Brighton: Sussex Academic Press, 2007, pp. 101–10.

this motif in detail in "The mystery of Marie Roget," the most voluminous of his detective stories. At the same time this story is the prototype of the utilization of journalistic information in the solution of crimes. Poe's Detective, the Chevalier Dupin, works not with personal observation but with reports from the daily press. The critical analysis of these reports constitutes the rumour in the story.[20]

Dupin, like Poe, reads the local newspapers. Like Joyce, they relish mystery stories in almanacs, sensational pamphlets and the tidbits of the penny press. Hence the length and repetitiveness of this tale, which curiously makes it look like an authentic police inquiry—the irony being, of course, that the investigation fails. Dupin's attempt to find his way through a printed maze of reports fails. The conflicting accounts about a highly visible murder turn into a paper trail that he will superimpose on the map of the city. Needless to say, the amateur detective will not succeed in this quest.

A degree of hermeneutic undecidability is added by Poe when he transposes the *fait divers* to Paris. His Parisians cross the Seine in ferry-boats, the children who discover the young woman's clothes gather sassafras bark.[21] Baudelaire excuses these blunders and notes that Poe never pretended to have been in Paris—it is only an allegorical translation. In fact, the corpse of Mary Rogers, the "beautiful cigar girl," had been found in the Hudson river after having been apparently sexually molested in the summer of 1841. She becomes Marie, a Parisian *grisette*, in Poe's tale. Suspects had been named: Daniel Payne, who was to marry her, but committed suicide out of grief in October 1841. Another, John Morse, was apprehended but cleared himself when he proved that he had been on Staten Island at the time, and not in Hoboken where Mary's body was found.[22] It is under the pretence of rational calculations of probabilities that the opening pages of "The mystery of Marie Roget" make a bold assumption: the death of Marie was a murder: "The atrocity of this murder (for it was at once evident that murder had been committed), the youth and beauty of the victim, and, above all, her previous

[20] Walter Benjamin, *Charles Baudelaire: A Lyric Poet in the Era of High Capitalism*, Harry Zohn (trans.). London: Verso, 1997, p. 43.
[21] Edgar Allan Poe, *The Complete Tales and Poems of Edgar Allan Poe*. Harmondsworth: Penguin, p. 198, hereafter CTP; and Régis Messac, *Le "Detective Novel" et l'influence de la pensée scientifique*. Paris: Honoré champion, 1929, p. 349.
[22] See Amy Gilman Srebnick, *The Mysterious Death of Mary Rogers. Sex and Culture in Nineteenth-Century New York*. Oxford: Oxford University Press, 1995; and for a more novelistic treatment, Daniel Stashower, *The Beautiful Cigar Girl: Mary Rogers: Edgar Allan Poe and the Invention of Murder*. New York: Dutton, 2006.

notoriety, conspired to produce intense excitement in the minds of the sensitive Parisians." (CTP, p. 171)

The tale was serialized in three issues of *The Ladies' Companion* in 1842 and 1843. Poe assumed that there was a single murderer, a man with whom Mary had a date; after the deed, the murderer would have been killed by a local gang. The idea combined two hypotheses developed by the penny press that attributed the crime either to a jilted lover, or to a collective rape by a notorious gang of New York. Yet Poe was not sure that his conclusions were right. He delayed the publication of the third instalment, and revised once more the text for his collected *Tales* of 1845. Later revisions made room for another hypothesis, namely that Mary had not been gang-raped or murdered by a jealous suitor, but had died after an illegal abortion. The publication of his *Tales* in 1845 was contemporary with a new abortion law. Well-known abortionists like Madame Restell had been named in connection with the death of Mary. In November 1842, a certain Mrs Loss, who owned a roadside inn close to the spot where the corpse was found, made a deathbed confession connecting Mary's death to a botched abortion. She becomes Madame Deluc in Poe's story. This might not have been Mary's first abortion, since there had been a suspicious event one year earlier, when Mary's admirers had been "thrown into confusion" by her absence from the cigar shop. An official investigation had started when Mary reappeared "in good health, but with a somewhat saddened air" (CTP, p. 171), or with "a slight paleness" (CTP, p. 192). She resumed her work without giving any explanation, but soon after left her job to help her mother manage their boarding house. The place did not have a great reputation. Mary seems to have behaved just like Polly, the loose and pretty daughter of Mrs Mooney in Joyce's story "The boarding house". As in the *Dubliners* tale, she was enticing men of means, getting at least one promise of marriage.

Poe's "mystery" started with an unverified assumption: it was not an accident, it was not a suicide, therefore it was a murder. And like every riddle, it had to find a solution. Symptomatically, Poe wrote that there was "nothing *outré*" in this murder (CTP, p. 180), implying that the scene of Marie's death did not match the gruesome ferocity of the two French women's deaths, their throats slashed by razors wielded by an ape, one whose body was violently stuffed in a chimney, that he describes in "Murders in the Rue Morgue." Poe surmised that this enigma would be easy to solve. It turned out differently. The deciphering of a mass of press documents led to an intractable illegibility. Indeed, one might say of Mary's story that *sie lässt sich nicht lesen*. This is why Poe has to insert qualifications: "There might have been a wrong *here*, or, more possibly, an accident at Madame Deluc's." (CTP, p. 200) Later, he grants equal probability to competing theses: ". . . either a fatal accident under the roof of Madame Deluc or a murder perpetrated in the thicket of the Barrière du Roule." (CTP, pp. 203–4) However, these modifications do not prevent him from looking for clues of murder until the end; he still seems intent on finding the guilty parties, "tracing to its *dénouement* the mystery which enshrouds her." (CTP, p. 206)

Poe's programmatic delusion is evident when we look at the police reports that he quotes. They mention "brutal violence," but shrink from explicit details of a very intimate nature. Like the newspaper accounts, Poe's analysis is both precise and purposefully vague: "The dress immediately beneath the frock was of fine muslin; and from this a slip of eighteen inches wide had been torn entirely out—torn very evenly and with great care. It was found around her neck, fitting loosely, and secured with a hard knot." (CTP, p. 174) Since the "slip" was not used to strangle her to death, the clean cut in the inner garments is incompatible with a savage rape performed by inebriated gangsters or with the murderous act of a single man. Poe's sagacity is at fault here; one reason that has been adduced was that he was afraid of bringing suspicion to the plausible father of a first aborted foetus, his friend John Anderson. Besides, all the evidence mentioning screams of terror and a gang of mischief-makers came from "Madame Deluc" or her friends who had an interest in diverting suspicions from what took place in the house.

In the last pages of his tale, despite his misgivings, Poe sticks to the hypothesis of a collective murder. Yet, he adds that one should take into account "coincidences" and "important miscalculations." (CTP, p. 207) Poe appears as a duped Dupin since, far from solving the riddle, he has added to the chronicle of Marie's demise another layer of commentaries that are as full of holes as the rest. The contradictions between his praise of the sleuth's search for clues and his rationalist "induction" come to a head when the detective appears blinded by an excess of evidence. The "facts" in the case of Mary's death were, from the start, tainted by melodrama—all the elements were combined: a promiscuous and beautiful young woman whose corpse is washed ashore, and the disappearance of a local beauty whose entourage counted at least three persons who had a reason to murder her. The popular press did not wait for Poe to invent the "mystery" of Mary Roger's death. From the start, it was couched in the stuff of popular epics, dated gothicism and urban melodrama. Dupin's rationalism is the reverse of tired journalistic clichés. Poe's romantic exchange between love and death was grafted on a popular culture that loved murdered *grisettes*, mad geniuses, and pipe-smoking detectives. The real upshot of the young woman's murder was a tightening of the anti-abortion laws, and the creation of a more efficient police-force in New York.

If this interaction is parallel to a drift towards modernity, Poe's confusions and equivocations had to acquire a more modern sense of style. Style, being unleashed in the way described by Rancière, could not but bypass its boundaries or overcome artificial categories, among which figured the opposition between the rational and the sentimental. In this process, Poe had to be relayed by Lautréamont's systematic and cold-blooded delirium. Poe's sentimentalism verging on kitsch has to yield to a deliberate recycling of kitsch as a literary medium. This defines Isidore Ducasse's aesthetic program, one that successfully integrated stylistic tensions by heightening them. Ducasse chose popular melodrama as the literary site that he would occupy more as an army does with an enemy's land, with massive amounts of destruction and by inflicting as much pain as possible, than by gentle colonization. This was the literary site that he set out to warp and pervert by lacing the positivism of the rationalist tradition with excessive gothic features. He exaggerated the link between melodrama, crime and *fait divers*. Poe was one of his choice models, although he more often pillaged Ponson du Terrail's endless *feuilletons*. His decision to copy and invert popular crime stories in the *Songs of Maldoror* was parallel to what he did in "Poésies": this sequence of quotes from moralists like Pascal and Vauvenargues was made up of sentences whose meaning he inverted and negated. Lautréamont, a figure of excess, would lead to Surrealism; Breton and his friends relished his concerted outrage against good taste, stylistic distinction, morality and aesthetics.

Ducasse specialized in the *outré* style that he absorbed from the *feuilletons*; he had read Poe's "The mystery of Marie Roget" in Baudelaire's translation. This pushed him to reach a climax of gratuitous horror in his prose poem. This is in the third book of the *Songs of Maldoror*.[23] This passage shocked even Water Benjamin. For Benjamin, Lautréamont was one of the three anarchists (the other two are Dostoevsky and Rimbaud) who detonated literary bombs all at the same time. They transformed the Romantic praise of crime and evil into political weapons. Here, we meet a crazy old woman dancing along the road. A stranger passes, she pulls out a roll of paper on which she has consigned the story of her life. She reads the account of her daughter's murder. The stranger then reads the text, which describes how the innocent little girl has been violently raped by Maldoror. This done, Maldoror commands his dog to bite her to death. Disobeying the order, the bulldog imitates his master and rapes the girl. She is still alive; Maldoror unleashes his devastating furor, and digs his knife into the child's vagina. The scene turns nightmarish: "From the widened hole he pulls out, one after one, the inner organs; the guts, the lungs, the liver and at last the heart itself are torn from

---

[23] Comte de Lautréamont (Isidore Ducasse), *Maldoror and Poems*, Paul Knight (trans.). London: Penguin, 1978.

their foundations and dragged through the hideous hole into the light of day. The sacrificer notices that the young girl, a gutted chicken, has long been dead."[24] The old woman who had narrated this adds that the maniac rapist must have been insane, and thus forgives him. The stranger faints, then comes to: he was none other than Maldoror himself, who had returned to the scene of his crime, although he had forgotten about it. Ducasse adds sarcastically: "how habit dulls the memory!" The paroxystic passage ends quietly, a strange quiver sends up the mock pastoral tone of the beginning. A quasi-Yeatsian tone of elegiac evocation suggests the deepening shades that will veil, quite conveniently, the gruesome transgression.

Songs of Maldoror exploits popular genres like *feuilletons*, narrating the exploits of invincible criminals, adding cheap gore in the tradition of the grand-guignol plays, which attracted the crowds along the "grands boulevards" of Paris (the meticulously documented site of the adventures of Maldoror) in which torrents of fake blood would spout at the least provocation. The mixture of melodrama and inflated rhetoric undermines itself and produces a dark poetry of pulp gothic. This verbal pop art *avant la lettre* bridges the gap between a debased mass culture and a new sensibility attuned to linguistic excess, jarring metaphors and the parody of conventional morality. Maldoror revisits English gothic tales and French *romans noirs*, adding grotesque twists that mimic convulsive hysteria in language. At the same time, he makes fun of Romantic aspirations to a "recollection in tranquility" by means of an immersion in bountiful Nature. Since Nature means crime, as Sade and Baudelaire knew it, there is no peace to expect from it. Like Rimbaud, Ducasse has read Poe and Baudelaire and absorbed the distilled spirit of Sade. Benjamin writes, commenting on Baudelaire's sadism:

> Nature, according to Baudelaire, knows this one luxury: crime. Thus the significance of the artificial. Perhaps we may draw on this thought for the interpretation of the idea that children stand nearest to original sin. Is it because, exuberant by nature, they cannot get out of harm's way? At bottom, Baudelaire is thinking of parricide.[25]

Ducasse, a systematic literary parricide, managed to dispatch his immediate predecessors, Baudelaire and Poe above all, by creating a poetic style that opened new doors of perception for André Breton and the Surrealists. The

---

[24] Lautréamont, see footnote 23, pp. 129–30.
[25] Walter Benjamin, *The Arcades Project*, Howard Eiland and K. McLau. Cambridge: Harvard University Press, 1999, p. 240.

most direct forms of address accompany the most bizarre images clamping together incompatible levels of style. This new hybrid style provides an equivalent of the Parisian arcades sung by Aragon and memorialized by Benjamin: they are outmoded, sooner or later condemned, already ruined from within. The remnants of another age, they contain the seeds of the future, announce new forms of change and exchange. Benjamin, who noted "The arcades as milieu of Lautréamont,"[26] knew that Isidore Ducasse had first lived near Passage Vivienne and died nearby, in another passage at 7 rue du Faubourg, Montmartre.

What is new in Ducasse's writing is that he explicitly quotes popular genres, reclaims their debased styles and cheap sensationalism for serious poetry while making a show of pithy condensation: "In a tale of this sort . . . there is no occasion for diluting in a godet the shellac of four hundred banal pages. What can be said in half-a-dozen pages must be said, and then, silence."[27] Like Joyce's *Ulysses*, Lautréamont's poem condenses countless interminable dime novels. By giving birth to such a monstrously magnificent abortion of an older literature, Ducasse and Joyce accomplished what Duchamp and Breton were aiming at, the reconciliation of high modernism with popular culture.

Samuel Beckett condensed the issue I have been grappling with in a pithy formula: "Mr. Joyce does not take birth for granted, as Vico seems to have done."[28] Admittedly, Beckett is discussing *Finnegans Wake* and not *Ulysses*; yet I believe that this insight applies to Joyce's entire *oeuvre*. At least since the *Portrait*, we have learned to superimpose the notion of a developing style with the organic account of the embryonic development of a soul. "The soul is born," he said vaguely, "first in those moments I told you of. It has a slow and dark birth, more mysterious than the birth of the body."[29] Indeed, Joyce doesn't take birth for granted—this is how he puts a distance between his writing and the biological metaphors that it appeals to. Not to take birth for granted means that one will not hold it as sacred, and perhaps, not even as "natural." Joyce was neither an eighteenth-century physiocrat nor a Catholic pro-life supporter. His ambition was to examine critically the conditions of possibility of the gift implied in the verb "granted." Then and only then can one "take" something or nothing out of the process of writing.

---

[26] Benjamin, see footnote 26, p. 847.

[27] Lautréamont, see footnote 23, p. 240. Translation modified.

[28] Samuel Beckett, "Dante . . . Bruno . . . Vico . . . Joyce," in *Our Exagmination Round his Factification for Incamination of Work in Progress*. London: Faber, 1972, p. 8.

[29] James Joyce, *A Portrait of the Artist as a Young Man*. New York: Viking Critical Library, 1968, p. 203.

Beckett was evidently the heir of Joyce's and Poe's meanderings through style considered as crime and destruction. This is why he famously decided to write in French in order to write "without style." He made that fateful decision in the fifties, just at the time when Roland Barthes was advocating the *Nouveau Roman* as a "blank" writing. Its pure writing would be writing without literature and without style. He made his position very clear in *Writing Degree Zero* (1953), a book with which Rancière's *Mute Speech* is often in dialogue. More recently, Ben Hutchinson has investigated the conflicted links between the main modernist writers and the concept of style in his brilliant *Modernism and Style*.[30] I can only pay homage to his magnificent synthesis. Among all the writers he examines in his survey of all those who identified style with crime, none has gone further than Beckett in his wish to "worsen" language so as to pave the way for a new subjectivity, capable of resisting in spite of all. This programme had been explained quite early by a minor character in his first play, *Eleutheria*. The speaker is Doctor Piouk, who has found a solution to solve the problems of the human species.

> Dr. Piouk: I would ban reproduction. I would perfect the condom and other devices and bring them into general use. I would establish teams of abortionists, controlled by the State. I would apply the death penalty to any woman guilty of giving birth. I would drown all newborn babies. I would militate in favour of homosexuality and would myself give the example. And to speed things up, I would encourage recourse to euthanasia by all possible means, although I would not make it obligatory. Those are only the broad outlines.[31]

No doubt, listening to this, we can only assert, as Madame Krap does in her reply: "I was born too early."[32] We too were born too early, yet the future remains open . . .

---

[30] Ben Hutchison, *Modernism and Style*. New York: Palgrave Macmillan, 2011.
[31] Samuel Beckett, *Eleutheria*, Barbara Wright (trans.). London: Faber, 1996, pp. 44–5.
[32] Beckett, see footnote 32, p. 45.

9

Universalism and its Limits
The reasons of the absurd

I have referred several times to Beckett's work in these pages, whether discussed by Badiou or Adorno, or in dialogue with Joyce and Kafka. He came to preeminence in the 1950s under the banner of the theater of the absurd. My focus in this chapter will be what has been called "the literature of the absurd," a term that has fallen out of fashion, and rightly it seems, but that can be read differently in the context of a theoretical horizon. In order to do this, we need to take the issues of a globalized theory into account. I would like to take a fresh look at the "reasons" of the "absurd" via authors like Camus, Beckett, and Kafka, in an effort at combining theoretical and literary approaches. My understanding of what can be called the "paradox of the universal"[1] will be by way of reopening critical debates concerning those authors. I will start by exploring an older controversy concerning Kafka's universal appeal, a discussion that is almost forgotten, yet full of meaning for today's concerns about globalization, particularism and the questioning of universalism.

Kafka between Greenberg and Leavis

The fierce debate opposed the American art critic Clement Greenberg, who was then the main exponent of modernism as Abstract Expressionism, and the British critic and Cambridge Professor, F. R. Leavis. Their discussion began in the Spring of 1955. Greenberg had translated a few short stories by Kafka, such as "Josephine," for a co-edited volume called *Parables*, published in 1947. In 1955, Greenberg published "The Jewishness of Franz Kafka: some sources of his particular vision," in which he strongly stated that Kafka's vision could not be dissociated from his being Jewish. For Greenberg, Kafka's

---

[1] I am indebted to the analyses of Monique David-Ménard about Kant in this respect. See her book *Les Constructions de l'Universel: Psychanalyse, Philosophie*. Paris: Presses Universitaires de France, 2009; and the excellent collection edited by Jelica Sumic, *Universel, Singulier, Sujet*. Paris: Editions Kimé, 2000.

main tradition derived from the Halacha, even if he, as an emancipated and enlightened Jew living in Prague, apparently did not believe in the promise of a Messiah. If the meaning of his texts could not be exhausted by Jewish mysticism, at any rate the form itself was Jewish. As in the Halacha, Kafka's tales and parables revolve around the interpretation of the law, and they do so "with a patient, if selective, circumstantiality that belongs more to description and logical exposition than to narrative."[2] Greenberg developed this as follows:

> This is why, in my opinion, his shorter efforts are generally more successful than his novels or extended short stories like "The metamorphosis." ... Beyond a certain point, the peculiarly stealthy, gradual movement in time and perception that Kafka is able to achieve tends to bore the reader—whose patience is further taxed by the insufficient promise of a resolution. ... States of being are what are conclusive here, and these for Kafka can have no beginnings or endings, only middles. What is more, these exclude moral issues, and hence no moral choices are made in Kafka's fiction. To the extent that this fiction succeeds, it refutes the assumption of many of the most serious critics of our day—F. R. Leavis is notably one of them—that the value of a work of literary art depends ultimately on the depth to which it explores moral difficulties.
>
> (CEII, p. 208)

Beyond the revealing admission that he found Kafka's novels boring, Greenberg was challenging Leavis's ethical type of criticism. This elicited a counter-attack from the British critic who reiterated his idea that good literature engages with ethical issues: Kafka was no exception. Leavis objected to the fact that Greenberg stressed the limitations of Kafka as a creative writer (CEII, p. 208). Was it that Greenberg was stating that the meaning of Kafka's works was opaque for readers not familiar with Jewish culture? Leavis was clearly on the side of the universal. He explained that, being neither Jewish nor Catholic, he felt that he could sense Kafka's greatness just as he could see the point of a Catholic novel by Graham Greene. For him, Kafka transcended both his local neurosis (which was doubted by Greenberg) and the Jewish tradition, a tradition that had the disadvantage of remaining a "particularist" or even a "non-Western" one (the latter phrase quoted Greenberg's terms).

---

[2] Clement Greenberg, "The Jewishness of Franz Kafka: some sources of his particular vision," *The Collected Essays, Affirmations and Refusals, 1950–1956*, John O'Brian (ed.). Chicago: Chicago University Press, 1993, p. 208, subsequently abbreviated as CE.

Greenberg counter-attacked by highlighting Kafka's humor, which he saw as a way of transcending his fragmentariness and his "imprisonment" in a tradition. Kafka's greatness appeared to him more in his mannerisms than in grand projects, schemes that often remained abortive. Stories like "Josephine," "Investigations of a dog," or "Hunter Gracchus" would give the full measure of Kafka's genius. There should be, he argued, a dialectical relationship between universal appeal and the specific conditions of production:

> What I cannot see at all is why the resemblances I find between the method of Kafka's imagination and Halachic logic should have any more *special*—that is, exclusive—an interest for "those familiar with Jewish culture and tradition" than Shakespeare's echoes of Montaigne have for experts in sixteenth-century French literature, or the cosmological scheme of the *Divine Comedy* has for Catholic medievalists. I hoped I was explaining the cause of an effect in Kafka's writings that those unacquainted with Jewish tradition feel as much as I do—who am not, in my ignorance of Hebrew and many other things, *that* familiar with Jewish tradition anyhow. The explanation of the cause was not intended to enhance one's opinion of the effect, nor was the Jewishness of Kafka's art expected to recommend it in any way that it could not recommend itself at first hand to any reader, Gentile or Jew.
>
> (CEII, pp. 212–13)

Greenberg had touched a nerve. A longer reply followed, in which Leavis insisted on a discrepancy between Greenberg's evaluation of Kafka and his account of the work (CEII, p. 213). Humor could not suffice to offset the absence of moral issues. Greenberg denied that our discriminations about art and literature have no bearing on "our future personal living," because he had fallen into the trap of aestheticism. This triggered a reply that marked the end of the exchange. Greenberg agreed that Leavis was right: he (Greenberg) rejected any form of moralism and preferred aestheticism to moralism. "I do hold with art for art's sake. ... If I agreed with Dr. Leavis, I would have to conclude that art was a substitute for life and experience." (CEII, p. 216) Greenberg flaunted a Kantian aestheticism. This is how the last letter ends—it has a lot to say about the "paradox of the universal."

> In his *Critique of Aesthetic Judgment* Kant demonstrated that one cannot prove an aesthetic judgment in discourse. Let Dr. Leavis see whether he can, in practice or theory, refute Kant's arguments. For what he [NB: Kant] is claiming in effect is that one can so adequately exhibit in *words* one's grounds for an aesthetic judgment that agreement with it is

compelled by the rules of evidence and logic. Kant holds that one can appeal only to the other person's *taste* as exercised through experience of the work of art under discussion.

. . . Morality is built into the mind, and works of art have to respect the limitations that morality imposes on fancied action; otherwise the reader's or observer's interest cannot be held, whether in high- or lowbrow literature. But this does not mean that we have to learn from literature in order to enjoy it properly, or that those who do not learn from it are in no position to judge it. Art, in my view, explains to us what we already feel, but it does not do so discursively or rationally; rather it acts out an explanation in the sense of working on our feelings at a remove sufficient to protect us from the consequences of the decisions made by our feelings in response to the work of art.

(CEII, p. 216)

The reference to Kant functioned as an absolute weapon (Greenberg would use it later to define modernism as such) and was enough to silence Leavis. Greenberg's catharsis left him no wiser than before, but he had made his point. The chain of reasons leads from a stylistic preference for Kafka's shorter texts to a general theory that lays down the laws of art and finds in Kant's third Critique a way of connecting modernism and theory. Curiously, Greenberg uses Kant to attack a universalist concept of literature, which is Leavis's position, a universalism that has to be backed up by the ethical function attributed to literature. Kafka's appeal is universal, he helps us make sense of the "human condition" and this understanding will in its turn make us better people. Literature contains "universals of fantasy" as Giambattista Vico would have it, thanks to which we imaginatively merge with other points of view. In the name of a postulated empathy with the other points of view (with people whose religion I do not share, for instance) the experience of reading literature offers tools for living better. Ethics—an Ethics of the Other, to be sure—remain as the *telos* and horizon of literary criticism, which is a position that has been taken more recently by deconstructive critics like Derek Attridge.

On the other hand, Greenberg insists on a Jewish particularism; it is a welcome limitation, and such a limitation will later echo with the idea that modernism is fundamentally defined by its limitations; indeed, these limitations, once accepted and understood can then be successfully transformed into aesthetic programs. Here, the limitations of Kafka's thought and origins send us back to a question of the judgments needed by literature. They should not be confused with aesthetic judgments since there is a specificity to aesthetic judgments, as Kant had shown in his third Critique.

We have accordingly moved from a Jewish reading of Kafka to a Kantian appreciation of the function of judgments (not *a priori* but reflexive in this case) about art. When you experience the beauty and the depth of Kafka's writings, you learn about yourself and the judgments you are bound to make when appreciating works of art.

Greenberg does not believe in the ethical power of Kafka's works, but he insists upon their beauty and aesthetic value. Kafka's works are powerful precisely because they skip the ethical mode. This they do by hesitating between the aesthetic and the religious, to use Kierkegaard's useful categories. The story aptly called "The judgment" would be a case in point. It presents a son condemned to death by his father for no other reason than perhaps having wished to supplant him in his role as a businessman. In spite of the fact that the son professes to love his father dearly, he is torn on the eve of an engagement that he has to disclose the news to his best friend, who happens to live in Russia. In deploying the convoluted dynamics of "judging" as a verdict invariably leading to a "death sentence," Kafka makes us become aware of how we still react to authority as "sons." Since we are always already caught up in Oedipal patterns of subversive and punishable desires, love for our parents is ambivalent, and love has to make room for hate, while the apparently unexpected condemnation can then be re-interpreted as the only logical resolution. This logical resolution—so effective when it allowed Kafka to dramatize his own inability to marry—is also, of course, a logical absurdity.

Camus, Kafka, and the aphoristic tradition

This is the point where I will want to turn to Albert Camus's famous analysis of Kafka in terms of the absurd. Here Camus is talking about *The Trial*.

By an odd but obvious paradox, the more extraordinary the character's adventures are, the more noticeable will be the naturalness of the story: it is in proportion to the divergence we feel between the strangeness of a man's life and the simplicity with which that man accepts it. It seems that this naturalness is Kafka's. And, precisely, one is well aware what *The Trial* means. People have spoken of an image of the human condition. To be sure. Yet it is both simpler and more complex. I mean that the significance of the novel is more particular and more personal to Kafka. To a certain degree, he is the one who does the talking, even though it is to us he confesses. He lives and he is condemned. He learns this on the first pages of the novel he is pursuing in this world, and if he tries to cope with this, he nonetheless does so without surprise. He will never show sufficient astonishment at his lack of astonishment. It is by such contradictions that the first signs of the absurd world are recognized. The mind projects into the concrete its spiritual tragedy. And it can do so solely by means of a perpetual paradox which confers on colors the power to express the void and on daily gestures the strength to translate eternal ambitions.[3]

Camus's main point in this vibrant and inspired reading (it was the only section of his book that was censored by the Vichy regime because it was about a Jewish writer when Camus asked for permission to print the essay in 1942; the Kafka analysis was completed in 1938[4]) that Kafka's constant strategy is to express "tragedy by the everyday and the absurd by the logical." (p. 127) Having posited the absurd as the central core of Kafka's works, Camus sees its universality in a new paradox, which apparently limits the scope of the absurd in view of the alleged universality of Kafka's meaning:

His work is universal (a really absurd work is not universal), to the extent to which it represents the emotionally moving face of man fleeing humanity, deriving from his contradictions reasons for believing, reasons for hoping from his fecund despairs, and calling life his terrifying apprenticeship in death. It is universal because its inspiration is religious. As in all religions, man is freed of the weight of his own life. But if I know that, if I can even admire it, I also know that I am not seeking what is universal, but what is true. The two may not coincide.

(p. 136)

I will want to test this welter of contradictions and paradoxes by looking at a few of Kafka's fragments—often thought to have condensed his most explicit views about faith, revelation, salvation, sin, and "the human condition." The very title given by Max Brod outlines such a quasi-religious program: "Considerations on sin, suffering, hope and the true path."

The view of Kafka as an absurdist author of parables was shared by Clement Greenberg, who had translated a few stories like "The building of the temple," "The sirens", "Couriers" and "Josephine" for *Parables and Paradoxes*. As we have seen, Greenberg believed that Kafka's shorter forms were more pregnant with meaning and offered a sort of Jewish revelation. Kafka's "aphorisms," in Richard Gray's thesis, mediate between the universal

---

[3]   Albert Camus, *The Myth of Sisyphus: Appendix, "Hope and the Absurd in the Work of Franz Kafka,"* Justin O' Brien (trans.). New York: Random House, 1991, pp. 125–6, translation modified.

[4]   See Albert Camus, *Essais*. Paris: Pléiade: Gallimard, 1965, Note on p. 1414.

and the particular.[5] These short fragments that are so enigmatic, belong to a genre that is often thought of as either "classical" (with the French moralists as a model) or "Romantic" (with the German Romantics) but may have serious claims to being called modernist. Kafka's aphorisms are akin to the "philosophemes" that we have already encountered, those pithy phrases full of meaning: tags, mottos and apophthegms that can be mentioned independently of their original context. (And this is a Kafkaian issue, with texts that come from the journals, which are then inserted in longer narratives to be, at times, detached again.) These statements are cryptic, dense, often paradoxical when not pure oxymorons.[6] Their characteristics include a notable syntactic compression,[7] a high dependence on German's amphibologies, which is what renders translation often impossible. This is exemplified by aphorism 46 in *Betrachtungen*: "'The word *sein* means two things in German: 'being' and 'belonging-to-him.'"[8] (*Das Wort "sein" bedeutet im Deutschen beides: Dasein und Ihm-gehören.*)

We note that "*Ihm*" in "*Ihm-gehören*" is capitalized, which may suggest God, or a higher person. What does this mean? Where did Kafka want to go with this? The obvious semantic amphibology (*sein* as the possessive pronoun "his" which doubles as the noun or verb for "to be" and "being") hides a deeper destabilization of ontology. This may be taken as Kafka's sense of ontological difference. My being is already a belonging. This has as foundational an impact as when Heidegger differentiates between *Sein* as capitalized "Being" and *Seiendes* as the "being" (lower case "b") of *Dasein* as existence. The tantalizing semantic ambiguity of these aphorisms will trigger proliferating commentaries. They lead into several directions at once and give the sense of inexhaustible riches in the expression. Here, too, ontology and the idioms of a given language are pitted against each other, placed at the extreme poles of a conceptual arc.

Kafka drafted the collections known as "He" (dating from Fall–Winter 1917 and 1918), and the Zürau aphorisms in 1920, at a moment when he had apparently renounced completing his novels. Thanks to an inbuilt logic of paradox, each aphorism leads to its own undoing. They are often to be seen as

---

[5] Richard T. Gray, *Constructive Destruction: Kafka's Aphorism, Literary Tradition and Literary Transformation*. Tübingen: Niemeyer, 1987. This is the title of Chapter 6, p. 264.

[6] See Mardy Grothe, *Oxymoronica: Paradoxical Wit and Wisdom from History's Greatest Wordsmiths*. New York: Harper, 2004. Kafka is quoted once: "Don't despair, not even over the fact that you don't despair." (p. 164)

[7] See my previous analysis, p. 151.

[8] Franz Kafka, "The collected aphorisms," in *The Great Wall of China and Other Short Works*, Malcolm Pasley (ed.). Harmondsworth: Penguin, 1991, p. 86. Hereafter abbreviated as GWC.

questions without an answer, or answers without a question. Or the question has been posed by another text. For instance, let us take the very first aphorism: "The true way is along a tight-rope, which is stretched aloft but just above the ground. It seems designed more to trip one than to be walked along." (GWC, p. 79) (*Der wahre Weg geht über ein Seil, das nicht in der Höhe gespannt ist, sondern knapp über dem Boden. Es scheint mehr bestimmt stolpern zu machen, als begangen zu werden.*) This fragment embodies the deconstructive energy of the Kafkaian aphorism. Kafka imagines a pure truth as an "above" reality and then deconstructs it. He first evokes the image of an ideal, lofty truth suspended in the air. The second stage inverts the image of a rope suspended above, the rope is brought just over the ground. Finally, the tightrope turns into a tripwire so as to juxtapose the image of a true path with its inverted parallel. The clear and visible transcendence of truth initially invoked is destroyed through negation, inversion and chiastic recursion.

But where does this trope come from? As Peter Sloterdijk has argued, the aphorism only makes sense if we understand it as Kafka's ironical response to Nietzsche's axiom from *Thus Spake Zarathustra* that "man is a rope over the abyss." This is in the "Prologue" to the book, when Zarathustra gives his first discourses. He asserts: "Man is a rope, fastened between animal and Superman—a rope over an abyss." (p. 43) (*Der Mensch ist ein Seil, geknüpft zwischen Tier und Übermensch,—ein Seil ueber einem Abgrunde.*) Even before he had expressed this idea, the crowd had called him a "tight-rope walker" (*Seiltänzer*, p. 43, "Prologue", section 3) and we do meet a real tight-rope walker in section 6. He walks between two towers in the village, but when he is in the middle, the devil appears, overtakes the first man, jumps over him and the tight-rope walker falls to his death. As the dying man sees Zarathustra kneeling next to him, he says that he knew the devil would trip him. Zarathustra refuses to pity him and mocks his belief in god or the devil.[9]

For Peter Sloterdijk, this marks a general shift from asceticism to acrobatics in European thought.[10] The dying tight-rope walker prefigures the dying "Hunger artist" of the story with the same name. Kafka manages to condense a tension already present in Nietzsche. After all, Zarathustra could take the acrobat as a disciple, even if a clumsy follower; but no, he berates the dying

[9]   Friedrich Nietzsche, *Thus Spake Zarathustra*, R. J. Hollingdale (trans.). Harmondsworth: Penguin, 1969, p. 48.

[10] Peter Sloterdijk, "The last hunger artist," in *You Must Change Your Life*, Wieland Hoban (trans.). Cambridge: Polity Press, 2013, p. 64.

man without any sympathy. This gives a more ominous overtone to the sentence he had previously uttered: "What is great in man is that he is a bridge and not a goal; what can be loved in man is that he is a *going-across* and a *down-going*." (p. 44) (... *ein* Übergang *und ein* Untergang *ist* ...)

Thus we see that if the aphorisms stage a tension between the particular and the universal, this tension should generate "dialectical images" (to quote Walter Benjamin). Their implied dialogism (here, between Nietzsche and Kafka, between Zarathustra and the acrobat, between rise and fall, etc.) prevents them from deploying a single thesis. Thus the apodictic structure of statements that sound as necessarily true, their authoritative aspects disguise more malleable and proliferating meanings. Fittingly, the aphorism's resistance to a single definition parallels the form itself, since it presents a set of cryptic, fragmented hermeneutical puzzles to be unwound. Yet this does not explain what makes an aphorism distinctly "Kafkaian." These fragments can be read as compressed fictions presenting a subject who struggles to balance language and reality. They point to a discrepancy between linguistic capabilities and the shock of a real perceived as foreign, opaque, threatening. A Kafkaian aphorism would be the shortest narrative form capable of capturing the interaction—at times quite aggressive—of Self and Other, while noting that the point of view is more often than not that of the Other.

The aphorisms can be serious, enigmatic, and even grotesque. There is often a weird sense of humor. They are bound together by a deconstructive dialectic that Richard Gray calls "constructive destruction" and Stanley Corngold "chiastic recursion." Each new term, consisting of elements syntactically and conceptually parallel to those of a previous term, arises by means of an inversion of these elements. Patterns of "chiastic recursion" construct parallel lines of inverted meaning within each aphorism, folding the text back on itself.

Arguing against Max Brod's thesis of a religious Kafka, Gray and Corngold think that Kafka's aphorisms move away from revelation. They pose hermeneutical puzzles, are shrouded in a willed obscurity attained in the name of a blinding truth. Groping for my "way," I will negotiate the paradoxes of Kafka's "Considerations" by focusing on the paradigm of movement.

14 If you were walking across a plain, had every intention of advancing and still went backwards, then it would be a desperate matter; but since you are clambering up a steep slope, about as steep as you yourself are when seen from below, your backward movement can only be caused by the nature of the ground, and you need not despair.

(GWC, 81)

15 Like a path in autumn: scarcely has it been swept clear when it is once more covered with leaves.

(GWC, p. 81)

18 If it had been possible to build the Tower of Babel without climbing up, it would have been permitted.

(GWC, p. 82)

21 As firmly as the hand grips the stone. But it grips it firmly only to fling it away the further. But the way leads into those distances too.

(GWC, p. 82)

26 (*second half*) There is a goal, but no way; what we call a way is hesitation.

(GWC, p. 83)

38 There was one who was astonished how easily he moved along the road of eternity; the fact is that he was racing along it downhill.

(GWC, p. 85)

76 This feeling: "Here I will not anchor," and instantly to feel the billowing uplifting swell around one.

(GWC, p. 91)

Here are two famous examples: # 87 "A belief like a guillotine, just as heavy, just as light." (GWC, p. 94) and # 93 "Never again psychology!" (GWC, p. 95) Why shouldn't there be any psychology? Because it indulges itself via easy transference projections, endless explorations of affective ambivalence, in short, because it presents a "bad infinite" and is thus too easy. It leads to an excess of comprehension or empathy. "Nausea after too much psychology. If someone has good legs and is admitted to psychology, he can, in a short time and in any zigzag he likes, cover distances such as he cannot cover in any other field. One's eyes overbrim at the sight."[11] Is this nausea or ecstasy? Excess brought about by psychology has to be reduced by a writing of the outside. Truth will be opposed to the field of psychological masks and disguises, fictions and lies about oneself and the others.

---

[11] Franz Kafka, *The Blue Octavo Notebooks*. Boston: Exact Change, p. 79.

103 You can hold yourself back from the sufferings of the world, that is something you are free to do and it accords with your nature, but perhaps this very holding back is the one suffering that you could avoid.

(GWC, p. 97)

109 (*second half*) It is not necessary that you leave the house. Remain at your table and listen. Do not even listen, only wait. Do not even wait, be wholly still and alone. The world will present itself to you for its unmasking, it can do no other, in ecstasy it will writhe at your feet.

(GWC, p. 98)

Thus, for Kafka, writing is capable of providing an inner progression or movement. Writing "moves" you, you can remain still, and read. Thus the world unmasks itself—here is the promise of a *jouissance* of the Other.

The abysmal aura of a Truth that will be withheld shines throughout. Given Kafka's fixation with lies and deception, which runs throughout the Aphorisms, revelation is inherently inaccessible although not impossible in theory. Kafka's texts circle around the absence of an expected revelation. In *The Castle* and *The Trial*, Kafka constructs an intricate labyrinth of relationships and possibilities, tracing the futile and seemingly endless journeys of the protagonists. *The Castle* concludes mid-sentence, lost in a tangle of narrative possibilities. *The Trial* ends with Josef K.'s humiliating death. K.'s death is an anti-revelation by removing any possibility of illumination or final understanding. It only obfuscates the plot further. The aphorisms correspond to a desire to reach the truth quickly and immediately— they derive from what Hermann Broch called the "impatience of knowledge," yet they do not produce this vision. Even when they thematize explicitly this impatience, the aphorisms debunk it:

There are two cardinal human sins from which all others derive: impatience and indolence. Because of impatience they were expelled from Paradise, because of indolence they do not return. But perhaps there is only one cardinal sin: impatience. Because of impatience they were expelled, because of impatience they do not return.

(# 3, GWC, p. 79)

Thus, driven by "impatience," Kafkaian aphorisms explore the metaphorical division between the material world and a higher state of being while challenging this barrier in its impossibility. It does not matter that the ground is limited to where the subject can stand: (# 24) "What it means to grasp the good fortune that the ground on which you stand cannot be greater than what is covered by your two feet." (GWC, p. 82) The tension between the local and the eternal, the trivial and the universal is central. Kafka's dialectical moves imply contrapuntal relationships in the flow from universal to trivial. The effect is one of deconstruction or demystification rather than revelation, yet the concept of Truth is not destroyed, on the contrary. Truth is a decentering tool, a hole in discourse. Yet this Truth devours all the rest, and ends up destroying both the world and the subject. The logical impossibilities deployed in Kafka's aphorisms evoke a principle of verticality that is denied, lost, obfuscated. The hope that a vision of truth will bypass the obscure labyrinths of *The Trial* and *The Castle* is always frustrated. The aphoristic style achieves a shortcut, but then literally puts an end to the narrative, and thus undercuts itself. Kafka jumps from an ethics of language to a perception of the Law as such. Singularity is not abolished but seen from the outside. The writing becomes the writing of the Real in so far as the writer has to side with the world and not with his subjectivity.

Three aphorisms converge as to the idea of a triumph of the world against the subject, who subsists only as an exception, an excluded center of values:

52 "In the struggle between yourself and the world, second the world.

(GWC, p. 87)

53 One must not cheat anyone, not even the world of its triumph.

(GWC, p. 87)

He has discovered the Archimedean principle, but he has turned it to account against himself; evidently it was only on this condition that he was permitted to discover it.

("He," GWC, p. 105)

Yet Kafka still needs the framework of messianic promise, Kierkegaard's or Pascal's overcoming of the ethical by the religious. It is not the Text but the Messiah who can embody the principle of the "to come"—it will come, as we know, not on the last day but on the day after the last day . . . "The Messiah will come only when he is no longer necessary; he will come only on the day after his arrival; he will come, not on the last day, but on the very last day."[12] This is why Kafka prefers to lose and never finishes the totalizing text. In a sense, he paves the way for Beckett's poetics of impotence and deprivation. Yet, all this

---

[12] Franz Kafka, *Basic Kafka*. Upper Saddle River: Prentice-Hall, p. 182.

presupposes a hermeneutic circle, a circle that has to be run through over and over again, in an endless mechanism best illustrated by the text "On parables." Here is how it ends, in the version proposed by Muir in 1947:

> Concerning this a man once said: "Why such reluctance? If you only followed the parables you yourselves would become parables and with that rid yourself of all your daily care."
> Another said: "I bet that is also a parable."
> The first said: "You have won."
> The second said: "But unfortunately only in parable."
> The first said: "No, in reality: in parable you have lost."[13]

The first speaker addresses the utopia of pure aestheticism, and if one agrees that the only life worth living is that of literature (as Proust suggests) then, indeed, one should be able to live happily ever after, since life will always be inferior to fiction. Yet, if the parables' true meaning yields simply a tautology, like the idea "that the inconceivable is inconceivable," then this fictional world seems too remote, too far from the need to battle every day with life's intractable concerns and dramas. Thus the second speaker is right to tell the first that he has only added one level of fiction to the problem and has not progressed toward the truth. The first one is obliged to concede that he has been beaten. But when the second speaker believes that he has won, the first one has to qualify the other's victory: he has won in reality and lost in parable, which means that he may have won a space for reality as distinct from fiction, but by doing this he has relegated the world of fiction to an "other" world marked by lies and alienation. He will be safer in his everyday life but will have lost the possibility of consolation in the name of literature—hence his life, deprived of the imagination, will be all the poorer ... Corngold wittily remarked that one can always add: "I bet that is also a parable ..."[14] The movement of what Sartre would call a "whirligig" (a *tourniquet*, in his book on Jean Genet) or what Barthes had called "bathmology" (the "science of degrees") is unstoppable. We can also quote Kafka's last diary entry: "Every word, twisted in the hands of the spirits—this twist of the hand is their characteristic gesture—becomes a spear turned against the speaker. Most especially a remark like this. And so on *ad infinitum*."[15] More enigmatically

---

[13] Franz Kafka, *Parables and Paradoxes*. New York, Schocken, 1961, p. 11.

[14] Stanley Corngold, "Kafka's later stories and aphorisms," in *The Cambridge Companion to Kafka*, Julian Preece (ed.). Cambridge: Cambridge University Press, 2002, p. 105.

[15] Corngold, see footnote 14, p. 106.

perhaps, we have the twisted logic of aphorism 29: "The beast wrests the whip from the master and whips itself in order to become master, not knowing that this is only a fantasy produced by a new knot in the master's whip-lash." (GWC, p. 83) Where can one find a better commentary on the Hegelian dialectics of the master and the slave?

From Camus's Kafka to Derrida's "Stranger"

Camus had also linked Kafka and Nietzsche in his 1938 essay: "... truly hopeless thought just happens to be defined by the opposite criteria ... the tragic work might be the work that, after all future hope is exiled, describes the life of a happy man." (p. 137) This explains the famous ending of the *Myth of Sisyphus:* "We have to imagine Sisyphus a happy man." In the essay on Kafka, he goes on:

> The more exciting life is, the more absurd is the idea of losing it. This is perhaps the secret of that proud aridity felt in Nietzsche's work. In this connection, Nietzsche appears to be the only artist to have derived the extreme consequences of an aesthetic of the Absurd, inasmuch his final message lies in a sterile and conquering lucidity and an obstinate negation of any supernatural consolation.
>
> (p. 137)

Thus Meursault appears similarly Nietzschean, but more as a suburban "overman," both in freedom and its caricature. Ending up in a jail after the senseless murder of an Arab, he is waiting for his execution, free at last, unredeemed and hating everybody. In a well-known "Preface" written for the English edition, Camus seems to praise his hero's sense of difference from all the others by saying that Meursault is incapable of lying. When asked why he shot the Arab to death, Meursault replies all too honestly that he felt more annoyance than regret—which condemns him to death.

> For me, therefore, Meursault is not a piece of social wreckage, but a poor and naked man enamored of a sun that leaves no shadows. Far from being bereft of all feeling, he is animated by a passion that is deep because it is stubborn, a passion for the absolute and for truth. This truth is still a negative one, the truth of what we are and what we feel, but without it no conquest of ourselves or of the world will ever be possible.
>
> One would therefore not be much mistaken to read *The Stranger* as the story of a man who, without any heroics, agrees to die for the truth. I

also happen to say, again paradoxically, that I had tried to draw in my character the only Christ we deserve.

(Dated January 1955—the novel itself was
published in 1942 in Paris)

We do not have to accept Camus's bombastic assessment—I really don't, for instance. In order to exemplify a second time the clash between universalist and particularist readings, I would like to survey a critical debate about this novel. It opposed Pierre Nora, who in 1961 published an incendiary book entitled *Les Français d'Algérie*. Nora is ferocious facing the political short-sightedness and racist prejudices of the French colons, the *pied-noirs*, and does not spare the leading intellectuals who were liberals like Camus. For him, there is no existential or metaphysical "absurd," but the absurdity of the colonial system: "Camus, who felt that he was like Robinson in Oran (where he drafted *The Stranger*) appears on a psychological plane as the truly sublimated expression of a real historical situation, a situation that has been simplified, decanted and streamlined."[16] The point of Camus's novel, "a masterpiece of Algerian literature" (FA, p. 208) is to denounce the way French citizens killed or terrorized the Algerians—what is surprising in the outcome is not that Meursault kills an Arab for no clear reason, but that he will pay for his crime with his life. In Nora's reading, the famous five shots that kill a young Arab on a beach in Algiers become the symptom of the "latent aggressiveness" of the French colons, which make Meursault much less a Sartrian Roquentin than a figure that could stand for any French man living in Algeria. "And the death sentence of the end, far from evoking any Kafkaian trial, turns into the disquieting admission of a historical culpability, and takes on an air of anticipation." (FA, p. 209)

Thus, in Nora's analysis, Camus becomes a symptom of a specific historical situation: a man from the Left, a journalist who denounced poverty in Kabylia, he also represents the moment when the French felt that their domination was threatened and contested. He was a militant for a Franco-Arab community. His novel gives shape to the nightmare haunting the bad conscience of the colonists.

But, a Frenchman from Algeria above all, Camus transfigures this relationship of domination on an unconscious plane, the only plane in

---

[16] Pierre Nora, *Les Français d'Algérie* (1961), new edition. Paris: Bourgois, 2012, p. 209, subsequently abbreviated as FA..

which Arabs can be represented in the psychological constellation of the French, who remain motionless like foreigners under the sun.

(FA, p. 210)

Yet, in the following chapter devoted to "the liberals," Camus is taken to task; he wishes to be above violence, he refuses to be "either a victim or a torturer" (this is the title of one of his collection of essays[17]) which leads him to play a disinterested role, refusing any class solidarity in the name of the tragic human condition (FA, p. 231).

> Camus could only revolt himself against history at the condition of suspending his judgment and to withdraw from the closed battle field. Now his disengagement was justified in the name of efficiency, as torture was at the time: "I have never stopped saying that these two condemnations could not be separated, if one wanted to remain efficient."
>
> (FA, pp. 231–2)

The rhetoric of the absurd or of the tragic rebellion of man against metaphysical fate only hides the real dilemma of the Left liberals, who could not agree to the armed struggle of Arab militants, and would not condone the terror campaigns of the *pied-noirs* or the French army.

The mention of torture in this passage is what triggered a no less violent attack by a former friend and school companion of Pierre Nora, Jacques Derrida. The main difference was that, although both were Jewish, Derrida had been born in Algeria and knew it intimately, whereas Nora was a Parisian who had just spent two years in Algeria. In the long (more than 42 pages) and impassioned letter published as an Appendix in Nora's book, Derrida, somewhat surprisingly, defends Camus. He first praises Nora for the remarks on *The Stranger*, even adds that his friend should write a whole book based on such brilliant insights (FA, p. 292). He agrees with Nora when the latter presents this book as an Algerian novel, and rejects—as Nora did, we have seen—the "critic-philosophical apparatus that Sartre has brought to bear artificially on it." He agrees with Nora that Camus's intentions have been pure even if his judgments could err. But he categorically rejects the imputation of any duplicitous acquiescence to torture:

> When he refuses to choose between the opposed violence in order to keep all its efficiency to his condemnation of all violence, the perfidy

---

[17] Camus, see footnote 4, pp. 331–52.

with which you write that "his disengagement was justified in the name
of efficiency, as torture was at the time" is really unworthy of Camus—
and of you. For either I am asleep or these are not the same things, the
same efficiency, the same means.

(FA, p. 293)

If Derrida does not appear as a "liberal" himself, he is also more skeptical
facing a purely Algerian nationalism in 1961. While Nora fully endorses the
"passionate" energy of nationalism in the struggle against colonialism,
Derrida keeps a critical distance facing such "passionate energy." (FA, p. 294)
Where does this leave us facing *The Stranger*? Derrida's reading would stress
both the historical determination, which makes of Meursault a symptom of
the imminent collapse of the French system, and a textual resistance to
ideology, whether pro- or contra-nationalism or internationalism. There is a
sudden metamorphosis of the hero in the last pages of *The Stranger*. He had
been so far entirely passive, unable to express or even feel any emotion, even
when his mother had died or his girlfriend asks whether he is in love with her.
All the features that are heaped up as so many proofs of his monstrosity, such
as the fact that he starts a happy sexual relationship just after his mother has
died, and that could be understood according to a psychoanalytic rationality
(he could not enjoy sex as long as his mother was alive, for instance) become
all of a sudden a new "truth": not just the inability to invent lies, but a global
rejection of false systems of values like the consolations offered by the priest.
The previous numbness and dissociation are replaced by a powerful upsurge
of emotions, a torrential discharge, at the outcome of which Meursault even
identifies empathically with his mother, who had found a companion in her
old age.

> So close to death, Maman must have felt free then and ready to live it all
> over again. Nobody, nobody had the right to cry over her. And I felt ready
> to live it again too. As if that blind rage had washed me clean, rid me of
> hope; for the first time, in that night alive with signs and stars, I opened
> myself to the gentle indifference of the world. Finding it so much like
> myself—so like a brother, really—I felt that I had been happy and that I
> was happy again. I had only to wish that there be a large crowd of
> spectators the day of my execution and that they greet me with cries of
> hate.[18]

---

[18] Albert Camus, *The Stranger*, Matthew Ward (trans.). New York: Random House, 1989,
pp. 122–3.

What Camus has done in this novel was to launch a style of indifference, a degree zero of writing in French—as Roland Barthes had observed—the style of the absurd, "flat and deep like a mirror."[19] Or to keep quoting his groundbreaking reading from 1944: With *The Stranger* "we see the beginning of a new style, style of silence and silence of style, in which the voice of the artist—equally removed from sighs, blasphemy and gospels—is a white voice, the only voice that can fit our unredeemable distress." (see footnote 19)

The Barthes of 1944 and the Derrida of 1961 agree. They accept the validity of Camus's ethical stance; not because they love moralism but because they see it as a new way of writing in answer to historical catastrophes. Writing in this styleless style is the only ethical answer to the dramas of WWII or the dead-end of colonialism. In 1961, Sartre and Camus had broken up, Barthes himself had deserted Camus in 1955,[20] most French radicals were on Sartre's side, espousing his neo-marxism. Derrida, true to his sense of the undecidability of ethical judgments, decided to defend Albert Camus. Perhaps, we will have to ask, is the "absurd" just another name for the undecidable?

Badiou versus Adorno on the value of Beckett

Among the French students who supported Sartre one would have found Alain Badiou, who remained a Sartrian leftist for a long time. This introduces my third critical debate, which I will have to sum up partly, opposing Theodor W. Adorno and Alain Badiou about Beckett. Both diverge when interpreting the presence of the "absurd" in Beckett's work. Badiou and Adorno have insisted on a serious need to read Beckett as a source of philosophical inspiration, but if one compares Adorno's and Badiou's interpretations of Beckett, there is a stark reversal in their starting points. Their general evaluations evince a dramatic shift from the negative to the positive. Spanning half a century of philosophical discussions of Beckett, their points of departure stand at antipodal ends while emphasizing the exemplarity of Beckett's work. Adorno begins with Beckett's negativity, a dialectical negativity that should not be confused with nihilism; Badiou brushes aside any suggestion of negativity, stressing instead the affirmative character of Beckett's philosophy.

---

[19] Roland Barthes, "Reflexion sur le style de *l'Etranger*" (1944), *Oeuvres Complètes*, Vol. 1 Paris: Seuil, 2002, p. 63.

[20] Barthes "Response to Albert Camus," see footnote 19, p. 479. Barthes rejects *The Plague*, finding fault with its ethical lessons.

Beckett and Adorno met several times, and a friendship ensued. At their first meeting in November 1958, Adorno noted that Beckett was making "reproaches" against Kafka, which surprised him and prevented him from developing the systematic comparison between the two writers he had planned. One of the most revealing notes he took then is: "Beckett (after Godot). Not abstraction but subtraction."[21] This underpinned Adorno's analysis of the way Beckett's position cannot be reduced to the absurd or to existentialist themes. On the contrary, *Godot* debunks existentialism while radicalizing the subjective foundation provided by phenomenology. Beckett derides the "existentialist jargon" that provides mystified images of the human condition. Its pathos essentializes it in a "process of abstraction that is not aware of itself." The value of Beckett is that it comes close to this position but parodies this abstracted vision of man.[22] Thus Adorno sees Beckett's work as a war machine against existentialism, that of Sartre and then of Heidegger. Beckett's absurdist "subtraction" fights against the "abstraction" of those who negate concrete life and its historical determination in the name of a reified concept of existence. Beckett reduces the subject to an utterly laughable absurdity. He derides philosophical abstraction by creating an impasse, a dead end from which one can only be saved by a regressive laughter that spares nothing.

Yet, this absurdist debunking keeps its political value. Adorno's essay about *Endgame* is a refutation of Lukacs's condemnation of "absurdist" theater as nothing but "petty-bourgeois nihilism." On the contrary, Adorno saw in Beckett's alleged apolitical stance a highly political position. Beckett exposes both the disingenuousness of Marxist humanism and the sterility of Heidegger's ontological difference. This transforms the so-called apolitical Beckett into a figure of resistance to totalitarianism.

Adorno's main theme is thus Beckett's post-phenomenological reduction of what has already been reduced ("With Beckett, positive categories as hope turn into absolutely negative ones. Here hope goes to the nothing."[23]) so as to explore the specific nature of Beckett's nothing: "Is the nothing only nothing? This is the central issue in Beckett. Absolute rejection, because hope is only where there is nothing to keep. Plenitude of the nothing. This is the explanation of his remaining in the zero-point."[24] The emphasis on negativity

---

[21] Rolf Tiedemann, "*Gegen den Trug der Frage nach dem Sinn*". *Eine Dokumentation zu Adornos Beckett-Lektüre, Frankfurter Adorno Blätter III*, Text+Kritik. Munich 1994, p. 25. All my quotes come from these pages. The translation is mine.
[22] T. W. Adorno *et al.*, "Trying to understand *Endgame*," in *Can one live after Auschwitz?*, R. Livingstone (trans.). Stanford: Standford University Press, 2003, p. 246.
[23] Tiedemann, see footnote 21, p. 44.
[24] Tiedemann, see footnote 21, p. 73.

refutes the "absurdist" allegiance in Beckett, who has nothing to do with Ionesco.

> Beckett's plays are absurd not because of the absence of any meaning, for they would be simply irrelevant, but because they put meaning on trial; they unfold its history. His work is ruled as much by an obsession with positive nothingness as by the obsession with a meaninglessness that has developed historically and is thus in a sense merited, though this meritedness in no way allows any positive meaning to be reclaimed. . . . Artworks that divest themselves of any semblance of meaning do not thereby forfeit their similitude to language. They enunciate their meaninglessness with the same determinacy as traditional artworks enunciate their positive meaning. Today this is the capacity of art: Through the consistent negation of meaning it does justice to the postulates that once constituted the meaning of artworks. Works of the highest level of form that are meaningless or alien to meaning are therefore more than simply meaningless because they gain their content through the negation of meaning.[25]
>
> (AT, pp. 153–4)

Beckett's absurd keeps a political impact even when he does not explicitly engage with politics. For Adorno, it was typical that the right-wing junta of colonels who had seized power in Greece banned Beckett's works: "Greece's new tyrants knew why they banned Beckett's plays, in which there is not a single political word." (AT, p. 234) Beckett's absurdism will exemplify resistance in art, testifying to a spirit of obstinate ethical perseverance facing barbarism. Such perseverance does not have to shout its name or be explicit. The idea is developed at the end of *Negative Dialectics*:

> Beckett has given us the only fitting reaction to the situation left by concentration camps—a situation he never calls by name, as if it were subject to an image ban. What is there, he says, is like a concentration camp. He spoke once of a lifelong death penalty, implying as only hope for the future that there will be nothing any more. This, too, he rejects. From the rift of inconsistency thus found, it is the imagery of the Nothing as Something that emerges, and it will then stabilize his poetry.[26]

[25] Theodor W. Adorno, *Aethestic Theory*, translated by Robert Hullot-Kentor, Minneapolis, University of Minnesota Press, 1997, pp. 153–4, subsequently abbreviated as AT.

[26] Theodor W. Adorno, *Negative Dialektik*. Frankfurt: Suhrkamp, 1970, pp. 371–2. I have modified the English translation of *Negative Dialectics*, E. B. Ashton (trans.). New York: Continuum, pp. 380–1.

Beckett would thus, like Paul Celan but with different rhetorical strategies, provide a possible answer to Adorno's self-imposed quandary: how to write "poetry" after Auschwitz? To write poetry or *Dichtung* after Auschwitz entails one central paradox. What Adorno praises in Beckett's "nihilism" is that it appears as the opposite of usual nihilism. Beckett is a "true nihilist" because he opposes the spurious positive values provided by post-Auschwitz restoration of an older order.

As we will discuss again later, Adorno returned to Kafka when he took the tale of "Hunter Gracchus" by Kafka as a way of understanding the specific negativity evinced by Beckett. Hunter Gracchus was a man who had missed his own death by accident. Even though he died, he was condemned to roam the earth, turning into an immortal being in spite of himself. In Adorno's reading, Gracchus was compared with the bourgeoisie that has failed to die. Gracchus adumbrates the more sinister meaning of "between life and death" that the death camps of the Nazis have enacted with a vengeance.[27] This finds an echo in Adorno's reading of *Endgame*. The tragedy does not derive from death as in a classical tragedy, but from the very "abortion of death." The pathos of the play derives from the sense that even after all is over, one has to go on. This would correspond to a post-holocaust situation, when the mechanization of death in the camps has generated a new level of the unspeakable. The idea, therefore, is that the best denunciation of a post-apocalyptic post-Holocaust situation, a predicament in which we are still caught, can be achieved by a dramatization of the non-death of the subject. Hamm's actions and speeches in *Endgame* do not betray a fear of death but a wholesale fear that "death could miscarry."[28]

Even when Badiou rejects these "negative dialectics," his starting point is similar. He begins by rejecting a common idea in the interpretation of Beckett portrayed as "a writer of the absurd, of despair, of empty skies, of incommunicability and of eternal solitude."[29] (OB, p. 38) On the back of the cover of the Beckett book we see a strong refutation: "No, Beckett's *oeuvre* is not what was always said about it—that it was despair, absurdity of the world, anxiety, solitude, decrepitude . . ."

Like Adorno, Badiou sees Beckett as straddling two schools, modern phenomenology and classical rationalism: wedged between Descartes and Husserl, he rereads Heraclitus, Parmenides, Plato, Kant and Schopenhauer.

---

[27] See Adorno, "Notes on Kafka", footnote 22, p. 227. See Franz Kafka, "The Hunter Gracchus", *The Complete Stories*. New York: Schocken, 1983, pp. 226–230.
[28] Adorno, see footnote 22, p. 289.
[29] Alain Badiou, *On Becket*, edited by Alberto Toscano and Nina Power, Manchester, Clinamen Press, 2003, p. 39, subsequently abbreviated as OB.

The dominant fashion in 1956 was to read Beckett as an existentialist nihilist, a pessimist or an absurdist: "a dark comedian whose metaphysical clowns wandering under an empty sky ruminate on the absence of god, expressing tersely the despair inherent to man's estate." Then Beckett was reframed as a modernist only interested in the problematics of language. As Badiou recalls, he tried to bridge the two views, combining a Sartrean reading insisting on man as a "useless passion" with the question of language in the name of ethics, commitment and politic. Badiou's program in the fifties aimed at reconciling Sartre's negative ontology with Blanchot's mysticism of an intransitive language, "complet(ing) the Sartrean theory of freedom through a careful investigation into the opacities of the signifier" (OB, p. 39).

Badiou always insists on the ethical dimension in Beckett. Beckett would embody an ethics of courage and fortitude, which yields a positive imperative, founded upon a theory of undying desire. Beckett teaches us never to yield on our desire, even when everything collapses. Beckett's lesson in ethical affirmation gives us the courage to keep on living and creating.

As both Adorno and Badiou argue, Beckett follows a "methodical askesis" that goes back to Descartes and Husserl in a wish to "suspend" everything that is inessential. Absurdity, clownish humor and devastating nihilism are instrumental. Beckett reduces human subjects to paralyzed cripples, ectoplasms in a jar, Winnie in a hole in *Happy Days*—this is his way of returning to a Cartesian and Husserlian *epoché* (OB, p. 44) exposing what is truly "generic" in man. Beckett thus initiates a systematic investigation of "thinking humanity." (OB, p. 44) His way of destruction discovers what resists, what remains indestructible. Such a fundamental indestructibility yields the only stable foundation for ethics.

Following insights provided by Adorno and Horkheimer in *Dialectics of Enlightenment*, one could even bring Badiou and Adorno closer by analyzing how *Watt* demonstrates the links between Kant's morality, capitalism, technology (Watt was the name of the inventor of the steam engine) and Marquis de Sade's erotic machines (the orgy, a complex montage of bodies that will leave no one idle, sexually speaking) buttressed by a rhetoric of excess and pain.[30]

The most absurdist text to examine in detail would be *Watt*, but I will refrain from doing so given the complexities of the plot and technique. I'll just say, to sum up a long analysis, that *Watt* is both a Sadian and a Kantian text.

---

[30] I develop this in "Watt/Sade: *Beckett et l'humain à l'envers*," in *L'Inhumain*, Marie-Christine Lemardeley, Carle Bonnafous-Murat and André Topia (eds). Paris: Presses Sorbonne Nouvelle, 2004, pp. 71–83; and in "Unbreakable B's: from Beckett and Badiou to the bitter end of affirmative ethics," *Alain Badiou: Philosophy And Its Conditions*, Gabriel Riera (ed.). Albany: SUNY Press, 2005, pp. 87–108.

In a sense, Beckett was trying to emulate the perverse logics of Sade in *120 Days of Sodom*. Here, we know that he had followed Maurice Blanchot's apt analysis of absurdity in Sade. Beckett jotted down in a draft *Texts for Nothing* a reference to the "Preface" written by Bataille for Sade's *Justine*. In this "Preface," Bataille was quoting Blanchot's superb 1949 book, *Lautréamont et Sade*.[31] In this, Blanchot meditates on "Sade's reason." This essay echoes deeply with the major preoccupations of Beckett in *Watt*. Blanchot describes the contradictory ambitions of Sade's work:

> At every moment (Sade's) theoretical ideas set free the irrational forces with which they are bound up. These forces both excite and upset the thought by an impetus of a kind that causes the thought first to resist and then to yield, to try again for mastery, to gain an ascendancy, but only by liberating other dark forces by which, once again the ideas are carried away, side-tracked and perverted. The result is that all that is said is clear but seems at the mercy of something that has not been said. Then, a little further on, what was concealed emerges, is recaptured by logic but, in its turn, obeys the movement of a still further hidden force. In the end, everything has been brought to light, everything has been expressed, but equally everything has once more been plunged into the obscurity of undigested ideas and experiences that cannot be given shape.[32]

There is no better evocation of the twisted logic of *Watt*, and this paragraph could also sketch Beckett's entire program in the *Trilogy*. Blanchot sees in Sade a provocateur whose uncontrolled excess leads him (and us) to think beyond the usual limits of rationality, thus moving also beyond literature in itself.

A later Beckett text also comes close to naming the event of the Shoah as a turning point. In the French version of *The Lost Ones* (*Le Dépeupleur*) we have an explicit reference to Primo Levi.[33] Levi's central question, provided by the title, *Se quest'un uomo*, is repeated at the end of *The Lost Ones*,[34] as

---

[31] I owe this reference to Peter Fifield, who in "'Accursed Progenitor!' *Fin de Partie* and Georges Bataille," in *Samuel Beckett Today/Aujourd'hui*, vol. 22, pp. 107–21, argues that Bataille's testimony about the demise of own father, who died blind, syphilitic and abandoned by all during WWI, gave Beckett the inspiration for Hamm's character in *Endgame*.

[32] Maurice Blanchot, "Sade's reason," in *The Maurice Blanchot Reader*, Michael Holland (ed.). Oxford: Blackwell, 1995, pp. 75–6. The essay was first published in *Les Temps Modernes* in October 1947 under the title "A la rencontre de Sade."

[33] Samuel Beckett, *Le Dépeupleur*. Paris: Minuit, 1970, p. 55.

[34] Antoinette Weber-Caflisch, *Chacun son dépeupleur: sur Samuel Beckett*. Paris: Editions de Minuit, 1994.

Weber-Caflisch has shown. "*Si c'est un homme*," used twice in the last section, reiterates Primo Levi's question.[35] Moreover the questers in the cylinder who are called the "vanquished" evoke those *Lager* prisoners who had abandoned all hope; they are the "*musselmänner*," as opposed to those who had kept the will to survive. This event cannot be described but only hinted at obliquely. Adorno saw a paradoxical silence at work in *Endgame*. For him the play had less to do with the cold war and the fear of a universal atomic annihilation than with:

> Auschwitz, which names an event that is so disruptive that it could not be named. The violence of the unspeakable is mirrored in the fear of mentioning it. Beckett kept it nebulous. About what is incommensurable with experience as such one can only speak in euphemisms, the way one speaks in Germany of the murder of the Jews.[36]

Badiou and Adorno agree when they see subjectivity as the end-product of a long "torture" associated with Western rationality. Adorno seems to have anticipated Agamben when he talks of reducing subjects to mere existence or "bare life," this in *Aesthetic Theory*: Beckett's novels ". . . present the reduction of life to basic human relationships, that minimum of existence that subsists *in extremis*." (AT, p. 30) I have attempted to approach Beckett via Badiou and Adorno together. I have pointed to points of convergence (the concept of reduction or subtraction, the anti-dialectical dialectics of a Nothing that reverts to a positive affirmation, the insight that Beckett bridges the gap between ontology and ethics, etc.). Adorno identified in Beckett's work a refusal of the idea of progress—a refusal duly allegorized by the lack of movement in his plays. "His work is the extrapolation of a negative Καιρ'ος. The fulfilled moment reverses into perpetual repetition that converges with desolation. His narratives, which he sardonically calls novels, no more offer objective descriptions of social reality than—as the widespread misunderstanding supposes—they present the reduction of life to basic human relationships, that minimum of existence that subsists *in extremis*. These novels do, however, touch on fundamental layers of experience *hic et nunc*, which are brought together into paradoxical dynamic at a standstill." (AT, p. 30)

Adorno will follow Badiou when the latter decides to transcend the absurd. Badiou aims at opening Beckett's texts to the "music of thinking," a

---

[35] Primo Levi, *Si c'est un homme*, Martine Schruoffeneger (trans.). Paris: Julliard, 1990. See *Chacun son dépeupleur*, pp. 41–3.

[36] Adorno, see footnote 22, pp. 245–6.

music for which form is as important as content: it is always a "brilliant" form capable of punching holes in knowledge. Badiou will thus assert that Beckett's texts always "think," even when they seem to play the bow and the fiddle of absurd metaphysical *ritournelles*. In a sense, Beckett repeats what Kafka had to bring to us. As long as these texts assert the force of a paradoxical desire for Otherness while allowing beauty to be felt in language, they help us understand that words can go counter to the demands of thought by celebrating the power of beauty and also give shape to thought, a thought haunted by an alterity in which the claims of universalism, never fully destroyed, are displaced and qualified.

10

After the "Altermodern"

In all the previous chapters, I have presupposed a convergence between theory and the literature and arts of modernism. This chapter begins by recapitulating the links between canonical modernism as defined by Clement Greenberg and Theory. I will then sketch a genealogy of the postmodern, since that term has been presented as a reaction to modernism. To this now discarded concept, I will oppose Nicolas Bourriaud's term of the "Altermodern," a term used to usher in an aesthetics that corresponds to a globalized Theory. First, we need to define modernism in a straightforward manner.

The concept of modernism and its theory

The canonization of modernism by poets like Ezra Pound and T. S. Eliot—by literary critics like Hugh Kenner and Marjorie Perloff, by art critics like Clement Greenberg, and philosophers like Adorno—has implied concepts and criteria that correspond with the tenets of what is recognized as Theory. To give a precise example, I will discuss Greenberg's recourse to Kant's philosophy for his imposition of an American modernism as a dogmatic rationale for the aesthetics of the new in the fifties. In the same manner, the emergence of high modernism in literature, architecture, film, and the other visual arts could not have happened without significant borrowings from philosophers' theories. Thus Yeats's version of Irish modernism would have been unthinkable without Nietzsche; Eliot's anti-romantic and neo-classical bias obscure his reliance on the neo-Hegelian Bradley as well as his readings of Husserl and Bertrand Russell; Beckett discovered in Descartes and then Geulincx philosophical sensibilities akin to his; T. E. Hulme or Wyndham Lewis meditated on Bergson's philosophy before criticizing it; Virginia Woolf and the Bloomsbury group paid attention to the redefinition of philosophy as logical theory brought about by Moore and Bertrand Russell. Even before the New Critics in America and F. R. Leavis in England put authors like Eliot, Joyce and Lawrence on the map of academic curricula, most modernist authors knew that their success depended upon their ability to form their own audiences, to explain what they were doing and why, and finally to shape the taste of the common reader. This strategy implied that they needed to introduce the terms by which they wanted to be read. If notions such as "epiphany," "mood," or "objective correlative" have lost some of their relevance and turned into academic clichés, they have been effective in promoting new habits of reading and introducing intellectual discernment. Joyce, for instance, fascinated his friends by the passion with which he controlled the discussion of his texts via critics who provided concepts for further discussion (he liked "plane of meaning" better than Eliot's "mythical method," tried to launch with Jolas "the new mythos," and "the language of the night"—phrases that did not become canonical but proved effective in the critical dissemination of his later experimental writings.

On the other hand, the affinity of leading theoreticians for modernist texts is attested. One can think of Adorno and Beckett, Derrida and Joyce, Foucault and Borges, Jameson and Wyndham Lewis, Cixous and Lispector, Deleuze and Proust, Žižek and Kafka, de Man and Yeats. There are also many hidden or latent links, as when one parallels Derrida's work on "difference" with Beckett's interrogations of the voice and writing,[1] or refer Deleuze and Guattari's critique of psychoanalysis back to D. H. Lawrence's essays and novels. And even if Virginia Woolf stated that she was not a feminist, one wonders what feminist theory would be today without her groundbreaking texts.

Excellent conversations about the links between modernism and theory have been gathered by Stephen Ross in *Modernism and Theory*.[2] The debates between critics about the links between modernism and theory have highlighted numerous aesthetic and methodological parallels. The dialogical presentation assesses the role played by theory in contemporary interpretations of modernism, providing numerous examples of intersections between modernist authors and the problematic of Theory. The modernist period's peak being in the second and third decades of the twentieth century, it can serve as a site for interrogating and reframing the practices of scholars and theorists. In our current conversation about modernism, no-one has done more to promote the interaction between theory and the cultural historiography of the "modern moment" than Walter Benjamin. It is no coincidence that his essays and books have been cornerstones of definitions of modernism.

---

[1] See Derrida's interview by Derek Attridge in *Acts of Literature*. London and New York: Routledge, 1992, pp. 60–2.
[2] Stephen Ross (ed.), *Modernism and Theory: A Critical Debate*. New York: Routledge, 2009.

Indeed, Benjamin's main effort, his unfinished compendium called the *Arcades Project*, delineates the fault-lines between modernity and modernism. Benjamin was not duped by the shrill claims of recent authors to be "absolutely modern" (a task that Rimbaud had argued would loom larger at the end of the nineteenth century[3]). He notes wryly that each epoch believes itself to be at the vanguard of the modern: "Each age unavoidably seems to itself a new age. The 'modern' (*das 'Moderne'*) however, is as varied in its meaning as the different aspects of one and the same kaleidoscope."[4] Benjamin is less asserting a reshuffling of moving elements caught up in a machine to imply that variety merely veils sameness, than quoting obliquely Baudelaire's famous phrase comparing the new subject of modernity to a "kaleidoscope gifted with consciousness." This phrase would provide a good description of what this collection would aim to be: an accretive and dialogic immersion in a domain that will be explored through multiple angles and points of view. This is also how Baudelaire defined the rapture of the subject of modernity, a new "man of the crowd," as Poe saw him, who is also a "lover of universal life" joyfully entering the mass of urban passers-by in order to tap this "immense reservoir of electrical energy."[5] Benjamin meditates at length on Baudelaire's concept of modernity, and brings it into close connection with the two important philosophies of history of the nineteenth century, those of Hegel and Marx. In the same chapter, he quotes Roger Caillois in French about Paris, this "modern myth." Caillois states that "modernity" (*modernité*) implies the "elevation of urban life to the level of myth," (AP, p. 555; PW, p. 689) a feature that we would tend to associate with Joyce, Eliot and Pound, but was surely present in Baudelaire. Is this a sign that *modernité* has insensibly led us to *modernism*? We could believe this when we reach this isolated sentence, a simple question: "How does modernism become *Jugenstil*?" (AP, p. 561; PW, p. 697)

Here, one should pay attention to a subtle shift in gender: what the translators have correctly translated as "modernism" is not in the neutral as before (*das Moderne*) but in the singular feminine, *die Moderne*. Benjamin also uses the term *Neuheit* (translated as "Novelty"), or the "New," but not yet

---

[3] I have discussed the ambiguity of Rimbaud's famous statement "One has to be absolutely modern" in *The Ghosts of Modernity*. Gainesville: University Press of Florida, 1996, pp. 194–5.

[4] Walter Benjamin, *The Arcades Project*, Howard Eiland and Kevin McLaughlin (trans). Cambridge, MA: Harvard University Press, 1999, p. 545. For the German original, see Walter Benjamin, *Das Passagen-Werk*, Rolf Tiedemann (ed.). Frankfurt: Suhrkamp, 1983, vol. 2, p. 677, subsequently abbreviated as AP and DW.

[5] Charles Baudelaire, *The Painter of Modern Life*. London: Phaidon, 1995, p. 10.

the masculine term of *Modernismus*. Beyond arbitrary grammatical rules, one may ask more pointedly what is the "gender of modernism."[6] There was a sense that the "high modernism" had to be masculine, hence "hard," aggressive, ferocious even, against an effeminate culture of decadence or, even worse, the production of mass culture for a dominantly feminine audience, allegedly the consumers of popular novels. Yet, even within the field of modernist theory, a number of authors like Peter Bürger have argued that modernism as such had kept elements of the "soft" aestheticizing touch, whereas the real revolution in the arts and everyday life was to be found only in the "historical" avant-gardes. We can remember that, not so long ago, as eminent and influential a critic as Hugh Kenner had refused to grant the epithet of "modernist" to Virginia Woolf, who was deemed too "soft" and not experimental enough, reserving the term to the group animated by Ezra Pound, a group including, it is true, Hilda Doolittle alias H.D.[7] And Gertrude Stein could state that all geniuses were men—which also included her as well! In all these discussions, gender and politics are inextricably mixed.

As for Benjamin, his use of a feminine term (*die Moderne*) may be linked with what he criticized in the "*Jugendstil*" moment, a movement which is often rendered in English as "art nouveau." It is the post-symbolist generation of 1890–1910, the lineage linking Baudelaire to Mallarmé, Laforgue, Wilde, Jarry and the younger Gide and Yeats. Odilon Redon and Beardsley would be its main artists. Needless to say, Benjamin who embraced the material, technological and ideological acceleration of modernity cannot but reject the legacy of the *Jugendstil*, a movement that he always associated with the decadent poetry of Stefan George, with whom he had fought at the beginning of his career. Sexual perversion and fake mysticism are the ways in which *Jugendstil* would attempt to bring back a lost aura: "*Jugendstil* forces the auratic." (AP, p. 557; PW, p. 692.) In other words, we see here that Benjamin points to possible links between modernism and regressive aestheticism, which leads to stillborn productions or bad art, simply put, to Kitsch. This will provide an exactly identical point of departure for Clement Greenberg.

---

[6] See Bonnie Kime Scott (ed.), *The Gender of Modernism: A Critical Anthology*. Bloomington: Indiana University Press, 1990.

[7] Virginia Woolf did not belong to international Modernism for she was above all "an English novelist of manners," writes Hugh Kenner in "The making of the modernist canon," *Mazes*. San Francisco: North Point Press, 1989, p. 37. Kenner excludes Wallace Stevens as well, but for different reasons (p. 40).

What remains of Clement Greenberg's impact today is that he succeeded in promoting modernism in the visual arts after 1945, and justified his preference by establishing a solid theory of modernism.[8] For this he had to invent a specific blend of philosophy, cultural critique and aesthetics that corresponds rather well with what we understand by "Theory" today. Like Benjamin, Greenberg was struck by the cultural scandal constituted by the coexistence of "Kitsch" (debased popular art in all its commercial dilutions) and modernist high art. Only clear and precise criteria will allow one to make necessary distinctions. What is bad in Kitsch is that it is subservient to the whims of the market, it generates an endless tide of debased objects that prevent one from seeing authentic modern art. In order to ward off this threat, often identified with capitalism, it is vital to define strictly the conditions of the possibility of true artistic judgments. One will have to distinguish between *a priori* conditions of any artistic experience and the value judgments that underpin it so as to build foundations for an accurate appreciation of taste.

Quite naturally, this position led Greenberg back to Kant, a philosopher whose concepts proved invaluable if one searched for a secure foundation in aesthetics. Greenberg insisted that criticism is based on judgments, which led him to place modernism durably in the context of neo-Kantianism. His problematic of modernism started from the fruitful opposition between Kitsch and the avant-garde, and it ended up promoting the New York school of abstraction in the fifties because this school embodied what his esthetics promoted. The reference to Kant in connection with the promotion of Abstract Expressionism corresponded to a strategy that was meant to debunk two rival theories: a parochial praise of American values, in which he recognized the language of exceptionalism and jingoism, and the blurred messianic promise of avant-gardist internationalism. Greenberg used Kant selectively: for instance, he never invoked the theory of the Sublime in his aesthetics. He took seriously Kant's axiom that "The Deduction of aesthetic judgments upon objects of nature must not be directed to what we call sublime in nature, but only to the beautiful."[9] The main concepts used to promote modernism are the idea of a Critique, of the Beautiful and of

---

8   I have analyzed this in *Given: 1) Art, 2) Crime—Modernity, Murder and Mass Culture*. Brighton: Sussex Academic Press, 2007, pp. 172–89.

9   Immanuel Kant, *Critique of Judgment*, James Creed Meredith (trans.). Oxford: Oxford University Press, 1952, p. 133.

Taste as a common discourse on art. This is how "Modernist Painting" (1960) begins:

> Modernism includes more than art and literature. By now it covers almost the whole of what is truly alive in our culture. It happens, however, to be very much of a historical novelty. Western civilization is not the first civilization to turn around and question its own foundations, but it is the one that has gone furthest in doing so. I identify Modernism with the intensification, almost the exacerbation, of this self-critical tendency that began with the philosopher Kant. Because he was the first to criticize the means itself of criticism, I conceive of Kant as the first real Modernist.
>
> The essence of Modernism lies, as I see it, in the use of characteristic methods of a discipline to criticize the discipline itself, not in order to subvert it but in order to entrench it more firmly in its area of competence.
>
> (CE IV, p. 85)

In this model, modernism inherits from the Enlightenment the wish to found each discipline by criticizing it, in a critique that does not come from outside but from inside: "The limitations that constitute the medium of painting—the flat surface, the shape of the support, the properties of the pigment—were treated by the Old Masters as negative factors that could be acknowledged only implicitly or indirectly. Under Modernism these same limitations came to be regarded as positive factors, and were acknowledged openly." (CE IV, p. 86) Consequently, modernism discloses a doctrine of the "purity" of art. Purity based upon "self-definition" depends upon a rigorous deployment of the formal properties of the medium. Cézanne's revolution came from the exploration of the "limits" of his art, and modernism begun at the end of the nineteenth-century.

Greenberg's logic can be called "plokheic," in the sense that it follows the trope of an emphatic repetition. He keeps urging: "Let painting be painting, and purely painting." This is the logic of the *bloss* (mere, as in "mere form") deployed by Kant in his third critique, when he discusses how judgments of taste rely on the "mere form of the object."[10] It should not be confused with the logic of "autonomy" as it is too often. The main effort is towards an intensive repetition; it applies to modernist music and literature as well. All these domains can only progress by exploring the properties of their own mediums. If Greenberg's "Avant-Garde and Kitsch" successfully blended

---

[10] See on this point, Rodolphe Gasché, *The Idea of Form, Rethinking Kant's Aesthetics*. Stanford: Stanford University Press, 2003, pp. 72–88.

Marxism and high modernism *à la* Eliot, his later essays embodied a synthesis of modernism and theory. Greenberg provided a solution to Eliot's postulation of an "ideal order" of culture destined to be changed each time a new masterpiece arrived. Do new artists coexist peacefully with the previous ones or do they murder each other? Greenberg would suggest that evolution comes from struggle, often to the death: one has to destroy other reputations if one's criteria are to shape dominant taste. This raises the issue of power, money, and politics, a social game that Eliot had learned to play as well.

My contention is that there is still a lot to learn from Greenberg's experiential model underpinned by theory. His theory faithfully enacts Kant's "finality without end," this *Zweckmässigkeit ohne Zweck*, a notion that defines the essence of art that imitates the functioning of nature. What it asserts, most fundamentally, is that if nature is not absurd, then neither is art: art is a social production that follows the form of nature, both presupposing something like a common taste shared by all. This is how Greenberg ends up defending modernism with formal judgments buttressed by a concept of history that includes the notion of progress. Both Adorno and Greenberg believed that there were "discoveries" in the arts; for Adorno, indeed, one could not or should not continue writing harmonic music after Schönberg and his disciples; this would be regressive or reactionary, and he believed that Stravinsky had been guilty of such a sin; in the same way, one should not continuing painting realistic landscapes or portraits after Mondrian and Picasso without regressing in aim and technique. Neither Adorno nor Greenberg wanted to imagine a cyclical return of genres, techniques and schools; they eschewed the notion of parodic returns, formal "revolutions" quoting each other in a vertiginous cycle, which is more or less what we understand by "post-modernism." Post-modernism presupposes the existence of artistic fields that have been saturated and finally homogenized by an "end of history" similar to what Kojève had read into Hegel. Then no progress was ever possible.

For Greenberg, the praise of abstraction in painting corresponds to an aesthetic of the common taste; it is therefore imperative to educate the public. There must be a social consensus about the idea of art, and artists who destroy the consensus, like Duchamp, are rejected because of their adherence to nominalist aesthetics. If Duchamp could be made to assert: "I call art whatever I do," Greenberg reintroduced the issue of an "objective" value. He prefers saying: "Here is what I like, and we can all agree that it is good art." He was the last American critic who could reign on the world of museums and gallery owners, collectors and rich buyers, only he could reconcile the influence of money with the taste of sophisticated connoisseurs. Kantian theory, as

invoked by Greenberg to promote modernism, led the New York school to
the pinnacles of the art market.

The history of art theory succeeding Greenberg has shown that, as Hegel
himself had to confess, there is no "end of history." This also means that there
is no end of theory, even if theories have moved on and if taste has changed.
Even the concepts that have been offered as an antidote to Kant's formalism,
such as Bataille's notion of the "formless,"[11] require definitions and new
deployments of concepts.

Bourriaud and the "Altermodern"

Nicolas Bourriaud became famous when he launched the concept of
"relational esthetics" in 1998, as he co-directed the Palais de Tokyo's new
contemporary art museum with Jerome Sans. This book already aimed at
reclaiming modernity, but its terms are very close to those of Jean-François
Lyotard:

> It is not modernity that is dead, but its idealistic and teleological version.
>
> Today's fight for modernity is being waged in the same terms as
> yesterday's, barring the fact that the avant-garde has stopped patrolling
> like some scout, the troop having come to a cautious standstill around a
> bivouac of certainties. Art was intended to prepare and announce a
> future world: today it is modeling possible universes.[12]

Bourriaud quoted Jean-Francois Lyotard when he mentioned a model of
participational activities proposed by artists such as Rirkrit Tiravanija,
Philippe Parreno, Vanessa Beecroft or Maurizio Cattelan. Art was presented
as a "social interstice" and led to an encounter based upon "social infra-
thinness" in this book. Bourriaud was expanding a key concept in Duchamp's
later theories, and I want to mention these given the fact that Duchamp was
the absolute adversary of Clement Greenberg in the sixties and seventies. I
will briefly discuss it.

In the Summer of 1937, Duchamp took a vacation in Denmark, where he
elaborated a definition of the "infra-thin." He offered many examples (a

---

[11] See the excellent catalogue by Yve-Alain Bois and Rosalind Krauss, *Formless: A User's Guide.* New York: Zone Books, 1997.
[12] Nicolas Bourriaud, *Relational Aesthetics*, Simon Pleasance, Fronza Woods and Mathieu Copeland (trans). Dijon: Presses du Reeel, [1998 French] 2002, p. 13.

spider-web with its moiré effect, the people who pass at the last minute through doors or turnstiles) and then added this:

> All the "identicals," as identical as they can be (and the more they are identical) come closer to this infra-thin separative difference. Two men are not an example of identicity (*identicité*) and on the contrary move apart from a difference that can be evaluated as infra-thin. . . . It would be better to try and pass through the infra-thin interval that separates two "identicals" than accept too easily the verbal generalization stating that two twins are like two drops of water.[13]

This first definition is full of riddles. It begins with the curious term of "*identicité*," a word that does not exist in French or in English. It sounds like an Anglicism in French, unless it is a pun on "authenticity" as a mark of identity. Duchamp seems to be elaborating a philosophy of difference that takes into account the minute differences that are commonly forgotten in everyday life—hence his remarks on forgetting and art as allegory. The Notes on the infra-thin begin like this:

> 1. The possible is an infra thin.
> The possibility for several tubes of color to become a Seurat is the concrete "explication" of the possible as infra thin.
> The possible implies becoming—the passage from one to the other takes place in the infra-thin.[14]

As other Notes suggest, the key concept deployed here is difference, difference used in all its contexts, from the differences in sensations or perceptions that can be easily overlooked because they are barely perceptible to conceptual or technological differences. For instance, people forget material differences as well as the difference between two images; if a naked woman coming from a well stands for Truth, the exact details of her face will not matter. One can also overlook minute discrepancies between the faces of two twins who will be branded as "identical" in a single representation.

Meanwhile, Duchamp and Walter Benjamin had probably met in Paris. Ecke Bonk refers to the Benjamin archive and quotes Benjamin's account of a meeting with Duchamp. This was in the Spring of 1937: "Saw Duchamp this morning, some cafe on Blvd. St. Germain . . . Showed me his painting:

[13] Marcel Duchamp, *Notes*. Paris: Flammarion, 1999, p. 22.
[14] Duchamp, see footnote 13, p. 21.

Nu Descendant un escalier in a reduced format, colored by hand *en pochoir*, breathtakingly beautiful, maybe mention . . ."[15] Whether this all-too felicitous encounter between the theoretician of reproduction (or better said "reproductibility") and its most visible practitioner happened or not has been debated. If this is a fact, Duchamp would have shown Benjamin one of the serial reproductions of his entire *oeuvre* destined to go into the *boîtes en valise*.

A year later, Benjamin went to Denmark in his turn for a last stay with Bertold Brecht in Svendborg, on the island of Fyn. He had come from Paris to spend two months with Brecht from June to August 1938. Because of growing theoretical disagreement between the two writers, Benjamin left Brecht for a week close to the end of his stay. He went to Copenhagen in order to finish writing his long essay on Baudelaire. He had discussed his theses with Brecht just before leaving, and Brecht had voiced important reservations about Benjamin's ideas, as we can see in his diary:

> Benjamin is here. He is working on an essay on Baudelaire. He demonstrates that literature was distorted after 1848 by the notion of an imminent, ahistorical epoch. . . . Oddly enough an eccentric idea enabled Benjamin to write it. He assumes something that he calls the "aura," which is connected with dreaming (daydreaming). He says: when you feel someone's gaze alight upon you, even on your back, you respond (!). The expectation that whatever you look at is looking at you creates the aura. Apparently this has started to disintegrate in recent times, along with rites and rituals. B. discovered this while analyzing films, where the aura is destroyed by the capacity of works of art to be reproduced. All very mystical, despite his anti-mystical attitude. This is the way in which the materialistic approach to history is adapted! It is pretty horrifying.[16]

I cannot go on at length here, I want merely to underline the curious chiasmus of the two thinkers: at the end of the thirties, Duchamp was moving from a theory of the ready-mades as "found objects" in a store, in an everyday setting, to a theory of infinitesimal differences even between two industrially made objects, while Benjamin was developing his meditations on the work of art at the time of its technological reproduction. Both were interested in repetition and differences, but the object attacked by Benjamin's repetition was the

---

[15] Ecke Bonk, "Delay included," in *Joseph Cornell/Marcel Duchamp . . . in Resonance*, Anne d'Harnoncourt (ed.). Philadelphia: Philadelphia Museum of Art, 1998, p. 102.
[16] Bertold Brecht, *Arbeitsjournal*, I. Frankfurt: Werner Hecht, 1973, p. 150.

ancient "aura" surrounding an authentic masterpiece, whereas for Duchamp there was an attempt to discover infinitely small auras. It may be that the diverging theories paved the way for a more foundational theory of art, that which was provided by Greenberg about the same time.

Thus, if "participation," the "infra-thin" and "transitivity" were key-words for Bourriaud in 1998, everything changed ten years later. By that time, he was a curator at the Tate Modern in London, and this is where he organized the ambitious collective show entitled "Altermodern." The show opened in the Spring of 2009. Bourriaud's keynote speech to the 2005 Art Association of Australia & New Zealand Conference had already explained the rationale in those terms: "Artists are looking for a new modernity that would be based on translation: What matters today is to translate the cultural values of cultural groups and to connect them to the world network." This consists in a "reloading process" of modernism according to the twenty-first-century issues. Bourriaud calls "Altermodernism" a movement connected to the creolisation of cultures and the fight for autonomy. It aims at offering the possibility of producing singularities in a more and more standardized world. Altermodern can be read as art produced in hypermodernity, hybridity, absorbing the ideas of canonical modernism while inserting these in a globalized context. The 2009 Tate exhibition included lectures, performances, films and manifestos. All of these attempted to define the main features of Altermodern. Bourriaud listed four main themes: (1) The end of postmodernism; (2) Cultural hybridization; (3) Travelling as a new way to produce forms; and (4) The expanding formats of art.

What has changed most in 2005–2009 was a belligerent tone that led to direct attacks on postmodernism. The postmodern was reduced by Bourriaud to a discourse of loss and mourning. Against this, he wants to reawaken a new "strategic universalism." (Manifesto, p. 12) It recirculates older modernist tropes such as Baudelaire's *flâneur*, but at the level of a globalized errancy. I will quote more of Bourriaud's manifesto for the Altermodern:

If today we can envisage a form of modernism, this is only possible starting from the issues of the present, and assuredly not by an obsessive return to the past, whatever its attributes.

Altermodernism can be defined as that moment when it became possible for us to produce something that made sense starting from an assumed heterochrony, that is, from a vision of human history as constituted of multiple temporalities, disdaining the nostalgia for the avant-garde and indeed for any era—a positive vision of chaos and complexity. It is neither a petrified kind of time advancing in loops (postmodernism) nor a linear vision of history (modernism), but a positive experience of disorientation through an art-form exploring all dimensions of the present, tracing lines in all directions of time and space. The artist turns cultural nomad: what remains of the Baudelairian model of modernism is no doubt this *flânerie*, transformed into a technique for generating creativeness and deriving knowledge.[17]

The *flâneur* turned nomad is a trope borrowed from Deleuze and Guattari, but Bourriaud cannot be called Deleuzian, since the term would be too "postmodern" for him. He prefers combining Althusser and Lyotard, Derrida and Lacan, Peter Sloterdijk and Alain Badiou. He sees three sorts of nomadism: in space, in time, and among signs, which accounts for the excessive production of contradictory signs among the artists he gathers. But this nomadism is also a formal nomadism:

> In a word, trajectories have become forms: contemporary art gives the impression of being uplifted by an immense wave of displacements, voyages, translations, migrations of objects and beings, to the point that we could state that the works presented in *Altermodern* unravel themselves along receding lines of perspective, the course they follow eclipsing the static forms through which they initially manifest themselves.[18]

The show at the Tate, with all its prologues and manifestos, its happenings and in-jokes (Simon Critchley was to read a text with novelist Tom McCarthy in order to discuss the issue of inauthenticity; the two authors did not come themselves but were replaced by hired actors who impersonated them) elicited mixed reviews in the specialized press. One of the most sympathetic witnesses was Edgar Schmitz writing for *Artforum* in May 2009. Noticing that Bourriaud wanted to create a new "modernism for the twenty-first century," Schmitz confesses to being baffled by the profusion of texts, declarations, new coinings, rushed events, overlapping theoretical conversations and the like.[19] Like all reviewers, Schmitz takes pains to contrast the overarching discourse predicated upon a modernity that finally take stock of a globalized world, and the "creolized" works displayed by artists coming from very different cultures and countries. Pascale Marthine Tayou

---

[17] Nicolas Bourriaud, *Altermodern*, London, Tate Publishing, 2009, p. 14.
[18] Bourriaud, see footnote 17.
[19] Edgar Schmitz, "Tate Triennial 2009," *Artforum* International, Vol. 47, No. 9, May 2009, p. 228.

fused African and European pop-cultures, Matthew Darbyshire recreated a Palace of Culture in the Warsaw of 1955, Subodh Gupta exhibited a cascade of shiny stainless steel utensils. Among the exhibits that struck me with full force was Lindsay Seers's *Extramission 6 (Black Maria)* in which she turns herself into a camera and then becomes a projector, and Nathaniel Mellors's delirious *Giantbum* where we enter a spiraling labyrinth with several video projections and a few realistic talking heads mounted on metal wires.

A 2009 blog entry by Jonathan Jones for the Guardian[20] captures well the panic experienced by most British visitors; they accused Bourriaud of theoretical arrogance, critical short-sightedness, verbal obfuscation and general pretention. Jones also points out the need for the knowledge of some theory if one wanted to grasp fully Bourriaud's intentions.

> Bourriaud's ideas deserve more than the knee-jerk "emperor's new clothes" accusations of some newspaper reviews. Anyway, his writing in the Altermodern catalogue is not some stereotype of obfuscating unreward. It contains terrific passages of pure eloquence: "It seems difficult, in retrospect, to define the postmodern otherwise than as . . . a marshy delta on the river of time. We can now identify those last 25 years of the 1900s as an interminable 'afterwards'; after the myth of progress, after the revolutionary utopia, after the retreat of colonialism, after the battles for political, social and sexual emancipation." Anger flares in these words—an anger recognisable to anyone who remembers the world-weary intellectual climate of the late 20th century. Postmodernism really was the fag-end of an age. Yet it has hung around. It's amazing that it has taken until 2009 for someone to formally conduct its funeral rites. For that alone, Bourriaud deserves our gratitude. But what does the Altermodern replace it with?

Then, Jones selects the one piece he deems really worthy of praise, the Mellors installation; I want to quote him as I entirely agree with his endorsement:

> Nathaniel Mellors's Giantbum is the last and best thing in the Tate Triennial. As the name suggests, it's daft. You walk into a coiling tunnel with soft brown walls where video screens show different excerpts from what might be a 1980s Doctor Who serial or a rival to Blake's Seven. Gradually, a story emerges from the grandiose dialogue: these characters are trapped inside a giant and have sent an old man, The Father, to find a

---

[20] Jonathan Jones's "OnArt Blog," at the *Guardian*, www.guardian.co.uk, April 8, 2009.

way out. But instead he's become a poo-eater, feasting on faeces. He tries to blame the Ploppen, the monstrous creatures he encountered in the giant's bum. All this is ridiculous, funny, absurd. There's a nihilism, too.

Yet, at the centre of the installation is a different component, of infinitely greater weight. This, too, is funny: three incredibly lifelike prosthetic heads speak and sing in unison. Are these cyborg faces the Ploppen? Yet, if they are funny, then they are creepy and eerie, too—the lo-fi joke has become a hi-fi reality. The three heads have a disturbing metaphysical presence. These three synthetic faces singing about "freedom" constitute the most convincing and troubling digital artwork I've ever seen. But they are presented within a deliberately risible charade of an installation.

The disparate quality of Mellors's installation is, if I understand rightly, part of what makes it Altermodern. There is, I believe, also a truth in that divided nature. Is the world at this moment funny or scary? As we enter the science fiction age yet at the same time live in the same old clutter as before, is this the future or a parody of it?

Indeed, Nathaniel Mellors manages to combine the creation of a new Joycean language, both arcane and regressive, in which the main issues are defecation and incest, with an astute allegory of the allegory given the self-reflexive and self-involved device, in which a variety of speakers, including the three animatronic talking heads all looking alike but saying different things, seem to comment upon themselves endlessly. It takes us several progressions into the labyrinth to reconstruct the plot, written by Mellors, in which medieval explorers get lost in the intestines of a giant. As Adrian Searle has expressed it pithily in *The Guardian*: "There is a lot of bad acting and declaiming, a succession of dreadful puns, gags about a time-travelling Doctor Poo and Father Shit-mass, and some mock golden showers. Imagine the 120 Days of Sodom redone as panto."[21] As most commentators have wondered, was it necessary to invent the term "Altermodern" to show these fantastic, zany and creative artworks?

My answer would be in the positive. There was a call for a decision to stop playing the game of the "post-post-post," and also to renounce a specific post-modern melancholia, as if it was mourning the "grand narrative" whose end has been repeatedly announced.[22] My own understanding of the term of

[21] Adrian Searle, "Altermodern review: 'The richest and most generous Tate Triennial yet,'" www.guardian.co.uk, 2 February 2009.
[22] See Nicolas Bourriaud, "Post-post, or Altermodern Times," in *The Radicant*. New York: Lukas and Sternberg, 2009, p. 182.

"Altermodern," a concept with which I am in sympathy, made me choose a different artist to exemplify what I think are the best features of "Altermodern." I found this in the video work of Stan Douglas.

Stan Douglas's "Vidéo," or how to bring Kafka and Beckett together

A black Canadian artist born in 1960, Stan Douglas belongs to the Vancouver school of conceptual art. His interest in Beckett goes back to 1988, when he organized a show of "Samuel Beckett's Teleplays" at the Vancouver Art Gallery, for which he wrote an excellent essay, "Goodbye Pork-Pie Hat."[23] Since then, he has produced several films, photographs, reenactments and videos based on Beckett's later work. The specific example I will analyze is "Vidéo," an 18-minute video loop from 2007, with a French cast, shot in La Courneuve. Douglas uses Beckett's *Film* as a grid, upon which he also splices Kafka's *Trial* and Jean-Luc Gordard's *Deux ou trois choses que je sais d'elle*.[24]

First, one needs to know what Beckett's *Film* is about to make sense of this video. The notes which explain the argument of *Film* state a thesis about the persecutory exemplified by old Buster Keaton caught fleeing from the camera's gaze, and from any sort of gaze: "*Esse est percipi*. // All extraneous perception suppressed, animal, human, divine, self-perception maintains in being. // Search of non-being in flight from extraneous perception breaking down in inescapability of self-perception."[25] *Film* rests upon a bold and original division between seen objects and the eye represented by the camera itself. It was almost impossible to endow the camera with this inquisitive and predatory quest, therefore Beckett has to imagine a subterfuge: when people would be seen at an angle of less than 45 degrees, they did not feel that they were being seen; if that angle exceeded 45 degrees, they would look horrified. The "camera eye" pursues Keaton, who has been storming along "in comic foundered precipitancy" and is discovered by the camera. The result is a sort

[23] Stan Douglas, "Good-bye Pork-Pie Hat," in *Stan Douglas*, edited by Scott Watson, Diane Thater and Carol J. Clover, London. Phaidon, 1998, pp. 92–9, subsequently abbreviated as SD.

[24] This last point has been made powerfully by Mieke Bal in an exemplary reading of "Vidéo," in Stan Douglas, *Past Imperfect—Works 1986–2007*, Hans D. Christ and Iris Dressler (eds). Stuttgart: Württembergischer Kunstverein, 2007, pp. 65–93.

[25] See *Film*, by Samuel Beckett, Complete scenario, Illustrations, Production Shots, with an essay "On Directing *Film*" by Alan Schneider. New York: Grove Press, 1969. Henceforth, *F* and page number.

of panic that makes him halt and turn towards the wall. When the camera reduces the angle, it releases him (*F*, pp. 14–15).

Director Alan Schneider evoked the numerous technical mistakes which led to a great part of the footage being unexploitable, while he had shot "more 180-degree and 360-degree pans than in a dozen Westerns." Beckett's rationale aimed at questioning the structure of the entire cinematographic apparatus; The plot climaxes when Keaton, alone in his room having got rid of his dog and his cat, covered the goldfish, the mirror and the bird, tears up one after the other his family photographs. After this effort, he seems ready to sleep or face death, but then discovers with a start that he is still seeing himself! In the last shot, Keaton wakes up from a trance in the rocking chair, seeing that the eye of the camera was himself, which is conveyed by a blurred shot of Keaton's face, with the same patch on the eye. These technical difficulties were not insuperable, but the embedding of the two visions is barely understood by spectators who have not read Beckett's notes. *Film*'s stilted and almost clumsy style saves the film from total opacity: the technique mimics Keaton's deadpan humor. There is a unity of technical means, where style and objects, wry humor and metaphysical anguish, lack of sound (except for a telling "shhh!") and black-and-white atmosphere converge. Moreover, the scene takes place around 1929 to call up both the Depression and Keaton's productive years.

In the same way as in *Film*, "Vidéo," remains silent until the end, when we hear a gunshot and then loud pop music. There are several visual echoes: the young black woman who goes home covers her bird with a blanket, she opens a folder very similar to the one Buster Keaton has, with photographs of himself at various ages; similarly, the young woman see herself younger, and then tears up all the pictures. Above all, it is the insistent presence of police officers who come in and out of her room that echoes with Kafka's work. One soon realizes that Douglas has grafted the plot of *The Trial* shot in 1962 by Orson Welles. Welles had freely adapted Kafka's famous novel. One morning, Josef K., a young bank clerk, finds threatening police officers in his bedroom who inform him that he is under arrest. They do not divulge the nature of the crime, but it seems that he can remain free for a while. K. discusses the issue with his landlady and then his attractive neighbor, whom he ends up kissing. When he goes to his office, he is reprimanded by a superior, and then returning later, after an evening at the opera, sees the police officers who first visited him whipped in a back room. K.'s uncle suggests that he should consult with a lawyer. Before, K. meets the hyper-sexual wife of a courtroom official, and passes a room full of condemned men waiting for trial. The lawyer is unable to help, but his wife sends K. to a painter, Titorelli, who has access to the court. He gives relevant tips, but the real disclosure comes from a priest in the cathedral who lets K. know that he has been condemned to death. Just on the eve of his thirty-first birthday, K. is seized bodily by two executioners. They lock arms with his, bring him forcefully to a quarry and give him a knife. When K. refuses to commit suicide, a stick of dynamite is thrown at him. K. laughs and picks it up. We see from a distance a huge explosion. From this bare-bones summary, one can see that there is not much in common with *Film*. Yet, Douglas manages to splice the two almost seamlessly. We see the crowd of people waiting for their trial, at the end the black woman is given a gun and a loud shot is heard.

From the start, Douglas wanted to correct the view of high modernism put forward by Adorno, who, according to him, had a limited view of Beckett's impact. Yet, it was Adorno who had linked Beckett and Kafka, as we have seen in Chapter 7, when he interpreted *Endgame* through the filter of "Hunter Gracchus." It is clear that Douglas mixes the two canonical modernist writers less to affirm their combined power as "great texts" or "epoch-making films" than to resist a sacralizing theory of modernism that has led in the past to ahistorical monumentalization. This is why he rejects the "ahistoricity, closure and the affirmation of a masculine academic canon" (SD, p. 92), reiterating that what interested Beckett was the resolute treatment of "ignorance and impotence." To explain more precisely what he rejects, he quotes a sentence that he finds "typical" of Adorno:

For the norm of existential philosophy—people should be themselves because they can no longer become anything else—*Endgame* posits the antithesis, that precisely this self is not a self but rather the aping imitation of something non-existent. Hamm's mendacity exposes the lie concealed in saying "I" and thereby exhibiting substantiality; whose opposite is the content disclosed by the "I." Immutability; the epitome of transience, is its ideology. What used to be the truth content of the subject—thinking—is still only preserved in its gestural shell. Both main figures act as if they were reflecting on something, but without thinking. (SD, p. 93)[26]

---

[26] In SD, pp. 92–3, Stan Douglas quotes Michael T. Jones's translation of Adorno in *New German Critique*, Vol. 26, Spring/Summer 1982, p. 143. The translation by Shierry Weber Nicholsen is different: "*Endgame* presents the antithesis to existential philosophy's norm that human beings should be what they are because there is nothing else they can be— the idea that this very self is not the self but a slavish imitation of something that does not exist. Hamm's duplicity points up the lie involved in saying 'I' and thereby ascribing to oneself the substantiality whose opposite is the contents that the ego synthesizes. The enduring, as the quintessence of the ephemeral, is in its ideology. But of thought, which used to be the truth content of the subject, only the gestural shell is retained. The two figures act as though they were thinking something over, without in fact thinking anything over." Adorno, *Notes to Literature*, vol. 1. New York: Columbia, 1991, pp. 267–8.

For Douglas, such analyses are "typical" not only of Adorno but also of post-war European ideology—the old subjectivity that existed once in Beethoven's times has been lost and is today nothing but a "grotesque of ossified form." (SD, p. 93) The "culture industry" prevents today's subjects from recognizing this condition, and they exhibit "a humanity that has become an advertisement for inhumanity." (SD, p. 93) While Douglas admits that this captures something of the ethos of plays like *Godot* and *Endgame*, he adds that by the late 1950s, Beckett has moved forward, and that his theatrical work, until then relatively conventional in the sense that it did not trouble the division between spectators and actors, moved closer to his prose. Doing this, Beckett started "articulating the mendacity of 'they' as an equivalent to the 'lie concealed in saying "I"—moving as it does from describing to *inhabiting* situations.'" He goes on: "In these theatrical settings, both audience and author are asked to admit their complicity in the visibility of the spectacle, and distanced judgments or interpretive 'explanation' becomes an uneasy pretence." (SD, p. 93)

In fact, in this extremely sharp and prescient analysis, Stan Douglas proves to be entirely right. Beckett, who started out as a "high modernist" slowly discovered the infinite potentialities for "othering," meaning that media such as film, radio, television, installation art, etc. could provide. One letter about *Film* stands out in his correspondence with Alan Schneider. This was written after Beckett had watched two screenings of *Film*, not yet given its final cut:

> After the first I was not too happy, after the second I felt it really was something. Not quite in the way I intended, but as sheer beauty, power and strangeness of the image. The problem of the double vision for example is not really solved, but the attempt to solve it has given the film a plastic value which it would not have otherwise.... from having been troubled by a certain failure to communicate fully by purely visual means the basic intention, I now begin to feel that this is unimportant and that the images obtained probably gain in force what they lose as ideograms and that whole idea behind the film, while sufficiently expressed for those so minded, has been chiefly of value on the formal and structural level.[27]

Here is an interesting admission from an author who was eager to keep his control on all the technical and intellectual aspects of his works.

---

[27] Beckett's letter from 29.9.1964 to Alan Schneider, in "No Author Better Served," *The correspondence of Samuel Beckett with Alan Schneider*, Maurice Harmon (ed.). Cambridge, MA: Harvard University Press, 1998, p. 166. This letter contains the notes, diagrams and explanations added to the scenario of *Film*.

In that sense, we can understand what Stan Douglas achieves when he modifies *Film* in such an apparently disrespectful way or in modernizing or politicizing moves. He wants to avoid the complacent tone of general critique that we find in Adorno's theoretical generalizations. Yet, very intelligently, he also avoids an easy recourse to identity politics based, as they could have been, on the rights of the oppressed or on the exception to the system embodied by excluded minorities. Here is how Douglas formulates his attitude, which rejects both post-war existentialism and cultural critique:

> In contrast to Beckett's persistently insufficient first persons, the philosophical existentialists and the critical theorists of the Frankfurt school often claimed for themselves a rhetorical self through which they could speak as the last instance of a subjectivity soon to be extinct. An *ideal* self. A victim of history who speaks with a tacit nostalgia for some presumed wholeness, describing, in minute detail, all that the historical moment refuses him—ignoring the way in which that history persists in himself, and ignoring as well all that has been left out of his dialectic.
>
> (SD, p. 93)

When Beckett is totally successful he is able to write against "this pathetic heroism." (SD, p. 93) Later on, he observes that the "heroic (if melancholic) identity" described by Adorno and staged by Beckett in the 1950s was always male, white, bourgeois and of European descent (SD, p. 98). Modernist nostalgia has to be both harnessed and undermined, read as symptom and made to serve a broader perspective. Douglas wants to retain Beckett's "persistent distrust of discrete self-identity" while rejecting the "potentially authoritarian subject that lies behind any such identification." (SD, p. 98) Beckett has delineated (or at least allows others to imagine) the shape of an activity of meaning which, for our culture and its institutions, is still dismissed or marginalized as "non-meaning." (SD, p. 98)

Why then the forceful hybridization of Becket and Kafka? Beckett would no doubt have been horrified by such a move, a splicing that destroys the purity of his original meaning; and he would conclude that even if one can admit that Buster Keaton be replaced by a black woman, to have her commit suicide at the end "kills" the meaning he had intended about perception and the "ineluctability of self-perception." But here, self-perception and perception are all inscribed within the domination of the eye of the surveillance camera that begins and ends, thus bringing about the circularity of the constant loop achieved by "Vidéo." Moreover, this hybridization of *Film + der Prozess* could be understood as a belated Adornian joke. Indeed, Adorno has always been wishing to compare the two writers, and this was a comparison that Beckett

had refused. At their first meeting in November 1958, Adorno was surprised to
see that Beckett was making "reproaches" against Kafka, which baffled him
and prevented him from developing a systematic comparison between the two
writers he had planned. The point is not that Douglas has spliced elements
from both plots rather seamlessly, but that in order to do so, he has had to take
another distance. This is the distance afforded by the third or fourth world
within the first world of high culture; thus he needs the black woman, the
hiding black man, several hints of political terror, and allusions to a French
scene dominated by unrest about paperless and homeless African *sans-papiers*
in Paris, in a context of social trouble spreading in the French *banlieues*, all that
decenters and hybridizes both works and authors.

Finally, it is a meditation on torture that connects Beckett and Kafka much
more than metaphysical or formal issues. We may remember that K. has
unwittingly sent two "wardens," the police assistants Franz and Willem, to a
horrible punishment by flagellation, a scene that he witnesses near his work
office. The scene of torture and unfair punishment already announces his fate,
since he lies to cover up the whipping by blurting out to his co-workers: "It was
only a dog howling in the courtyard,"[28] which, much later, generates the famous
"Like a dog!" of the ending (T, p. 229). As to Beckett, a single look at "Rough for
Radio II" (written in French in the late sixties) or "What Where" (1984) will
persuade readers that the question of torture is of prime importance for the
later work. Following Adorno's and Horkheimer's insights in *Dialectics of the
Enlightenment*, but with very different concepts, Stan Douglas also links
Beckett with Sade:

> Superficially, Beckett's work resembles that variety of Modernism,
> initiated by Sade, which exacts from its culture extreme instances of
> rational form in order to parody tacit contradictions. But unlike the
> Sadean libertine who in self-satisfied egoism is content to catalogue the
> limits of his world, Beckett admits that the limits of his culture are not
> the limits of possibility. An unfortunate consequence of the Sadean
> method is that it is often only capable of replicating, in inverted form, the
> authority that it had intended to criticize—maintaining as it does a
> theological notion of centre or hierarchy which appropriates certainty
> for its blasphemy and authority for the blasphemous subject. The
> difference in Beckett is that, in place of this closed world (which had

---

[28] Franz Kafka, *The Trial*, Willa and Edwin Muir (trans.). New York: Schocken, 1984, p. 87,
hereafter T plus page number.

been invented in order to be mastered), he imagines an uncertain one: the residence of an even less certain subjectivity.[29]

We now understand better what Stan Douglas means when he states that he is interested in exploring the "failed utopias" of modernism, while remaining true to one central aspect of modernism: its "exploratory nature."[30] His art of the "interform" plays on the broader mutliculturalism of today and tomorrow while critically revisiting our modernist heritage, making it indeed "Altermodern."

---

[29] Stan Douglas, "Goodbye Pork-Pie Hat," in *Stan Douglas*, Scott Watson, Diana Thater and Carol J. Clover (eds). London: Phaidon, 1998, p. 92.

[30] See "Stan Douglas in conversation with Diedrich Diederichsen and Nora Alter," Slought Foundation Audio-visual Archive, February 14, 2011.

11

Conclusion

The long-lasting joke of the future
(Marx and Kafka, Althusser and Antigone)

Le soleil se couche en des confitures de crimes,
Dans cette mer plate comme avec la main.[1]

In "Post-post, or Altermodern times," his conclusion of *The Radicant*, Nicolas Bourriaud alludes to the thesis developed by Peter Sloterdijk in a 2005 book[2] that offers a general "philosophical theory of globalization."[3] In this ambitious and far-ranging synthesis, Sloterdijk retraces the history of the shrinking planet, when the world was conceived as a "globe," a globe that would be unified more and more under the aegis of international capitalism. The steady development of technology has contributed hugely to the acceleration process: it all began in the middle of the nineteenth century, when the model of progress was seen as a series of explosions in an engine using oil or gas. The rapid release of energy in the air became the paradigm for a speeding modernity that felt like the divine impetus of the new age.[4] Sloterdijk's remarkable book explores the counterpart of the scientific dogma as a progress dependent on universal scientific progress: the retreat of the subject who inhabits an "inner world" expanded to the dimensions of the universe. This he finds in a poetic phrase borrowed from a poem by Rilke, "Every Thing beckons us to feel it." The fourth stanza begins like this:

Through all creatures *one* space expands:
World interior space. Birds at flight still

---

[1] "The sun is sinking into marmalades of crimes // In this sea flattened as if by a hand." From the sonnet "Outwards" by Henry J.-M. Levet (1900), in Henry J.-M. Levet, *Cartes Postales et autres textes*, Bernard Delvaille (ed.). Paris: Gallimard, 2001, p. 93.

[2] Peter Sloterdijk, *In Weltinnenraum des Kapitals, Für eine philosophische Theorie der Globalisierung*. Frankfurt: Suhrkamp, 2005.

[3] Now translated into English, see Peter Sloterdijk, *In the World Interior of Capital: Towards a Philosophical Theory of Globalization*, Wieland Hoban (trans.). Cambridge: Polity Press, 2013.

[4] In *The Radicant* (New York: Lukas and Sternberg, 2009, p. 177) Bourriaud quotes Peter Sloterdijk, see footnote 2, pp. 351–2.

Fly through us. O, that I want it to grow,
The tree I see outside now growing *in* me.[5]

To speak of a refuge in an "inner space" or a "world interior" is misleading, since Rilke always appeals to the principle of the "Open" that we discussed briefly in Chapter 5. This "Open," that is both an inner and an outer space, acquires more importance given the development of the technologies of instant communication. Here, with the vision of a complete interpenetration of nature (birds, trees) and lyrical subjects, Rilke provides an instant counter-utopia to capitalistic globalization. The date of the poem's writing is not a coincidence, as Sloterdijk notes.[6] We have not forgotten that it was Rilke to whom Freud tried to explain that the impending disaster of a world war, and the death of all beautiful things, should be not a reason to fall prey to melancholy.[7]

What I would add to Sloterdijk's compelling philosophy of globalization is that the model of a future predicated on more and more rapid releases of energy, from oil erupting in gushes to immensely powerful computerized engines, rockets and drones, which accomplishes the unleashing of an exploding but "convulsive beauty" dear to Breton, this futuristic future taking war as the ultimate form of the new art because it will cleanse the old world of all its hangovers, all this can also be construed as a Freudian theory of laughter. Indeed, laughter implies a pent-up energy suddenly released in the air by verbal means; it rests upon a whole economy of saving and expenditure, and it connects several persons or groups of persons engaged in social interactions.

This is why I conclude by presenting a series of vignettes focusing on laughter and theory. In my 2002 book, I had alluded to Hans Blumenberg's idea of the laughter of the Thracian maid as a key to the role of theory throughout the ages.[8] Going back to Plato, Blumenberg's brilliant book, *The Laugh of the Thracian Maid*,[9] examines the long tradition of commentaries on the fall into a well of Thales—the philosopher who could observe the stars in the sky but could not see where he stepped on the earth. Since Plato, it was narrated by authors such as Chaucer and Montaigne. Heidegger returned to

---

[5]   Rainer Maria Rilke, "*Es winkt zu Fühlung fast aus allen Dingen*" (1914), in *Werke in drei Bänden*, Band II. Frankfurt: Insel Verlag, 1966, pp. 92–3. I translate literally.
[6]   Sloterdijk, see footnote 2, Note 219, p. 308.
[7]   See Sigmund Freud, "On transience," in *Writings on Art and Literature*. Stanford: Stanford University Press, 1997, p. 176.
[8]   Jean-Michel Rabaté, *The Future of Theory*. Oxford: Blackwell, pp. 2 and 136–7.
[9]   Hans Blumenberg, *Das Lachen der Thrakerin: Eine Urgeschichte der Theorie*. Frankfurt: Suhrkamp, 1987.

the anecdote in "The question toward the thing," arguing that science and philosophy should part their ways. For Blumenberg, on the other hand, one should reconcile the feminine laughter of a maid and the explorations of the older philosopher: laughter brings a corrective limit to the claims of Theory and, above all, it spares nobody in the end. Here, by moving back to a similar notion in Althusser, I will shift the emphasis to the issues of futurity and community. What can a future laughter mean, how can we laugh at the future? We will have to begin with one of the first thinkers of a global future, Karl Marx, as re-read by Lacan, a psychoanalyst who pays attention to symptomatic manifestations like laughter.

The laughter of the capitalist

When Lacan was reading Marx, quite early on his attention was attracted to a specific type of laughter. In a seminar from the Winter of 1968, Lacan reminisced about his discovery of Marx's works when he was about twenty. He was reading the first chapter in *The Capital*, Book III, Marx's rather involved account of the production of surplus-value. Lacan, who would read *Capital* while taking the metro to go to his hospital like all other Parisian blue-collars, was suddenly struck by a passage. This is when the capitalist, who sees how absolute surplus-value can be generated, stops in his account and laughs. Lacan comments on this: "This feature may seem superfluous, yet this is the point that had struck me at the time of these useful readings. It seemed to me at the time that this laughter derives from what Marx is unveiling, that is the essence of surplus-value."[10] Marx is indeed launching a whole Introduction to the theory of value at that point of *Capital*:

> The capitalist paid to the laborer a value of 3 shillings, and the laborer gave him back an exact equivalent in the value of 3 shillings, added by him to the cotton: he gave him value for value. Our friend, up to this time so purse-proud, suddenly assumes the modest demeanor of his own workman, and exclaims: "Have I myself not worked? Have I not performed the labor of superintendence and of overlooking the spinner? And does not this labor, too, create value?" His overlooker and his manager try to hide their smiles. Meanwhile, after a hearty laugh, he re-assumes his usual mien. Though he chanted to us the whole creed of the economists, in reality, he says he would not give a brass farthing

---

[10] Jacques Lacan, *Le Séminaire, livre XVI, D'un Autre à l'autre*, session of December 4, 1968, Jaques-Alain Miller (ed.). Paris: Seuil, 2006, pp. 64–5.

for it. He leaves this and all such like subterfuges and juggling tricks to the professors of Political Economy, who are paid for it. . . . The circumstance, that on the one hand the daily sustenance of labor-power costs only half a day's labor, while on the other hand the very same labor-power can work during a whole day, that consequently the value which its use during one day creates, is double what he pays for that use, this circumstance is, without doubt, a piece of good luck for the buyer, but by no means an injury to the seller.

Our capitalist foresaw this state of things, and that was the cause of his laughter. . . . The trick has at last succeeded; money has been converted into capital.[11]

The capitalist's laughter accompanies the disclosure of a fundamental principle: the value that labor-power possesses on its own and the value that it creates differ in nature and in quantity. The capitalist laughs because he is both exposing his trick and enacting it; he does so both obviously and covertly, and in the end nobody understands his game. This is the essence of capitalism: the unholy conversion of money into capital, of work into surplus-value. This laughter has literary echoes and philosophical predecessors; it covers up the silent and monstrous work of metamorphosis:

This metamorphosis, this conversion of money into capital, takes place both within the sphere of circulation and also outside it; within the circulation, because conditioned by the purchase of the labor-power in the market; outside the circulation, because what is done within it is only a stepping-stone to the production of surplus-value, a process which is entirely confined to the sphere of production. Thus "*tout est pour le mieux dans le meilleur des mondes possibles*." ["Everything is for the best in the best of all possible worlds."—Voltaire, *Candide*] By turning his money into commodities that serve as the material elements of a new product, and as factors in the labor-process, by incorporating living labor with their dead substance, the capitalist at the same time converts value, i.e., past, materialized, and dead labor into capital, into value big with value, a live monster that is fruitful and multiplies. (see footnote 11)

There is something satanic in the process, and in another section, Marx quotes Goethe's *Faust*. This instant of disclosure of the secret is a Freudian

---

[11] Karl Marx, *Capital: A Critique of Political Economy*, vol. I (1867), translated into English by Samuel Moore and Edward Aveling. Moscow: Online version, Americanized spelling. For the original text, see Karl Marx und Friedrich Engels, *Das Kapital, Werke*, Band 23. Berlin: Dietz, 1970, pp. 207 and 208.

Witz. Truth has been expressed in an apparent joke that was in fact exhibiting a secret.

Here is, for Freud, the paradigm of the joke, Heine's *Witz* about the poor Hirsch-Hyacinth explaining that Baron Rothschild has treated him quite "famillionairely."[12] In his account, Freud sees a principle of verbal economy at work, which also brings out something hidden (p. 5). Collapsing "familiarly" and "millionaire," one follows the law of condensation, one of the mechanisms of the dream. The laugher of the capitalist is a sleight-of-hand exposing the mechanism of surplus-value, just as the laughter of the joke is triggered by a short-circuit. Economy and spending clash with each other in a burst of hilarity. Why does the capitalist laugh? Because he knows that he makes money without having to work by milking the unfair system of production based on surplus-value. Why does the joker laugh, thus making the others laugh? Because he can attract sympathy without having to do anything, just by letting the potentialities of language work for him, exploiting for an instant of verbal triumph a mechanism that is available to all, in their dreams at least. Hence we will have to conclude that the unconscious of capitalism functions like the unconscious of language.

Lacan loved the most outrageous slogans and mottos painted in red letters on the walls of Paris in May 1968, not only because a few quoted him indirectly but also because they disclosed hidden truths ironically: "It is forbidden to forbid," "Be realistic: take your desires for realities," "Take down structures into the streets," etc. When his seminar resumed in November 1968, it was devoted to the elaboration of new mathemes, concepts and formulas. Alluding to Althusser's groundbreaking reading of Marx in *Reading Capital* (*Lire Le Capital*), Lacan was thinking more of "*Rire Le Capital.*" Laughter defines a libidinal economy combining Freud and Marx. Thus Marx paves the way to a new understanding of how the "object a" (the part object cause of desire in psychoanalytic theory) is caught up in an economy of *jouissance.* Lacan coined the term "*Mehrlust*" (surplus enjoyment) as parallel to Marx's *Mehrwert*, surplus-value. If capitalism is the modern way of dealing with production (everything hinges around the means of production), psychoanalysis inverts the process of capitalism: one pays to work on oneself, which generates a truth that speaks, eschewing capture by the dialectical twists of surplus-enjoyment. Inverting the usual links between truth and knowledge, Lacan takes knowledge beyond the field in which it serves the "exploitation of men by men." But if communist is, in the famous joke, "just

---

[12] Sigmund Freud, *The Joke and Its Relation to the Unconscious*, Joyce Crick (trans.). New York: Penguin, 2002, p. 4.

the reverse," Marx points to the circular link between the concept of "revolution" and that of capitalism.[13]

It is in this context that Lacan elaborated his Freudo-Marxism. It culminated with his theory of the four discourses developed in the Fall of 1969. This theory mediated between Althusser's revision of Marxism (the critique of economism, the rejection of humanism and the new theory of ideology) and Foucault's critical historicism called "genealogy." Without entering into the details, I'll stress that the theory of the four discourses is founded upon the term of "surplus *jouissance*." The coining dates from 1967, combining Freud's *Lust* with Marx's *Mehrwert*, and accounts for the social function of symptoms as well as for the libidinal energies invested in social labor. Two couples are opposed, or better embraced: the Master and the Hysteric who appear complementary as they replace the old Hegelian category of the master and the slave, and the Psychoanalyst and the Academic, also opposed and complementary, replacing the couple of psychoanalysis and philosophy.

Later, Lacan would add the "discourse of capitalism" as well as the "discourse of science" to the four discourses. Science would be associated with the discourse of the Hysteric in so far as the latter aims at procuring new knowledge, while it is linked with the discourse of the University when this knowledge is merely catalogued and transmitted. Similarly, the discourse of capitalism falls under the sway of the discourse of the Master, since it is also the discourse of power, of the institutions, of the State. Society is caught from the specific angle of psychoanalytic practice, a practice in which everything is reduced to language and its effects. It is a practice that highlights what is most commonly forgotten in these issues: the place of the subject's enjoyment asks what is the main signifier that can provide ideals or a program, and looks for a dialectization of knowledge (understood as "unconscious knowledge") and *jouissance* under the shape of an elusive or impossible object, this "surplus enjoyment."

In "Radiophonie,"[14] Lacan introduced a "discourse of capital," examining Marx's desire as a thinker:

> For Marx, with the plus-value that his chisel detached so as to restitute it to the discourse of capital, paid the price one has to put to negate, as I do, that any discourse be pacified by a meta-language (of Hegelian formalism in that case); this price, he paid it by forcing himself to follow the naive

[13] Lacan, see footnote 9, p. 333.
[14] Jacques Lacan, "Radiophonie" (1970), in *Autres Ecrits*, Jacques-Alain Miller (ed.). Paris: Seuil, 2001, pp. 403–46. Abbreviated as AE and page number.

discourse of ascendant capitalism, and by the hellish life he gave himself thereof.

This verifies what I say about the *plus-de-jouir*. The *Mehrwert* is the *Marxlust*, that is Marx's own *plus-de-jouir*.

(AE, p. 434)

The joking "displacement of discourse" that Lacan elaborated was far from the utopian hope that society could be changed after a revolutionary strike or as the outcome of a civil war. Lacan refused another temptation, that of the revolutionary's abnegation, the polite disappearance of a militant's desire for the greater glory of "a rosier tomorrow." Subjects cannot disappear to enact the logic of History. Those who do, end up playing the role of "baby-sitters of History": "When one will acknowledge the kind of *plus-de-jouir* that makes one say 'Wow, this is somebody!', then one will be on the way toward a dialectical matter maybe more active than the Party fodder (*chair à Parti*, punning both on '*chair à canon*,' cannon fodder, and on '*chair à pâté*,' patty filling) commonly used as baby-sitter of history (*baby-sitter de l'histoire*)." (AE, p. 415) Even if the combination of the four discourses can never be immune to what Hegel had called the "cunning of Reason," a reason underpinning a History that arranges and accommodates everything, a clearer understanding of its logic should make us aware that "the future lasts for a long time." It becomes crucial to refuse to turn into "cannon fodder" for its slaughter-bench, as well as to be wary of not playing the nice but deluded role of "baby sitter" of History, while the grownups continue laughing up their sleeves, secure in their magical tricks and accumulating more power and capital. But will the baby-sitter of History be male or female?

Antigone's laughter

Hegel has an answer: the baby-sitter is a woman. Rather than being called the first philosopher of desire, Hegel is the first philosopher of sexual difference. In the *Phenomenology of Spirit*, this appears in the discussion of Sophocles' *Antigone*. Antigone faces her two dead brothers: one is a hero for the city of Thebes, the other is a traitor. Yet they belong to the same family. Hegel sums up how sexual difference works within the unity of the family: "The difference of the sexes and their ethical content remains, however, in the unity of the substance, and its movement is just the constant becoming of that substance."[15]

---

[15] G.W.F. Hegel, *The Phenomenology of Spirit*, A. V. Miller (trans.). Oxford: Oxford University Press, 1977, p. 276.

Hegel has posited the community and the family as separate horizons, one of which is suited to man, the other to woman. This ethical substance, however, is immediately blown to bits by the battle to the death between Eteocles and Polyneices, on the male side, and by the challenge Antigone represents to Creon's law, on the female side.[16]

Creon embodies the political values of the city, Antigone embodies the ethical values of the family. Creon honors the defender of Thebes, Eteocles, but leaves Polyneices's body unburied. He prevents anyone from rendering the rites to him upon penalty of death. Antigone defies his law when she covers Polyneices's body. For Hegel, the conflicting value systems have equal rights. Creon wishes to separate "the good from the bad" in the name of a logic of inclusion and exclusion, Antigone stresses a more fundamental respect for the dead that admits of no division—hence we can think that she reasserts the universality of these "unwritten laws": no-one should be allowed to have his or her corpse devoured by wild beasts in the open, everyone should be allowed to be buried.[17] Nevertheless, one passage has caused wonder. Antigone presents the universal duty owed to all the dead, but distinguishes between other members of her family and her relationship to one particular brother. She expresses this in the poignant lamentation before she walks into her tomb:

> O but I would not have done the forbidden thing
> For any husband or for any son.
> For why? I could have had another husband
> And by him other sons, if one were lost;
> But father and mother lost, where would I get
> Another brother? For thus preferring you,
> My brother, Creon condemns me and hales me away,
> Never a bride, never a mother, unfriended,
> Condemned alive to a solitary death.[18]

Goethe expressed the wish that these lines were an interpolation, as Lacan reminds us.[19] Yet, Hegel is not shocked: "The loss of the brother is therefore irreparable to the sister, and her duty towards him is the highest."[20] Evidently, Lacan relishes the "odor of scandal" that these lines contain (S7, p. 256). One

[16] Hegel, see footnote 14, p. 284.
[17] Sophocles, "Antigone," in *The Theban Plays*, B. F. Watling (trans.). Baltimore: Penguin, 1968, p. 140.
[18] Sophocles, see footnote 16, p. 150.
[19] Jacques Lacan, *Seminar VII, The Ethics of Psychoanalysis*, Dennis Porter (trans.). New York: Norton, 1992, p. 255. Abbreviated as S7 and page number.
[20] Hegel, see footnote 14, p. 275.

of the main issues implied by this "scandal" concerns the concept of "generation," both in the sense of the ability to procreate, here refused to Antigone, and in the sense that the succession of generations has been perverted after Oedipus's transgression. Antigone's very name suggests a movement "against" generation, something like a manifesto for "No Future." It is as if her fate was linked to a deliberate or enforced sterility. Moreover, in this passage, she contradicts the universal command that one should respect all the dead, whoever they are. Her shocking personal preference for one slain brother can lead to an obvious psychoanalytic reading that would detect an incestuous love linking brother and sister.[21] This has been expressed wittily by Gérard Pommier:

> We all love Antigone, don't we, this magnificent heroine who braves the laws of the city in the name of higher laws that appear to be placed even higher than our modern humanitarian human rights. But we should ask ourselves a question: would Antigone have reacted so bravely if she had been in analysis? Would she have acted in the same way knowing that her desire to bury her brother with her own hands was the other side of her desire to kill him, or the result of her ambivalent incestuous love for him? You see then how psychoanalytic discourse can be hated and how there are perhaps good reasons to resist it! And if Antigone had said: "I realize that my passion to bury my brother is as great as my passion to kill him with my own hands, but nevertheless, I will not give up on my desire and keep obeying the higher laws"—then this would probably not have made a very good drama.[22]

However, Hegel interprets this absolute singularity differently:

> The brother ... passes from the divine law, in whose sphere he lived, over to human law. But the sister becomes, or the wife remains, the guardian of the divine law. In this way, the two sexes overcome their (merely) natural being and appear in their ethical significance, as diverse beings who share between them the two distinctions belonging to the ethical substance.[23]

---

[21] Patrick Guyomard writes: "Lacan's praise of Antigone is the application of a theory of desire in which death names the power and effect of the signifier, but at the same time it is a praise, although denied, of incest." *La Jouissance Tragique*. Paris: Aubier, 1992, p. 59.

[22] Gérard Pommier, "New resistances to psychoanalysis," in J-M. Rabaté, *Lacan in America*. New York: The Other Press, 2000, p. 81. See also George Steiner's *Antigones*. Oxford: Oxford University Press, 1984, pp. 156–62, for a treatment of the incest theme.

[23] Hegel, see footnote 15, p. 275.

228   *Crimes of the Future*

Hegel's reading of *Antigone* presupposes not just a clash between the law of the city and the moral code of individual, but also a meditation on the ethical (and political) function of sexual difference. This explains why Creon is afraid of looking weak in front of a mere woman: "Better be beaten, if need be, by a man, // Than let a woman get the better of us."[24] (A, p. 144) The family is the site of a transition between the hidden laws coming from the gods and the written laws of the city. The brother emerges from the family and moves into the public domain, while the sister can choose to remain in the house, as Ismene does, or go out into the open and act, as Antigone does. Hegel seizes on this and on the subversive factor represented by Antigone: insofar as she is not merely the representative of the unwritten law of the gods, but also of an extreme singularity of desire, she embodies the "perversion" of the universalist values upon which Creon's order is based.

> Since the community only gets an existence through its interference with the happiness of the Family, and by dissolving (individual) self-consciousness into the universal, it creates for itself in what it suppresses and what is at the same time essential to it an internal enemy—womankind in general. Womankind—the everlasting irony (in the life) of the community—changes by intrigue the universal end of the government into a private end, transforms its universal act into a work of some particular individual, and perverts the universal property of the state into a possession and ornament for the Family.[25]

Hegel thus stresses the guilt inherent in Antigone's action. She transgresses the law knowingly: "By the deed ... it becomes guilt. .... And the guilt also acquires the meaning of *crime*; for as simple, ethical consciousness, it has turned towards one law, but turned its back on the other and violates the latter by its deed."[26] Antigone embodies ethical consciousness because of her awareness of her crime. Hegel quotes the line:

> Because we suffer we acknowledge we have erred.
> (Antigone, I, p. 926)[27]

This is the only line in which Antigone hesitates for an instant; she is on the threshold of death since she has just been condemned to be entombed alive.

---

[24] Sophocles, *Antigone*, in *The Theban Plays*, translated by E. F. Watling. Baltimore: Penguin, 1968, p. 144.
[25] Hegel, see footnote 15, p. 288.
[26] Hegel, see footnote 15, p. 282.
[27] Hegel, see footnote 15, p. 284.

This statement has been glossed by a translator as meaning: "If the gods regard this right (so that I, though pious, am thought impious), I would confess, having been taught by suffering (according to the maxim παθος μαθος) that I have done wrong."[28] Other commentators refuse to give undue emphasis to a single line. Most of the time, Antigone seemed adamant that she was right to act as she did.[29] She may be arguing that the gods will finally declare her right, since she postulates that their decrees should be valued above human laws.

Hegel, having paired off Creon and Antigone as both "wrong" in some way, concludes that the only possible outcome is a total annihilation of each party:

> The victory of one power and its character, and the defeat of the other, would thus be only the part and the incomplete work which irresistibly advances to the equilibrium of the two. Only in the downfall of both sides alike is absolute right accomplished, and the ethical substance as the negative power which engulfs both sides, that is, omnipotent and righteous Destiny, steps on the scene.[30]

Once more, death will remain the "absolute master." Death will mediate, allowing a movement toward a definition of ethical life (*Sittlichkeit*) as a substance reconciling the universal and the singular in the community. We see Hegel contrasting the ethical law, founded on the universal, with desire, which is always particular.[31] Thus the relation of the sexes cannot be abstracted from power relations. This is why it is not enough to pit the unwritten law of the Family against the written law of the State. The *Unterschied der Geschlechter*, the difference of the sexes, has to traverse both the ethical and the political realms. This leads to a generic difference between tragedy and comedy.

A conflict between passion and duty would too quickly develop its comic overtones, as Hegel notes,[32] whereas authentic tragedy relies on the conflict between one duty and another duty, when each group knows immediately what is to be done. Hesitation and irony function as hindrances to pure

---

[28] Sophocles, *Antigone*, Martin L. D'Ooge (ed.). Boston: Ginn and Co., 1887, p. 113.
[29] See Patricia Jagentowicz Mills, "Hegel's *Antigone*," in *Feminist Interpretations of Hegel*, Patricia Jagentowicz Mills (ed.). University Park: Pennsylvania State University Press, 1996, pp. 68–71.
[30] Hegel, see footnote 14, p. 285.
[31] Hegel, see footnote 14, pp. 274–5.
[32] Hegel, see footnote 14, p. 279.

tragedy. If you wait, you are tempted to smile or snigger. This is how Hegel watches, as a disenchanted observer, the ethical substance of the *polis* crumble to pieces. The main culprit in this irremediable dissolution is Antigone, who embodies a new version of sexual difference: feminine irony.

> Since the community only gets an existence through its interference with the happiness of the Family, and by dissolving [individual] self-consciousness into the universal, it creates for itself in what it suppresses and what is at the same time essential to it an internal enemy—womankind in general. Womankind—the everlasting irony [in the life] of the community—changes by intrigue the universal end of the government into a private end, transforms its universal activity into a work of some particular individual, and perverts the universal property of the state into a possession and ornament for the Family. Woman in this way turns to ridicule the earnest wisdom of mature age which, indifferent to purely private pleasures and enjoyments, as well as to playing an active part, only thinks of and cares for the universal. She makes this wisdom an object of derision for raw and irresponsible youth and unworthy of their enthusiasm.[33]

Undermined from within by feminine "petulance" fueled by sexual difference, the age-old bonds become moribund laws and the ethical world of unified substance implodes. The irony of woman who fights against hoary wisdom with the weapon of ridicule unleashes the cult of the younger ones, which subsequently allows for relentless individualism. Single individuals replace a universal community. Such a collapse explains how one moves on to the world of the unhappy consciousness and the Enlightenment, in short, to modernity: "… the simple compactness of their individuality has been shattered into a multitude of atoms."[34] When verbal atoms fly everywhere, we reach the zany world of American slapstick. Antigone has won thanks to what is both a Pyrrhic and a Marxist (but in the sense of the Brothers Marx) victory.

Kafka and the jokes of the future

The archives of modernity contain other disrespectful and debunking laughs, also linked with the question of femininity. This is where Kafka's specific glee

---

[33] Hegel, see footnote 14, p. 288.
[34] Hegel, see footnote 14, p. 289.

comes into play. It follows the pattern outlined by Hegel, combines regressive and progressive elements while remaining conscious of the decorum that has to be debunked. In a letter to Felice, Kafka describes how he fears to be overtaken by sudden fits of convulsive laughter; this is his specific form of hysteria. What triggered it in this case was the official speech of thanks he had to give to the president of the insurance company in which he worked. First, the president took a ridiculous pose to listen better, crossed his legs, laid a hand on the table, lowered his beard on to his chest, forcing his protruding stomach to heave. This sight elicited a burst of giggles from Kafka, but they might pass for a tickle in his throat. The president stared at him, and then Kafka could not contain the devilish laughter surging from the depths. As the President responded with his own speech of thanks, Kafka lost control altogether:

> At first I laughed only at the president's delicate little jokes; but while it is a rule only to contort one's features respectfully at these little jokes, I was already laughing out loud; observing my colleagues' alarm at being infected by it, I felt more sorry for them than for myself, but I couldn't help it; I didn't even try to avert or cover my face, but in my helplessness continued to stare straight at the president, incapable of turning my head, probably on the instinctive assumption that everything could only get worse rather than better, and that therefore it would be best to avoid any change. And now that I was in full spate, *I was of course laughing not only at the current jokes, but at those of the past and the future and the whole lot together*, and by then no one knew what I was really laughing about.[35]

To hide the rest of the colleagues' embarrassment, a co-worker extemporized a speech in his turn, but because of his effort, he became too animated, and his exertions proved too much for Kafka who this time roared with wild laughter: ". . . the world, the semblance of the world, which hitherto I had seen before me, dissolved completely, and I burst into loud and uninhibited laughter of such heartiness as perhaps only schoolchildren at their desks are capable of." (LF, pp. 147–8) Utter silence greeted this outburst. The president nobly exonerated the culprit by blaming it on his jokes, before dismissing everyone hurriedly. Yet, it was impossible to stop Kafka: "Undefeated, roaring with laughter yet desperately unhappy, I was the first to stagger out of the

---

[35] Franz Kafka, *Letters to Felice*, James Stern and Elisabeth Duckworth (trans). New York: Schocken, 1973, p. 147, italics mine. Abbreviated as LF and page number.

hall." (LF, p. 148) Coughing and wheezing, he rushed to his desk to write a letter of apology, believing that he would never be pardoned.

We need to take seriously the scene of Kafka laughing at the jokes "of the past and the future and the whole lot together." Here is hearty apocalyptic laughter, a messianic glee calling up Sara's giggles in the Bible. Kafka's pervasive laughter was witnessed by friends like Gustav Janouch or Max Brod. He laughed out loud when reading *Metamorphosis*. Kafka laughed most at figures of authority. When he was tempted to join Rudolf Steiner's anthroposophical movement, he met the founder himself in March 1911. Kafka asked Steiner whether one could be a writer and a theosophist at the same time. We don't know Steiner's answer. Kafka merely observed that, while listening, Steiner kept "working his handkerchief deep in his nose, one finger at each nostril."[36] The diary does not offer further comment: Steiner is reduced to a nose-picker, not a mystic, and Kafka thumbs his nose at him.

Social farce just generates writing. Numerous testimonies have been given of Kafka's sense of humor, of his pleasure in telling jokes, and of his fits of laughter when reading his own texts. Max Brod mentions the fact that Kafka laughed so much when reading the first chapter of *The Trial* to his friends that he had to stop reading.[37] Numerous writers have explained why they find Kafka funny.[38] They generally see a combination of religious elements and of profane release of libidinal energies. What is sure is that Kafka's laughter is never simple, it always combines a duality of affects or a tension between incompatible concepts. A good example would be the moment of hilarious release when Gregor Samsa finally learns to discover the possibilities offered by a new animal body after his "metamorphosis," even taking some pleasure in dancing head down from the ceiling, only to collapse on the floor:

> He especially liked hanging from the ceiling; it was completely different from lying on the floor; one could breathe almost freely; a faint swinging sensation went through the body; and in the almost happy absent-mindedness which Gregor felt up there, it could happen to his own surprise that he let go and plopped onto the floor.[39]

---

[36] Quoted by Frederick Karl, *Franz Kafka, Representative Man. Prague, Germans, Jews, and the Crisis of Modernism*. New York: Fromm Editions, 1993, p. 266.

[37] Max Brod, *The Biography of Franz Kafka*, G. Humphreys Robert (trans.). London: Secker and Warburg, 1947, p. 139.

[38] See for instance David Foster Wallace, "Laughing with Kafka," *Harper's Magazine*, July 1998, pp. 23–7.

[39] Franz Kafka, *Metamorphosis*, translated and edited by Stanley Corngold. New York: Norton, 1996, p. 21.

This is not simple slapstick, since the apparent "entertainment" Gregor has found leads to a series of complex actions and reactions: first when the sister claims that his room has to be emptied of all furniture, only to realize that she is too weak to move a heavy chest of drawers by herself; then by the mother, who argues that it is better to leave the room as it was, since it connects her son to his former human past. The two women finally begin to clear the room, until Gregor decides to keep, in spite of all, a portrait of a woman in furs to which he clings fiercely. A scene of slapstick ensues, in which the mother faints at the sight of this "gigantic brown blotch on the flowered wallpaper."[40] The reader, at this point, does not know whether to laugh or to cry.

This painful hesitation often implies the presence of some form of eroticism; Kafka is never sure whether love-making is a sign of enlightening progression or childish regression. We see this in *The Castle* with the meeting of K. and Frieda. This could be called love at first sight, were it not so fraught with tensions and ironies. K. has just learned from her that she is Klamm's mistress, and tries to conquer her in spite of her apparent mistrust. He achieves this all at once by saying something that he meant ironically ("You see right through me . . . I wanted you to leave Klamm and become my love instead. Well, now I can go."[41]) but is taken at face value by Frieda. After K. hides under the counter where she serves drinks, she comes to him; they kiss and enjoy an extraordinary moment of love-making:

> They embraced one another, her little body burned in K.'s hands, they rolled, in a semi-conscious state from which K. tried constantly but unsuccessfully to surface, a little way on, bumped into Klamm's door with a hollow thud, then lay there in the puddles of beer and the rubbish covering the floor.[42]

This instant of loving unconsciousness is so strong that it is enough for Frieda to refuse to heed the imperious call of her previous master, Klamm.

Similar ironical turns of phrase then taken seriously, or serious statements taken ironically, recur in Kafka's correspondence with Felice. They met at Max Brod's on August 13, 1912. Kafka wrote to her a month later to remind her of the promise she had made to accompany him on a trip to Palestine. Here is

---

[40] Kafka, see footnote 38, p. 26.
[41] Franz Kafka, *The Castle*, Anthea Bell (trans.). Oxford: Oxford University Press, 2009, p. 37.
[42] Kafka, see footnote 40, p. 40. The original connects the term for "rubbish," *Unrat*, with the term for "semi-consciousness," *Besinnungslosigkeit*: "*Unrat*" usually means "filth" or "garbage," also the negation of "*Rat*" (advice, counsel). Heinrich Mann named the anti-hero of his novel *Professor Unrat*. One will have recognized the unlucky male protagonist of *The Blue Angel*.

how his first letter ends, offering a magnificent example of the technique of stream of consciousness writing he would resort to once in a while:

> And yet, and yet—the only advantage of using a typewriter is that one easily loses the thread—if doubts were raised, practical doubts I mean, about choosing me as a traveling companion, guide, encumbrance, tyrant, or whatever else I might turn into, there shouldn't be any prior objections to me as a correspondent—and for the time being this is the only thing at issue—and as such, you might give me a trial.
>
> (LF, p. 5)

A trial this was, or would turn out to be. They would soon be entangled in a web of projects, counter-projects and obstacles, in a frustrating dance of longing and rejection that included plans of many other trips together they didn't make. The letters are marked by the same ironical tension and ambivalence. For instance, in the first letter in which Kafka addresses Felice with the more intimate *Du* instead of the formal *Sie*, he states first: "I belong to you; there is really no other way of expressing it, and that is not strong enough." (LF, p. 37) but ends with "Did I think of signing myself *Dein* (yours)? No, nothing could be more false. No, I am forever fettered to myself, that's what I am, and that's what I must try to live with." (LF, p. 37) One cannot help thinking of the aphorism on *Sein* as being and belonging;[43] we see how the metaphysical tension can be an ironical contradiction between a perverse seduction ploy followed by a plea to renounce it and abandon everything as idle and worthless, an impossibility to live without being devoured by writing disguised as an amorous farce. This is why Kafka's bursts of laughter were addressed, as he writes to Felice, at all the jokes of the past and the future. His laughter is supposedly produced in the no-time of an instant, yet in some cases, it implies a sense of history, as Hegel suggests, and more specifically a sense of the future. Laughing at a good joke is the best way we have of uniting past and future in a verbal flash, which allows us to connect a "now," Benjamin's apocalyptic *Jetztzeit*, with the shared hilarity of a collective subject grammatically produced as "we." Yet, such a "we," as Vivian Liska shows, is problematic.[44]

Glancing back at his correspondence with Felice, Kafka compared that period to World War I. It was a lovers' war,[45] marked by sudden advances and

---

[43] See Chapter 9, p. 177.
[44] See Vivian Liska, *When Kafka Says We: Uncommon Communities in German-Jewish Literature*. Bloomington: Indiana University Press, 2009.
[45] See Kafka, footnote 34, pp. 308–419.

huge losses or stalemates; we find one example of these self-defeating tactics in the scene—again, a scene of travel—he imagines in a letter mailed to Felice on New Year Eve 1913. Regretting once more that they cannot be together, Kafka spins out a fantasy of reunion. He imagines that he and Felice finally meet in Frankfurt. To celebrate this, they will go to the theater. But when the night comes, Felice, who would have rushed to be on time, would not find Franz at the theater. She would then have to go back to their hotel to see what's happening. In their room, she would discover Kafka still lying in bed even though it is 8.00 pm. He would explain why he has been unable to leave his bed:

> ... I maintain that I have been incapable of leaving my bed, complain about everything and insinuate even worse complaints; I try to make amends for the terrible wrong by stroking your hand, by seeking your eyes, lost in the dark room, and yet my whole behavior shows that I am quite prepared to repeat the whole thing at any moment. Although I am at a loss to explain myself in words, I am aware of our situation in every detail, and if I were in your place, standing at my bedside, I wouldn't hesitate to raise my umbrella and in my anger and despair break it over my head.
>
> (LF, p. 136)

The hypothetical scene is hilarious and infuriating while testing Felice's resolve even more sharply. What he enjoys in the writing of these letters is the distance that they presuppose, and moreover the uncanny ability he has found to torture a woman who loves him. The same New-Year letter adds some wry humor to the scene; Felice had written that they "belonged together unconditionally." Kafka snaps back that this is true: they should be bound together by the wrists of her left hand and his right hand. Bound like that, they would become a couple led to the guillotine during the French Revolution (L, pp. 136–7.) Marriage was indeed capital punishment for Kafka. This may have been true for Althusser too.[46]

Althusser's joke: Is the future lasting forever, or just for a long time?

Here are two bad jokes about Louis Althusser, both scribbled on the walls of the institution in which he spent most of his life, the École normale supérieure in

[46] One could adduce Althusser's early text, the pamphlet on "Conjugal obscenity" (1951), in Louis Althusser, *Écrits philosophiques et politiques*, Vol. 1, François Matheron (ed.). Paris: Stock/IMEC, 1994, pp. 327–39.

Paris. The first dates from 1968: "*Althusser à rien.*" The second dates from 1981: "*Althusser trop fort.*" The first can be translated as "Althusser: no use," and comes from a Leftist student disappointed with Althusser, who, even though he was a whole generation's guru, refused to leave the French communist party. He never gave his support to the Maoists who would quote him fervently. The second can be translated as "Althusser squeezes too tight." It refers to the tragedy of November 16, 1980, when the philosopher strangled his wife, Hélène Althusser (born Hélène Rytmann), in their apartment at the École normale supérieure. Admittedly, these jokes are in terrible taste; they stem from a similar disappointment. Many former disciples tried to interpret this crime as a symptom of the end of communism as rigorously redefined by Althusser. The unseemly murder marked the collapse of his theory of ideology, or of his theory of State Apparatuses, like a fall of the Berlin Wall of Theory. Those who knew Althusser a little better were less taken aback: his sudden fit of madness, a true acting out, corresponded to a peak in regular cycles of mania and melancholy depression that went back to after the war, which had made Althusser go back and forth between his prestigious teaching institution and all sorts of psychiatric wards in which he was given first shock therapy, then sleep therapy.

When Althusser wrote a memoir attempting to come to terms with the enormity of the drama condensed in his outcry "I've strangled Hélène!,"[47] his admission was candid but blurred: he had strangled her but did not know why or when exactly. It would be wrong to say that Althusser writes his memoirs to justify his murderous "insanity." The marvelous book, *The Future Lasts Forever: A Memoir*, sheds as much light on his own personal plight as on the evolution of Theory in the last century. I note that the French title (*L'Avenir dure longtemps*) should rather be translated as "The future lasts a long time," which reminds me of the quandary in which I found myself when Francois Dominique and I, having founded a small press called "Ulysse fin de siècle," had reached the end of our planned tenure in the year 1999. The "end of the century" was approaching, and we were not sure whether we had the funds to continue our publications. We had been helped by a number of "perpetual subscribers," and were grateful for their support and trust. We calculated that, by receiving our regular publications, they had more than quadrupled the amount of money they had given us to launch the press. We decided to write to them, arguing they had reached "half perpetuity," and brazenly asked them to give us the same amount to restart a press in the new century. We were convincing in our pitch, all our former subscribers sent us a check for a renewed subscription. Was Althusser thinking of some such

---

[47] Louis Althusser, *The Future Lasts Forever: A Memoir*, Richard Veasey (trans.). New York: The New Press, 1993, p. 16.

condemnation "to perpetuity" for the murder he had committed, even if he was freed on grounds of insanity? Was he thinking of the eternity brought about by posterity, the agency of History to which we entrust the final judgment for those who have impacted the thought of a whole period?

What is remarkable in this beautifully written memoir is the extraordinary lucidity displayed by the philosopher when he analyzes his family background, his various symptoms, and the intellectual debates from the thirties to the seventies with an unrivalled sharpness and clarity. The result is one of courage for the future, predicated on the philosophy of Feuerbach. Althusser put Feuerbach back on the map of French philosophy in the after-war years. He presented Feuerbach in those terms:

> Feuerbach, an astonishing and largely unknown figure, was the real originator of phenomenology (with his theory of the intentionality of the subject–object relationship). He also influenced some of the views of Nietzsche and of Jacob von Uexküll, the extraordinary philosopher-biologist much admired by Canguilhem, who reinterpreted Feuerbach's concept of *Welt* as *Lebenswelt*, etc. I owe a great deal to the close reading of his work.[48]

An immersion in Feuerbach's forceful critique of Hegel, which had paved the way to the young Marx of the *1844 Manuscripts*, was essential for Althusser as he gradually abandoned his juvenile Catholicism and turned to Marxism. One of the phrases he owes to Feuerbach is his very title, since it obviously derives from the idea of a "philosophy of the future." Let us recall the last paragraph in this text that Althusser had translated into French:

> So far, the attempts at philosophical reform have differed more or less from the old philosophy only in form, but not in substance. The indispensable condition of a really new philosophy, that is, an independent philosophy corresponding to the needs of mankind and of the future is, however, that it will differentiate itself in essence from the old philosophy.[49]

This is what is meant, more or less, by Althusser with his title: "The future lasts for a long time," which is also why it cannot be translated as "for ever," as this

---

[48] Althusser, see footnote 45, p. 207.
[49] Ludwig Feuerbach, *Principles of a Philosophy of the Future*, Manfred Vogel (trans.). Indianapolis/Cambridge: Hackett, 1986, p. 73. See also in Louis Althusser's edition of Feuerbach, *Manifestes philosophiques (1839–1845)*. Paris: Presses Universitaires de France, 1960, "Principes de la philosophie de l'avenir", pp. 131–204.

would ring too religious or "absolute." One can imagine that it is the young Marx who is writing this—and indeed, Marx's famous last thesis on Feuerbach ("The problem is not only to interpret the world, but to change it.") had been criticized by Althusser himself, as we have seen in Chapter 1. Althusser writes pointedly that "*all great philosophers* have sought to transform the world, or to make it regress, or to preserve and reinforce the status quo so as to avert the threat of changes, perceived as dangerous. On this point I still think I was right, despite Marx's bold and celebrated remark."[50]

We are here on the slippery ground of Althusser's serial re-readings of Marx, and of his notorious palinody, since he had started by asserting that all in Marx was due to Hegel and the Left-Hegelians like Feuerbach, and then had shifted abruptly in the sixties, asserting that if Marx was "scientific" then he must have had to break with Hegel's idealism, practicing an "epistemological cut." Without reopening this huge file, which corresponds to the several "Marxes" one can reconstruct, I want to draw attention to a singular feature of *The Future Lasts Forever*, which is its highly comic effect. Few readers have been sensitive to this, even though the editors of the original version warn us: "*The Facts* belongs to the comic and *The Future Lasts Forever* to the tragic mode."[51] One exception is Gérard Pommier, who has devoted a whole book to Althusser's "case." He has one excellent chapter on what he calls "Comical features of maniacal speech."[52] Most of his examples (and there are many) come from the first autobiography, *The Facts*, written in 1976, that is before the "drama," and rewritten as *The Future Lasts Forever* in 1985. There we discover a really manic philosopher who tells the truth in an often hilarious and inimitably furious and fast style. Here is the account of a meeting with Charles de Gaulle:

> I met De Gaulle, whom I did not know personally, in surprising circumstances in a street in the Seventh arrondissement. A tall man with a cigarette dangling from his mouth asked me for a light, which I gave him. He then immediately asked who I was and what I did. I replied: I teach at the École Normale. He remarked: the salt of the earth. I said, of the sea, the earth isn't salty. Or do you mean it is salacious? No: it is dirty (*sale*). He then said: you have quite a way with words. I said: it's my job. He replied military men don't have it to the same extent. I asked him what he did and he said: I am General de Gaulle.[53]

---

[50] Althusser, see footnote 45, p. 172.
[51] Althusser, see footnote 45, "Editors' Foreword," p. 8.
[52] Gérard Pommier, *La Mélancolie: Vie et Oeuvre d'Althuser*. Paris: Aubier, 1998, pp. 247–63.
[53] Althusser, see footnote 45, p. 347, translation modified.

There are similarly zany dialogues with Pope John XXIII, who apparently needed an intermediary to obtain his reconciliation with Brezhnev. Althusser lectures him on the relative positions of the communist parties and the Church. Yet he leaves the Pope "with a feeling of distress, having failed to convince him that I was not in fact the only person concerned."[54] There is the hilarious account of how Althusser, in a moment of maniacal jubilation, tries to steal an atomic submarine. The narrative becomes more and more like a story-board for a burlesque film by the Marx brothers:

> I took off my borrowed cap and telephoned a gangster who wanted to get hold of a nuclear submarine in order to do a deal for international hostages or with Brezhnev, telling him he could take delivery of it. During the same period I staged a first-rate non-violent hold-up in the Bank of Paris and The Netherlands to win a bet with a friend . . .[55]

While confessing to bouts of kleptomania, Althusser continues reeling off improbable tall tales: "I stole many other things as well, including a grandmother and a retired cavalry officer, but this is not the place to discuss such things as it might cause difficulties with the Vatican . . ."[56] Althusser was indeed famous for his one-liners and jokes about students and colleagues. I still remember his mock praise for Derrida—whom he liked, nevertheless—as "a world-record jumper; only he thinks he is a long-jump world record, whereas in fact he is a high-jump world record." The glee of someone who had "a way with words" as de Gaulle observed makes for a curious mixture of comedy and tragedy in the end. But this is the price Althusser had to pay for being a philosopher next to a discipline—historical materialism—that he considered as scientific. He develops this comic aspect of his job in his 1967 seminar on "Philosophy and the spontaneous philosophy of scientists." In his introduction, he is ready to play the part of a Thales derided by a Thracian maid:

> Let us be good sports. Philosophers at work! It is well worth going out of your way to have a close look at such a spectacle! What spectacle? Why, comedy. Bergson (*Le Rire*) has explained and Chaplin has shown that, ultimately, comedy is always a matter of a man missing a step or falling into a hole. With philosophers you know what to expect: at some point they will fall flat on their faces. Behind this mischievous or malevolent hope there is a genuine reality: ever since the time of Thales and Plato,

---

[54] Althusser, see footnote 45, p. 346.
[55] Althusser, see footnote 45, p. 349.
[56] Althusser, see footnote 45, p. 350.

philosophy and philosophers have been "falling into wells." Slapstick. But that is not all! For ever since Plato philosophy has been falling within its own realm. A second-degree fall: into a philosophical theory of "falling." Let me spell it out: the philosopher attempts *in* his philosophy to descend from the heavenly realm of ideas and get back to material reality, to "descend" from theory and get back to practice. A "controlled" fall, but a fall nevertheless. Realizing that he is falling, he attempts to "catch" his balance in a theory of falling (a descending dialectic, etc.) and falls just the same! He falls twice. Twice as funny.[57]

However, Althusser added that his hope was to be able to vanish in this hole, to become one with the work accomplished for the future:

> In truth, you have not come here solely for the pleasure of seeing us perform our comically clumsy acrobatics. For my own part, I agree with you that we have come to "fall flat on our faces," but in an unexpected manner that distinguishes us from the majority of philosophers and knowing it perfectly well: *so as to disappear into our intervention.*[58]

The philosopher as clown, we meet again the old trope of Thales, and Althusser used it as well against Lacanian psychoanalysis, conflating the dogmatic verbosity of Lacan's school and the Communist party in the same joke of History. The issue then was who would decide how long a psychoanalytic session would last. Althusser writes: "Who will decide in the debate in which the 'Lacanian' analyst, following the master, is alone in disposing of the language and the use of discretionary decision making, being, as one likes to say but above all to joke in the (Communist) party, 'unitary for two'?"[59] Will the Future last for ever, or just for a very long time? Or should it be treated in Lacanian fashion as a "variable session"? Don't we have all, somehow, to be "unitary for two" in order to decide how long the Future will last? Yet, as we say in French, the best jokes that we can share are also the shortest.

---

[57] Louis Althusser, *Philosophy and the Spontaneous Philosophy of Scientists* (1967), Warren Montag (trans.). London: Verso, 1990, p. 76.
[58] Althusser, see footnote 45, p. 78.
[59] Louis Althusser, "In the name of the analysands . . .," in *Writings on Psychoanalysis*, edited by O. Corpet and F. Matheron, and translated by Jeffrey Mehlman. New York: Columbia University Press, 1996, p. 143.

Index